THE LADY IS A CHAMP

CAROL B. POLIS
with RICH HERSCHLAG

THE LADY IS A CHAMP

Copyright © 2012
CAROL B. POLIS with RICH HERSCHLAG

Senior Editor PETER M. MARGOLIS
Editor AMY PRINZO
Designer DENNY ANDERSON

ISBN: 978-1-4675-0100-2

Velocity Publishing Group, Inc.
638 Lindero Canyon Road
Ste. 136
Oak Park, California 91377

www.velocitybooks.org
1-877-318-8007

Printed In U.S.A

CONTENTS

Preface

Tribute To Joe Frazier

CHAPTERS

PREFACE

The 1970s were a time of great upheaval for women. There was *Roe v. Wade* and the Equal Rights Amendment. There were Gloria Steinem, Billie Jean King, Golda Meir, and Carol Polis. Who is Carol Polis?

In 1971, Carol Polis married a part-time professional boxing referee. Within two years, she went from being a squeamish spectator to a professional boxing judge—the first woman ever to do so. As luck would have it, not only was this period the golden age of women's rights, it was also the golden age of boxing. Carol Polis had a ringside seat for all of it. Sometimes she was the main event.

From cutting her teeth on three-round undercard fights at the gritty Blue Horizon in Philadelphia to finding herself at the center of a riot at Madison Square Garden; from being schooled in Joe Frazier's sweat drenched gym on North Broad Street to officiating in a Don King tournament and being investigated by the FBI; from following the careers of local fighters like Boogaloo Watts, Willie "The Worm" Monroe, Benny Briscoe, and Eugene "Cyclone" Hart, to becoming a personal guest of Muhammad Ali; from speaking at the nearby Rotary Club to appearing as a contestant on *What's My Line?* and *To Tell the Truth*, five-foot-one, 115-pound Carol Polis, for better or for worse, was treated as an ambassador for all women, a novelty, and even a misfit.

Polis was bound by none of these labels. First and foremost, Carol Polis was a mom. When her marriage breaks up in 1977, Polis's life becomes more a matter of survival than knockouts. It is while keeping a roof over her kids' heads and later raising her grandson that Polis earns her heavyweight belt. The ultimate challenge, it turns out, comes not from attaining stature as a world class sports figure but from becoming a world class juggler.

At ringside judging a fight.

Carol Polis outdistances the '70s. Then the '80s and '90s, eventually officiating at a staggering twenty-seven title fights in nine countries. Like the era she leaves behind, she leaves the uncomfortable title of women's libber in the dust. Polis is, rather, an accidental pioneer—someone who attains greatness not by seeking celebrity or confrontation but rather by being herself. *The Lady Is A Champ* is a sports story that will inspire women and a woman's story that will floor boxing fans.

TRIBUTE TO JOE FRAZIER

The publication of this book is, for me, bittersweet. About the time we were going to press, we lost the great Joe Frazier. Joe was one of the good guys. One of the truest tests of a good guy is how he stands up to the pressures of life. The pressure he withstood in the ring—remarkable as it was—was perhaps the least of it. The media circus surrounding Frazier's bouts with Muhammad Ali was not like anything seen since. At the crux of it were disparaging remarks about Frazier's character, worthiness and toughness.

Nothing could have been more off the mark. Joe Frazier fought his way up from abject poverty to the top. Along the way, he not only remained humble but went out of his way to help the less fortunate, especially kids. Cloverlay, Frazier's world famous gym, was located on North Broad Street in a bleak working class section of Philadelphia. That was no accident. Joe's goal was to give young men an opportunity to get off the streets and into something that would give them a sense of pride and self-discipline.

Joe was never too busy for those young men. And he was never too busy for me. When I showed up unannounced at Cloverlay with my family at the height of Frazier's fame, we all got the royal treatment. My kids, especially my boys, were in awe. I was in awe, too, but for different reasons.

I learned a lot about what it really took to step into the ring with confidence—the endless, seemingly thankless hard work involved. But most of all, I was in awe of Joe Frazier. What were the odds of anyone rising to the top of the most competitive and often brutal game in the world and not only remaining a perfect gentleman, but building his life around the idea of being modest and giving back? That is what I call character,

worthiness, and yes, toughness.

In his later years, every once in a while Frazier worked the corner during a fight. That always brought cheers from the crowd, especially in Philadelphia. After the smoke cleared from the life of Smokin' Joe, what remained was his heart, and in Philadelphia folks can see right through to it.

Surprisingly, at least one more thing remained—his amazing physique. I always referred to him as a cement slab because of his rock solid legs. While he walked the Earth—or ran it—Joe Frazier never stopped training. Those of us who miss him like to think the training of both kinds—the physical and the spiritual—are already helping him go the distance in the next life.

— *Carol Polis*

Me and Don King

CHAPTER ONE
UNITED STATES V. POLIS

I pushed open the large oak door. It was about eight feet tall and so heavy I had to lean into it with all 115 lbs. It was about four inches thick, and if it were steel it could have been the door to a bank vault. There was, in fact, a lot of money behind the door, but it was in the form of Don King, the world's most successful boxing promoter.

Don King grew up a hustler in Cleveland. He was a tall, robust black man with an ebullient, circus-like demeanor that could turn quickly. It turned deadly once when a man robbed his gambling hall and King shot him in the back. It turned deadly again when King stomped an employee to death for the sin of owing him six hundred dollars. That act of retribution landed Don King in jail for four years.

When King got out of jail, he got into the fight game. As someone who fought with the heel of his shoe, he didn't know very much about boxing. But he knew how to sweet talk people and lure them with money. His rise as a promoter was nothing short of meteoric. He signed names like Ali and Foreman and everyone on down to managerial contracts while at the same time wearing the promoter's hat. He packaged the "Rumble in the Jungle" in 1974 and the "Thrilla in Manila" in 1975.

The Rumble was made possible by a payment of ten million dollars King solicited from the President of Zaire. In the fight, Ali played rope-a-dope with George Foreman for seven rounds before sending the exhausted heavyweight champion to the canvas with a barrage of punches Foreman could no longer defend. A billion people around the world watched on satellite TV as the aging Ali underscored his legend yet again. All one billion of them saw my mentor, Zach Clayton, referee the fight and give the final count.

Few of them knew what Clayton was actually saying during the count. I was one who did: "One, two, buckle my shoe, three, four, get off the floor . . . ." That was one of Zach's trademarks. He had left his post as Commissioner of the Pennsylvania State Athletic Commission after completing his term and was replaced by Howard McCall. No one, of course, could replace Clayton in the ring or in my esteem. I was even prouder of him than he was of me.

The "Thrilla" in Manila was another Don King coup. As the rubber match between Muhammad Ali and Joe Frazier, it was a lot more than a world heavyweight championship fight. It was the final meeting between two titans whose whole was still greater than the sum of their parts. The bad blood between Ali and Frazier was real, and the "Thrilla" captured a kind of intensity and desperation that could probably never be recaptured.

By the twelfth round, the two fighters were trading dozens of last gasp blows, any one of which could have killed a man. By the fourteenth round, Frazier couldn't see and Ali looked like he might expire. Eddie Futch, Frazier's manager, wouldn't let his fighter come out for the fifteenth and final round. Afterward, Futch was bombarded with criticism but explained calmly that he had seen too many men die in the ring to let it happen again. Ironically, it was Ali who said after the fight that he now understood what it was like to die.

And now the man responsible for those epics, and whose only bruises were to his reputation, sat across the room from me. Don King's office in New York was as huge as his ego. The distance was perhaps fifty feet, but it seemed to take forever for me to approach his massive mahogany desk.

For a long moment, I wasn't so sure this had been the right plan of action. I was judging fights regularly and was approaching three hundred and fifty bouts altogether. But as of November 1975 I wasn't going where I wanted to. I hadn't gotten a single New York fight since the debacle at the Felt Forum the summer before, and I couldn't imagine how I was ever going to make the leap to a title fight, let alone a title fight overseas. So I applied a bit of chutzpah in calling Don King's office and making an appointment. King had leapfrogged over a hundred other promoters to get where he was. He was the king of chutzpah, so it was entirely possible he would appreciate my brazen gesture.

Don King smiled widely as his massive hand shook mine. His hair stood up like a ring of Christmas trees, as it always did.

"You the lady boxing judge?" he said.

"The first," I said. "Carol Polis. It's a pleasure to meet you, Mr. King."

"So tell me, what can you do for me?"

"Well," I said, "to be perfectly honest, I'd give my right arm to do an Ali fight."

"Ho-ho, now!" King laughed. "Don't go giving no arm away, lady judge. You might get that fight for a lot less than an arm. You from Philly?"

"Fort Washington, Pennsylvania."

"One thing for sure, lady judge," he said. "I may not tell you yes today. But I certainly ain't gonna tell you no! I'm a black man who kicked a man to death and here I am. Ain't nobody bigger than me in this game, and there's two reasons why. You know what they are?"

"What are they?" I asked.

"First is I got God on my side. Second is I got just the right combination of wit, grit, and bullshit. I pulled myself up from my bootstraps. And I got the feeling that's something you can dig. Look at me! I got three strikes against me already—I'm black. I'm an ex-con. And I'm under investigation."

"I'm a woman, I'm Jewish, and I'm five-foot-one." Upon hearing that, King let out a belly laugh that somehow still came out high-pitched, like his speaking voice.

"Oh, that's just beautiful," he said. "Sounds like we're two kings in a ring. I'll tell you what. You know what you ought to do? Apply to the Maryland State Athletic Commission. I can't tell you exactly why, but apply. There's going to be something doing down there at some point. And like a good fighter, you want to be ready."

"Well," I said, "I appreciate the advice. Is there anything else you think I might do at this time?"

"Be sure to leave your name and how we all can get in touch. You see my assistant right up front, right up there. Now I'm gonna have to take this phone call . . . "

I left knowing I was on Don King's radar, at least at the outer reaches. I was not a 747. Maybe I was a single-engine jet used for short commuter flights. NBC News had recently done a short piece on me. In it, I mused about separating myself from any concern over who might win a fight. While footage ran of me looking on like a hawk ringside at the Spectrum, I discussed how names, backgrounds, and personal reactions to the fighters had to mean nothing once the first round bell rang. I sounded sober as a judge, and of course that was the idea.

This dry look at Carol Polis was balanced by footage of me serving dinner to my sons, Jimmy and Kenny, in my kitchen. We shot for hours just to get a few seconds that looked pretty much like all the rest. The conversation was stilted, and the food looked like prison gruel. There would be no guest spot on *The Galloping Gourmet*. But as a judge, I sounded like I really knew what I was talking about.

Balance was definitely the operative word and the reason athletes believed in far-fetched concepts like biorhythms to enhance their performance. I had fine-tuned my own rhythms as time went on. As they entered high school, Jimmy and Kenny were well-adjusted and didn't need much prodding from me. Jimmy was the more serious one, and Ken the more outgoing one with girls. With my own girls, Margie and Carol Paula, I tried to be less demanding academically and overall—not because they were girls but because they were younger and I had learned where to be less of a drill sergeant.

But beneath the production of this innocuous mini-documentary was an imbalance no camera was ever going to catch if I could help it. The kids were afraid of their step-father. And they had every right to be. Bob had a temper and let it fly often. I couldn't say for sure if the marriage was actually getting worse or if by failing to improve after so much time it just seemed worse. I found myself looking for turning points, but there were no obvious ones, just a long gradual downhill run.

We were doing our classic boxing films shtick one evening at a B'nai B'rith. There were about 800 men in the audience, which was more than some of the fights I had judged in recent months. Otherwise, there was nothing that exceptional about this gig until Bob finished introducing me. I heard the words from his mouth, into the microphone, bouncing around the hall with a little feedback, and then laughter. Tremendous, booming laughter. I knew I was the butt of the joke, but it took a few seconds to hear it clearly in my mind.

"And I have the privilege of being the first man in the country to have ever slept with the first lady boxing judge."

I was humiliated. I could take a joke, but this felt sleazy and a little creepy. It was maybe a six foot walk for me to the microphone, but it felt as long as the walk to Don King's mahogany desk. My eyes scanned the parquet floor looking for a little trap door to fall into and hide. There was nothing in my brain in the way of a retort. At least nothing I could hear over the laughter. Strangely, as I held the microphone, it came like a parry.

"That's what *he* thinks!"

Now the B'nai B'rith roof nearly fell in. The laughter had paused for an instant, only to double. I could hear individual gasps of delight piercing through. This was vaudeville for them. It was George and Gracie in the flesh and better than any grainy black and white footage of two men beating each other senseless ever could be. I liked it and carried on triumphantly as soon as I sensed the slightest lull. But I knew the bout wasn't over. I knew what I would have to face when I was done—him.

The slights and one-ups were forgotten for a bit in March of 1976, when we received a letter from Jack Cohen, Executive Secretary of the Maryland State Athletic Commission. Bob and I had applied in tandem for a license, which probably was a first, not just for Bob and myself, but for anyone. The letter stated that Don King had "testified to your ability as a boxing judge and your husband's as a referee." It went on to say that there were no openings at this time but that "signs point to an increase in boxing activity in Maryland within the next year or two." Apparently the black ex-con under investigation had remembered the feisty Jewish woman.

For exactly what purpose became clear in January 1977. I received a telephone call from James Farley, Jr., Commissioner of the New York State Athletic Commission. Strangely, it was not for an event taking place anywhere inside the state of New York. Don King had put together a tournament called the United States Boxing Championships. The idea was simple. Numerous countries around the world had a national boxing title at every weight division, but the United States did not. King proposed to fill that void with what he hoped would be the first annual tournament crowning the U.S. champs. He had the backing of ABC television, which in exchange for the sum of $1.5 million would own the broadcast rights.

I was assigned to judge a heavyweight fight in the third round of the tournament between Scott Ledoux and Johnny Boudreaux. It would be an eight round contest broadcast worldwide from the Halsey Field House at the U.S. Naval Academy in Annapolis, Maryland. There would be no five-point must system as in Pennsylvania, just a winner in each of the rounds. As in my home state, however, there would be myself, another judge, and a referee, each of whom would score the fight. I would receive a grand total of $100 for my efforts, plus $32 for expenses.

Bob had not received a phone call for that or any other fight in the tournament. Had he gotten such a call, and had it been on the same weekend, we would have gone down on separate trains. It was over for us. We were in the process of filing for divorce. To his credit, Bob had suggested we go for marriage counseling. I flat out refused. Here was a man who went into a tirade over how a car was parked in the driveway. Here was a man whom I caught in lie after lie regarding money he was sending to his ex in-laws. But that was just the beginning.

I had a friend named Judy. Her husband was Max Patkin, the Clown Prince of Baseball. In 1944, during an army exhibition game, Patkin was an unknown pitcher who served up a long ball to Joe DiMaggio. As DiMaggio went into his homerun trot, a mock-angry Patkin decided to follow the Yankee Clipper around the bases. The crowd loved it, and a clown was born. Patkin worked thousands of professional games stateside, often utilizing his rubbery face to send the fans rolling in the aisles.

Patkin was now in his late fifties, and Judy was clowning around on him. She was about twenty years his junior, and 5'10" with long blonde hair. Her build and fake eyelashes reminded people of Dolly Parton, except Judy had no buttocks to speak of. What she did have was Bob, more than once. I had found out about their affair recently, and now, like Max Patkin, my life was a circus.

That wasn't the final act for Bob, however. He had also slept with Judy's friend, Harriet, in some sort of kinky doubleheader. Harriet was a ringer, a pro, or in non-baseball terms, a prostitute. Bob apparently had a thing for prostitutes. I found out he had ordered up a Chinese hooker at work for a private affair in the conference room. My source for this juicy tidbit was Bob himself, who in almost the same breath mentioned his boss, Marv, was having an affair.

Betrayed though I was, I was not about to fall into the hell-hath-no-fury-like-a-woman-scorned trap. I had integrity and a life of my own. Still, one afternoon in a fit of anger I couldn't resist calling Marv at work. "Marv," I said, "Bob told me about the Chinese hooker he had in the conference room. Bob talks a lot. He told me about your affair, too. How many other people do you think he might have told, Marv? Any idea?" This was me hitting bottom, and I resolved it wouldn't happen again.

Bob was still living in the house, and as far as I was concerned he couldn't leave fast enough. The sooner he got out, the sooner I could stop worrying about what he might do to my kids. We were now in the thick of straightening out financial matters. It wasn't going to be easy. I had put Bob's name on the deed for my house. I owned half of a plot of land Bob had purchased in Las Vegas.

In exchange for getting my house back free and clear, I had to sign away my rights to the Vegas property. Amidst these matters were smaller ones like a joint savings account and a safe deposit box. I was on a tight schedule to get down to Annapolis and figured I'd deal with these issues when I returned. Before I left to catch my train, Bob accused me of having a boyfriend. If only.

Train rides can be better than car rides for clearing your head.

Without the responsibility of driving and all the directions, you were meditative. It was just you, the passing scenery, and your private thoughts. I knew I had a hand in the breakup of my marriage. I was a "hundred-and-ten-percenter." I gave a hundred percent of myself and then some and expected the same in return. Hardly a man was up to the hundred percent, let alone the extra ten. The result was a feeling of pressure or even suffocation for the male half, and when they feel any of that, they are wont to flee.

After checking into the Holiday Inn in Annapolis, I attended a reception thrown by the Naval Academy. The banquet hall was filled with some of the best dressed, best looking officers in the world, so in hanging around with gorgeous men I at least tried to make an honest man out of my soon-to-be-ex-husband. But the admiral hosting the event was as boring as a boat drifting slowly out to sea. Once he was done discussing the Army-Navy football game held very often in Philadelphia, the admiral's conversational artillery was exhausted.

Howard Cosell, who was covering the U.S. Boxing Championships for ABC, was at my table, too, with his wife. A media survey was done in which viewers rated the various well known sportscasters. Cosell came out both the most loved and the most hated of them all. Emotion meant viewers for ABC, even if many of those viewers simply loved to hate Cosell. There was a certain arrogance in his delivery, his hyperbole, and his know-it-all attitude. As far as Cosell was concerned, he wasn't simply reporting on the event. He was the event.

In the flesh, Cosell was a somewhat less secure version of his on-air persona. He had bad posture and reminded me overall of the actor, Walter Matthau. His hairpiece was present as always, vastly exceeding the amount and density of natural hair one could have allowed for a man of his age and complexion in his wildest dreams. We spoke a few times, and he kept calling me "Chris." Who was I to correct the great Howard Cosell?

The following afternoon, February 13, the Halsey Field House was packed with about 7,500 spectators. They generally weren't paying spectators, but that hardly mattered. The money was coming in from network advertisers. The venue had to be filled in order to avoid embarrassment on worldwide television. So about half the place was occupied by midshipmen, with various non-uniformed fight fans occupying the remaining seats. The first round of the tournament had been held on an aircraft carrier in Florida, and the second at Don King's alma mater— the Marion Correctional Institute in Ohio, where he had spent four years of his life. King undoubtedly had a flare for mixing the noble with the ignoble and somehow making it all look great.

The referee was Joe Bunsa and the other judge, Harold Valan. Both were well known in the sport of boxing. Scott Ledoux, age twenty-eight, from Minnesota, was the favorite. He was inching up near the top ten heavyweight fighters as ranked by *Ring* magazine and had a professional record of nineteen wins, four defeats, and one draw. His more recent fights included a few against some of the upper echelon heavyweights, such as Duane Bobick and former champion George Foreman.

LeDoux's fight with Foreman over the past summer ended in a three round technical knockout with Foreman the winner. But LeDoux fought furiously for about two-and-a-half rounds and surprised just about everyone, including Foreman. LeDoux was fair-skinned with a bushy, droopy mustache. Weighing in at around 225 pounds, there was a sluggish, paunchy, punch-drunk look to him, but that look could be deceiving. Foreman, at least for the moment, had moved on to better things, as he was sharing duties behind the microphone with Howard Cosell. Foreman was well groomed, wearing a light colored turtleneck sweater with a bright yellow ABC sport jacket over it.

Johnny Boudreaux of Houston, Texas was twenty-four and an up-and-coming heavyweight. He brought a record of nineteen wins, one defeat, and one draw to the ring. Only recently, however, had he begun fighting outside of Texas and facing high-ranking opponents. Boudreaux was the underdog in today's fight.

The first two rounds were unremarkable. LeDoux threw dozens of punches and few were effective. Most of them bounced off of Boudreaux's arms, glanced off his shoulders, or missed altogether. Boudreaux threw very few punches and maybe one or two were effective. Neither fighter looked particularly sharp or skilled. Neither took command of the round. That changed in the third round when LeDoux came alive with a flurry reminiscent of his fight with Foreman. A left-right-left combination landed Boudreaux on the canvas. Boudreaux pulled himself up quickly, and so it was a knockdown for LeDoux. The remainder of round three was even, and so I gave it to LeDoux.

The remaining five rounds were a lot like the first two. I scored the fight four rounds for Boudreaux, three for LeDoux, and one round even. It was not a fight I would have paid to see. I found out shortly that Valan had it five to three for Boudreaux, and referee Bunsa had it three rounds to two for the same fighter, with three rounds even. Scoring three rounds a draw was a more significant comment about the scorer than the fighters. In the Zach Clayton school of officiating, it was tantamount to a dereliction of duty. But with the decision unanimous, it hardly mattered.

The fighters, their managers, and the corner men milled about the audience as the scoring was read. Instantly, there was loud booing and protestations from the crowd, including presumably a lot of unhappy midshipmen. They were brave, smart, and handsome, but they didn't necessarily know boxing. Answering the call from the television people, Johnny Boudreaux stepped through the ropes and down out of the ring toward Cosell and Foreman. I was perhaps ten feet away and could hear snippets of dialogue. Still in the ring, Scott LeDoux looked like he had been hit in the ego. He shuffled and brooded like a drunken sailor.

As the interview with Boudreaux got underway, I saw Ledoux walk almost perfunctorily around the perimeter of the ring over to where the interview was taking place below. And suddenly there he was, the loser, leaning out of the ring and taking swings at the crowd. A dainty right jab caught Boudreaux's attention, sending him a breeze but failing to make contact.

Boudreaux and one of his ring men reacted like members of a street gang challenged in front of their friends. Meanwhile, Ledoux continued to lean out over the ropes and throw a flurry of off-balance punches. If not for the kicks he threw in, it was an instant replay of the mediocre Ledoux-Boudreaux fight of three minutes ago. I didn't want to have to score this again.

A melee ensued at ringside, with people grabbing other people. While personnel in the ring stopped LeDoux from losing a second time as a kick-boxer, George Foreman restrained Johnny Boudreaux and provided on-air candid microphone counsel for the benefit of the young heavyweight and six continents: "Be cool, don't fight. What you got to prove? The fight is over. You won."

But those same six continents were simultaneously witnessing something far more riveting. In the frenzy, one of Ledoux's swipes had taken Howard Cosell's hairpiece right off his scalp. His chrome dome exposed for the masses, Cosell went down like the fighters he had covered for so many years rather than let the shiny exhibition continue. When he emerged, petting his rug like a long lost friend, Cosell told his audience he had now seen everything in his lifetime. As he signed off, I heard someone I thought was LeDoux's manager say, "Let's find the judges!"

That was my cue. I somehow doubted they wanted to discuss the fine points of scoring in Maryland versus Pennsylvania, and though my hair was real, I didn't need my head knocked to the floor with it. So, like Cosell, I signed off, which I accomplished by running out of the arena for my life.

When I returned home by train in the evening, Bob was gone and the LeDoux-Boudreaux fight was all over the news. Bob had cleaned out his dresser drawers and his side of the closet. The Sunday TV sports wrap-ups were full of accounts of the fracas and charges by LeDoux that the fight was fixed. It was going to take a while to sort through all the allegations and what they might mean for me. In the meantime, however, I knew two things—one, that LeDoux had lost the fight all on his own, and two, I had to get to the bank before Bob did.

Monday morning at the train station I picked up as many newspapers as I could. It didn't take long to find out that Carol B. Polis was a possible witness in an extended FBI investigation into Don King's tournament. It didn't take much longer than that to read that Carol B. Polis was also a possible target of the same investigation. There was talk of the United States Attorney General setting up a grand jury in Baltimore.

Only an idiot or a hermit could have believed that Don King was anything this side of clean. I had pushed that heavy oak door and walked into his office with eyes wide open. What I hadn't fully understood, at least perhaps until now, was the extent of the web King had spun. King had made sure that not only was he the promoter of the tournament, but that he effectively owned almost every fighter in it. That, of course, was a conflict of interest, but Don King was all about conflict if it served his interest.

For starters, King had hired Al Braverman and Paddy Flood to serve as his "boxing consultants." A couple of Damon Runyonesque characters with cigars, disfigured noses, and leathery skin, they were in charge of recruiting talent for the tournament. Recruitment in this case meant boxers signing with Braverman or Flood as a manager.

In some cases, the boxers were already signed to either of the two men prior to the King tournament. In other cases, signing was a precondition to entering the tournament. In many such cases, the original manager of a given fighter had little choice but to watch the talent he had developed over a period of years vanish with the stroke of a pen. The chance at winning forty thousand dollars or more in the tournament coupled with the chance to be tied in with the powerful Don King—in the same company as Muhammad Ali and George Foreman—was just too enticing.

While Don King called these men consultants, they were really his employees. They even had an office in his townhouse on the east side of Manhattan. Other fighters in the tournament were held even more closely by Don King. Rising heavyweight contender Larry Holmes was managed by Carl King, who just happened to have an ex-con father name Don. Carl's brother, Eric, managed heavyweight boxer Stan Ward. When Don King ran out of sons, he pulled other close associates into the web. And where there is full control by a single power, kickbacks can't be far behind.

Some fighters and their managers, however, wouldn't give in. Mike

Ayala, the number two ranked featherweight in the United States, was never even asked to participate. It was well known that Ayala was loyal to his manager, who also happened to be his father. But Don King's people claimed they couldn't find Ayala's address. The result of a succession of such willful oversights was a tournament not worthy of the name U.S. Boxing Championships.

The cards had to be filled somehow, though. Where King's people couldn't find a worthy opponent, they invented one. Ike Fluellen was a cop from Bellaire, Texas who fought part time but called it quits in 1976. Not long after, Don King Productions representative Chris Cline, offered Fluellen a spot in the tournament. Soon, Fluellen found himself ranked tenth nationally as a junior middleweight in *Ring* magazine. Not long after that, his ranking shot up to third as the result of two fights in Mexico. Neither of the fights, however, had ever taken place, but why quibble? Fake rankings needed fake fights.

One of the biggest disappointments in all of these disclosures was the participation of *The Ring* magazine. Under Nat Fleischer, boxing's bible had been the pillar of the sport—fair, honest, and reliable even when the fight game was being dragged into the muck by scandals. In 1977, however, *The Ring* had been paid a consulting fee by who else, Don King, and the effect was readily apparent. Even James Farley, Jr., the New York State Athletic Commissioner, was under fire. Though his services were supposedly pro bono, his hotel rooms, travel, and all sorts of expenses were paid for by Don King Productions.

With everyone else seemingly in King's pocket, it wasn't much of a stretch to assume the officials were, too. But I wasn't. Not even close. What I had to show for accepting Don King's offer was a hundred bucks and a hole burning in the pit of my stomach that got worse with each stop on the train to Philadelphia.

There was $1,600 in our joint savings account at Continental Bank. I withdrew exactly half, $800, and deposited it into my personal checking account. I could have taken more money out, but this was no time to stop being a scrupulous person. At least not for me. When I went over to our safe deposit box, a bunch of little diamonds I had kept were gone. There was still time to go back and get the other $800 out of the savings account, but instead I walked out the door.

On my walk back to the train station, I was aware that I was passing beneath the building where Bob worked. I looked up at his fourth story window, and strangely he was at the window looking down. I could only hope someone bigger than both of us was looking down at him.

You can usually tell when the ring at your front doorbell is not a good one. There is a certain deliberateness about it. This was one of those. I was in jeans and sneakers early on a Thursday afternoon. I fixed my hair a little on the way to the door and straightened up. I opened the door and found two neatly dressed men in their forties. The short haircuts, the plainness of their dark suits, and the wing-tipped shoes told me a lot about who they were before they even tried. But when they flashed their badges, I knew for sure they were FBI.

I invited them into the dining room and clung to the only comforting thought I could find, that all my kids were in school. Naturally, the agents were investigating the U.S. Boxing Championships and Don King. With venues spread out across the country, it was an interstate matter. The agents sat down but didn't remove their jackets. It took them only a few minutes to inform me that they had subpoenaed my bank records. Blinking once or twice, I thought about the $800 deposit I had made only days earlier. That was just my luck—not enough money to do much with, but just enough to raise suspicions.

But this was my home, and so without ever letting my guard down I was at ease, sort of. I had to tell them the story of my life, from how I got into the fight game to how I knew Don King. I kept the Bob stuff to a bare minimum and realized I had reason to be thankful he never got an assignment in the tournament. Suddenly, one of the agents asked, "Do you have a record of your payment from Don King Productions?" I certainly did. Saving everything was saving my life.

I ran upstairs and came back down with two receipts—one for $100 and another for $32. This seemed as unrehearsed as it was. I also brought down any other documentation I could find, dating all the way back to my original appointment in Pennsylvania. I could sense we had turned a corner when the agents both took off their jackets.

Late in the second hour of questioning, we sounded more like old friends than law enforcement and suspect. I told them candidly that the LeDoux-Boudreaux fight was a unanimous decision and nothing to write home about as a sporting event. That crowds and the fighters themselves often saw the fight differently than the officials, but the officials were typically internally consistent for one main reason—we were professionals who knew what we were doing. That seemed to make an impression on the agents, but with these guys you really never knew for sure.

When they left I was relieved, though I felt like I had been hit by a Mack truck. They said the investigation could take months and told me to expect further contact. All I could think was that I would eventually be called to take the witness stand. At that point, under the lights and insisting my own innocence, and despite even the eventual outcome, all anyone would ever remember was that Carol B. Polis was part of that whole Don King scandal. I would be damaged goods. Then I considered how sloppy the house happened to look when the agents had arrived unannounced. And I suddenly realized I did have a little good luck once in a while.

As in the ring, some fights end with a whimper instead of a knockout. I had spent 1977 determined to win the fight for my reputation. I hired a lawyer, Stephen Yusem, who had been a friend since high school and who also happened to be an admiral in the naval reserve. In any matter involving Annapolis, that couldn't hurt. I hired a second lawyer, David Sorin, who came highly recommended for dealing with the U.S. Attorney General's office. Our approach was that the best defense was a good offense, and so among other things we were looking into suing Scott LeDoux for defamation of character. Sorin also utilized an inside contact in the U.S. Attorney's office to get a handle on which way the grand jury investigation was going.

As the year wore on, little bits of not so monumental news broke. ABC, who had finally cancelled the U.S. Boxing Championships in April, opened their own private investigation and found both themselves and Don King blameless. Don King couldn't have done it better himself. There was no point in my suing LeDoux, because his pockets were about as deep as Don King's conscience. And as David Sorin was informed later that year, the grand jury had no intention of calling me as a witness. Finally, on December 27, my father's birthday, the grand jury closed its investigation without handing down a single indictment. Knowing Don King was sleazy was one thing, proving it was another.

Relief for me was neither immediate nor complete. I continued to replay the LeDoux-Boudreaux fight in my mind, round by round, minute by minute, blow by blow. My bad luck had returned. I had to be nearly indicted and ruined over a truly mediocre fight. I considered quitting, but hundred-and-ten-percenters didn't do that, and I still dreamt of traveling overseas. For the time being, I traveled to North Broad Street in Philadelphia to judge a fight card at the Blue Horizon.

The fights on that cold winter night were a mixture of competitive and run of the mill. My night was now about getting to the parking lot to get my car, get home, and pay the babysitter. I was not more than a few steps down the aisle in the arena when eight or nine black men encircled me. "I noticed you didn't go for Jones," one of them in a beret said.

Jones. I recognized the name but couldn't recall a single thing about whatever fight Jones was in. My mind was a blur, but not in spite of having concentrated to migraine status pain while judging six consecutive fights—rather, *because of it.* "I'm sorry your man didn't win," I said. "I couldn't have known he was your man. I call them as I see them. Better luck next time." With that I flashed the peace sign. It worked the night I was almost killed at the Felt Forum and it worked here, too.

Outside the Blue Horizon, on the pavement, a small crowd had gathered near the corner. Two large black men were fighting. They were both adorned with gold chains, bracelets, and earrings. They were immaculately dressed in shiny silk suits. Their shoes were pointed. It was an even match in size and in style except for one thing—one man was standing and the other was on the ground. The one standing was kicking the other in the temple repeatedly, and the pointy shoe drew blood like an open fire hydrant.

Beneath a frigid January full moon, the crowd warmed themselves around the carnage while a police officer, also quite large himself, stood two steps from the assault and looked the other way. Four hundred fights and I had never seen anything in the ring one tenth as macabre or sad. I wanted to do something, but out here I was not an official or even the wife of an official. I was just a diminutive lady hoping to make it back to her car in one piece.

So I walked on with my back to the carnage and felt sicker with every step. After a year of waiting for the other shoe to drop, it finally had. I was alone and felt it. I needed someone right now but dwelling on it wasn't going to help. I had to remember the flipside, the saving grace— that my kids needed *me*.

CHAPTER TWO
I HATE BOXING

I am disconnected from reality, in another world, a world that is profane and barbaric. Inside a squared circle illuminated by beams of blinding incandescent light—with canvass reeking of mildew, resin and disinfectant—stand two prizefighters. Fists fly fast and furious like a cyclone, the fighters fiercely engaged in a life and death battle of brawn and brutality.

A fighter connects with a violent right hook and his opponent's head snaps back. Crimson and sweat spray the ring. A gaping cut opens up under the opponent's puffy left eye and the crowd explodes at the sight of blood trickling down his cheek. The blows are vicious and land with such force that it makes me want to look away. But I just can't help myself.

* * *

My only real memories of boxing were as a teenager in the early 1950s watching my family's black and white television set on a Friday night in Jenkintown, a suburb of Philadelphia. My father was watching along with my younger brother, Arthur. One of the fighters in the ring was a fellow by the name of Sugar Ray Robinson. I could tell he was a quick, graceful, amazing fighter. I could sense the excitement, at least secondhand. The brutality seemed suited to black and white. It made the action seem dramatic. But baseball was more my style. Or tennis. Or swimming, or diving. Anything but this.

Here in 1972, in living color, live from the second row of the Spectrum in Philadelphia, there was blood—coming from a fighter's mouth, nose, around the eyes. Some of it was landing on the canvass, and I thought for sure, any second some of it was going to land on me. If this was out in the street somewhere, the cops would be breaking it up, making arrests, and taking people to jail. As it was, the referee was letting it go on, merely moving the fighters apart for a moment—not to stop the cruelty, but only to let it continue more efficiently. Though I didn't know much about boxing, I knew there was a ring doctor somewhere. What was he doing? Waiting to see how close to death the patient got? Or was he not so much a ring doctor as a ring mortician?

Between rounds, I got Bob's attention at the edge of the ring and asked him what was the matter. Why weren't they stopping this thing? Why wasn't *he* stopping it. He explained the rule: The only way they would stop a fight on account of bleeding was if the blood interfered with the fighter's vision. So, I supposed, if you could still see at the official time of death, the fight would be allowed to continue. But I had to be satisfied with that answer for the time being. Bob wasn't just the referee—he was my husband.

Bob's first wife had introduced us a couple of years earlier. I was in my early thirties, a divorced mother living in a Cape Cod style house in the Philadelphia suburb of Fort Washington and raising four children. A bunch of my friends, most of whom were married, were taking their families to the Jersey shore. To join them, my kids and I were going to have to raise some money. So we held a garage sale and not only took in a few hundred dollars, but also got rid of countless no-longer-in-active-service strollers, cribs, highchairs, tricycles and anything else we could find.

I was down by the pool at the Ocean Bay Motel in Longport with my girlfriends. I happened to be on the phone, and a woman maybe a few years older than most of us came over and started talking. She wasn't with our group, so I figured one of my friends had met her down here. I soon realized that no one had met her before now. Her self-introduction was somewhere between friendly and rude with a slight lean to the rude side. She just kind of pushed herself on us, and we were all too polite to break away. The other thing was—not that I cared that much—she wasn't very attractive.

When she told us her husband was coming down to the pool, I was expecting Frankenstein to the bride thereof. But her husband, it turned out, was a handsome guy. Bob was in his mid-forties, about six-foot-two with a broad athletic build, dark hair, and rugged face that reminded me a little of a young Spencer Tracy. He was a charmer and very quick with a punch line. For the life of us, my girlfriends and I couldn't figure it out.

A few days after we got back to Fort Washington, I got a call from Bob Polis. I had to think for a second. It was the good looking guy, Bob, from the Ocean Bay Motel. I didn't think I had made that much of an impression. But he started telling me how at this point he was married in name only. He called back a few more times, and it wasn't just to talk about his defunct marriage. I told him flat out, however, that my parents raised a lady and I absolutely did not go out with married men. There was no way we were going out even to a simple dinner until he was officially separated and out of that house.

That took about a year, and we finally had our first date. Bob was born in Philadelphia and was twelve years older than I was. He was an athlete at Olney High School and then majored in physical education and lettered in football, basketball, and lacrosse at West Chester State College. He also boxed a little on an intramural basis. World War II interrupted his varsity career, and in 1943 he was commissioned as an officer in the Navy. He served as both a navigator and athletic officer in the Pacific.

After the war, he finished his degree at West Chester and added a master's in 1950. He taught physical education and math at Norristown High School, where of course he also coached. But he wasn't happy teaching and wasn't making the kind of living he would have liked to support his growing family. So in 1957, he left teaching for good to work as a stock broker for the E.W. Smith Company, where he had stayed ever since.

One aspect of his earlier life Bob didn't quit was boxing. In the early 1950s, he got into the ring professionally, but not as a fighter. He was a referee, licensed by the Pennsylvania State Athletic Commission. For years he worked relatively low-level professional prize fights, mostly in the Philadelphia area at venues like the Arena. The pay wasn't as good as that of a stock broker or even that of a teacher. A referee might make anywhere from twenty-five to fifty dollars for the night, and that might include six or more separate fights on the card, one after the other.

But Bob loved refereeing. As a part-time avocation, it got him out of the house two or three nights a month to do something he loved. He was the center of attention, more or less, without having to get his brains knocked out. And yet the skill required to referee, though not the same as a boxer's, was immense. You had to be on top of the fight, making sure there was no unfair advantage for either fighter while at the same time not interfering with the flow of the fight or interjecting yourself where you shouldn't. This was something I had, of course, never given a thought to, but as Bob explained it to me, I could see it was really an art form.

And he got very good at it. Over the years, he had refereed numerous championship fights and non-title fights involving middleweights and heavyweights ranked at or near the top of their division. One of those fights was Sugar Ray Robinson versus Joey Giardello. I didn't know who Giardello was, but I certainly knew who Sugar Ray Robinson was. And if *I* did, probably everyone did. For all I knew, Bob was in the ring on one or more of those Friday nights when I watched, barely interested, with my father and brother.

Bob refereed the middleweight title fight at the Spectrum between Joey Giardello and Rubin "Hurricane" Carter in December 1964. That was as close as Carter would ever come to a championship, as Giardello beat him handily. Bob recalled the details of the fight like it was yesterday. But I recalled hearing about how Hurricane Carter was convicted of a triple murder committed during a robbery in 1966 and how that conviction was fought for many years, and the cause joined by numerous celebrities.

On top of that, Bob had refereed more than one fight involving heavyweight Joe Frazier, who was a homegrown Philadelphia product and eventually the champion. In 1970, boxing fan or not, you couldn't avoid hearing three things on the nightly news—what was happening with and who was protesting the Vietnam Conflict, when the next moon shot was, and if and when Joe Frazier and challenger Muhammad Ali were finally going to have the showdown everyone was waiting for. Considering all this, it felt like I was having dinner with a virtual celebrity.

Bob and I were married on September 1, 1971. I had four children and so did Bob. Together, we made the Brady Bunch look like a quaint nuclear family. My kids were James Lawrence, 11; Kenneth Benjamin, 9; Marjorie Lynne, 8; and Carol Paula, 7. The first three were from my first marriage, the fourth from my second marriage. Bob's children, all four from his first marriage, were Jim, a junior in high school; John, 13; Andy 10; and Kathy, 8.

At first, most of Bob's kids were living with their mother in Elkins Park. But Jim quickly moved into our basement and hibernated. Bob was trying to get custody of John but was having a tough time of it. The three younger kids would go back and forth between our house in Fort Washington and their mother's house in Elkins Park. They were difficult at times. And whenever they went home to see Mommy, they came back worse.

Bob found out that the judge handling his custody case happened to live around the corner from us in Fort Washington. So he put me to work. I wrote a fifteen page letter to the judge on why Bob's son belonged with us in our lovely neighborhood and then hand delivered the letter to the judge's mailbox. I felt terrible doing it for more reasons than I could count, but for some reason I did it anyway.

We wanted something more in common than just a house full of kids. I had begun preparing for my stock broker's license, which gave me something to talk about with Bob. I was studying hard and had every intention of passing, even though once I passed, I had no idea in the world how I'd have time to actually get out of the house and work.

As far as boxing was concerned, I now had about twelve minutes of experience as a spectator, and the sum total of what I knew beyond the blood and brutality was the names of the boxers. It was Cyclone Hart versus Denny Moyer, though I couldn't tell which one was bleeding more.

And now, with Bob in the ring doing his best to chase after them, both of them—Hart and Moyer, sounding more like a songwriting or dancing duo—went flying out of the ring together. They landed on the arena floor in a twisted mess of leather and muscle. Lucky for me, they landed to my right about twenty feet. But I doubted I would ever forget that it could have been me under there, Carol Polis, all five-foot-one, 115 lbs. of me.

Denny Moyer climbed back into the ring. Cyclone Hart wasn't moving. Moyer looked dazed. Hart still wasn't moving. The ring doctor was hovering over him. Bob declared Moyer the winner, and a stretcher came for Hart. Word was he might have a cerebral concussion.

My night out with Bob at the fights was wearing thin after a few months. We were back at the Spectrum on this evening, and Bob was back in the ring. Bob knew he had to shake things up to keep me even pretending to be interested. At least I wasn't a kid. Kids didn't bother to pretend. So Bob taught me how to keep score. We talked about it here and there, at home, in the car. It wasn't like keeping score at a baseball game, where a run was a run. In boxing, there were guidelines, but the scoring was highly subjective.

Each round was scored separately, as if the preceding rounds had never occurred. Pennsylvania used the five-point system, whereby the winner of each round was awarded five points. The loser of the round was usually awarded four points, so that a typical round was scored 5-4. In a typical round, one fighter dominated the other—maybe not by a lot, but in some appreciable way. Maybe that fighter landed more effective blows than his opponent. Maybe he wasn't the aggressor but defended well, so that he not only blocked punches but used footwork and upper body movement to get into position and return blows solidly.

A good judge was not out there counting blows. A good judge looked for aggressiveness, clean hitting, and defensive skill. Above all, a good judge tried to determine who was the "ring general" in a given round. If there was a knockdown—one fighter knocking the other to the canvass—the judge was supposed to subtract a whole point from the final score of the round from the fighter who fell. That was how the final score for a round became 5-3. That was a relatively rare occurrence. You generally didn't score a round 5-3 just because one fighter landed a lot more effective blows than the other. That was usually still a 5-4 round. On the other hand, if a fighter was knocked down early in the round, it wasn't a signal for the judge to relax and score the round 5-3. There was still the rest of the round to consider.

Bob explained that the judge wasn't the one to decide what was and wasn't a knockdown. That was the referee's call. Sometimes a fighter's knee grazed the canvass. Sometimes he dropped and rested on one knee. Sometimes he went flat on his back for a referee's count. There were "soft" knockdowns and "hard" knockdowns. Regardless, a knockdown was a knockdown, and there was no knockdown unless the referee indicated to the judges that one had indeed occurred.

It was possible for a round to be scored a 5-5 tie. But that was discouraged by the Pennsylvania State Athletic Commission. The underlying notion was that virtually every round had a true winner, and if the judge was paying close attention, he would spot that winner. Of course, there were exceptions—true stalemates in a period of 180 seconds inside the ring. The first round could be especially difficult to judge as the two fighters were often feeling each other out. Nonetheless, if a judge turned in too many draws, it was an indication that he wasn't really doing his job.

At the other end of the scale was a knockout, as opposed to a knockdown. A knockout was exactly what every fan and non-fan thought it was. A fighter was down for the count of ten, and the referee declared the fight over. A technical knockout—where a fighter remained on his feet but was deemed by the referee to be physically unable to fight effectively—meant the same result. The fight was over, and the judges were freed from their responsibilities of scoring the fight. Their scores for the rounds were still a matter of record, but practically no one was going to criticize a judge after a knockout.

In Pennsylvania, there were two judges outside the ring, with the third judge being the referee. That left the referee with an awful lot to do at once. As good a view as he had of the fight, his priority had to be keeping the fight a fair contest. Keeping a running score could impede that effort. Not to mention that working hard to keep the fight fair could hurt the referee's scorekeeping. When the referee put himself literally between two fighters to break up a clinch, the running score in his mind could get knocked out faster than one of the fighters in the ring.

There was another problem with the referee serving as a judge. The idea that the same person who was responsible for maintaining order in the ring was also responsible for helping to decide the outcome represented too great a concentration of power for some in the fight game. In the United States of America, there was separation of church and state, and separation of the powers of government—executive, legislative, and judicial. So, as some states had already done, the Commonwealth of Pennsylvania was considering adding a third judge and making the referee just a referee.

The bottom line in a fight that wasn't decided by a knockout was the total score of the three officials. Each official's score was tallied with the total determining the official's decision. A fighter needed at least two of the three officials deciding in his favor to be declared the winner. All three made it a unanimous decision.

So here I was at the Spectrum ready to keep score round by round on the back of a program. I had a lot to focus on and a lot to remember, but the night would probably go by a lot faster this way. And it wasn't as if there was any pressure on me. The pressure was in the ring—on the fighters, on my husband, and on the judges not far from me with very stern looks on their faces. What they did actually counted.

I was glad what I did that night didn't count, not that it ever in a million years could. I did my best to look up, keep my eyes on the fighters, and follow the punches. Sometimes they were thrown so fast and in such flurries I wasn't sure who hit who or what really landed. Still, it really did seem to me more often than not, one of the two fighters dominated the round. Or maybe I was off in dreamland somewhere. In any case, I made sure I had the fighters' names spelled correctly, made sure I knew who was wearing which trunks, and marked down a score for each round the best I could. There were a lot of 5-4s.

With the last fight on the card over, Bob was out of the ring now and checking in with his bride, the amateur judge. As he looked over the back of my program, he seemed amused and encouraged that I had followed through with our game plan. "You know," he said, "these aren't half bad."

"Does that mean they're better than half good?" I said.

Even with the frenzy in the ring, Bob was a pro and of course had a very good idea of who won the rounds. So when Bob looked up again from my program, he had an idea.

"I'm going to turn these in to the commissioner," he said.

"Are you out of your mind?" I said. "You will do no such thing!"

But he was dead serious. I wasn't sure if his motive was to embarrass me, amuse himself, amuse the commissioner, or some combination of the three. I didn't want to find out. As Bob's eyes found newly appointed Commissioner Zach Clayton on the other side of the ring and his body began to move in the commissioner's direction, I did what any self-respecting wife, mother of four (or eight), and aspiring stock broker at the dawn of the age of women's liberation would do—I begged. It didn't work, and with Bob literally twice my size, I wasn't about to add another bout to the card.

Zach Clayton was well known to Philadelphia, to Pennsylvania, and beyond. In an era where civil rights were just beginning to move out of the political arena and into the board room, he was the first black commissioner of the Pennsylvania State Athletic Commission. Now in his early 50s, he was one of those overnight successes who worked at it for thirty-something years, and who every year managed to get a year younger in print.

He played basketball, football and baseball for Temple University in Philadelphia but had to drop out for financial reasons. Soon after, he was playing baseball in the Negro Leagues with the likes of Jackie Robinson, Larry Doby, and Roy Campenella, before they all were eventually allowed into the Major Leagues to display their talents to the whole country. Zach Clayton, however, went on to play professional basketball with several teams including the Harlem Globetrotters.

Clayton settled down in the world of sports he loved so much by becoming a boxing referee. He worked countless fights in the Philadelphia area, and slowly but surely, his reputation as a great third man in the ring grew. He was known as strict but fair and the fighters, whether black or white, respected him. In 1952, not long after his thirtieth birthday, he got the nod—that moment every professional hopes for in one way or another but learns to push to the back of their thoughts. Zach Clayton was selected to referee the heavyweight title fight between the champion, Jersey Joe Walcott, and the challenger, Ezzard Charles. The honor was extra special for Clayton, because he was the first black man in America ever to referee a title fight.

Now I looked around to the other side of the ring, through the ropes, and saw my husband Bob talking to this esteemed, illustrious man with the clean shaven head and the dapper, well trimmed moustache. I saw Bob handing him my slightly damaged program, which I had tried unsuccessfully a few minutes earlier to wrench from my husband's hand. I saw Zach Clayton looking carefully at the back of the program. And I wanted to hide.

It was too late for that now. With Bob right behind him, the commissioner was walking toward me, around the front row and stepping gracefully as possible past members of the crowd who still lingered and argued about the fights they had just witnessed. The best I could do at this point was to pretend to be looking elsewhere. But the fights were over and I didn't have my scorecard to look at anymore. He had it.

"Lady!" The commissioner spoke. It was to me. *I* was a lady. Even though I spent my evening watching guys bashing each other's brains out, I was a lady.

"Hello, Commissioner Clayton."

"It's Zach. Is this your scorecard?"

"I think it is."

"Well, lady," he said, "I gave this a good looking over, and if these here are the same fights I just saw on tonight's card, I'd say you did pretty darned well."

"Really?" I said.

"In fact," he said, "I like this better than what the men did."

"Well, I'll certainly take that as a compliment," I said. "Wow. How do I follow up something like that?"

"Keep doing it," he said. "That's all. You'll be back, I'm sure." He looked over at Bob for a moment and looked back at me. "You're definitely doing something right, and you'll only get better. I'd love to see your next effort. And one more thing—have your husband over here get you some regulation scorecards. I don't want to be looking at the back of a program."

Our next "gig" at the Spectrum was a few weeks away. At home, there were dishes to clean, beds to make, and cake crumbs to pick off the cushions. There were a few fights to referee, but they were mostly between eight-year-olds over who got the Bosco first. Between time, I thought about Zach Clayton. When I pictured him telling me to keep doing it, I remembered the twinkle in his eye. It stood out. He was a lot more than a tough guy or a master of the ring, and that twinkle somehow told the whole story.

One night, when the kids, and the hermit, and even the ref had gone to bed, I was wide awake at the kitchen table. Eleven o'clock was a good hour to cram in a little studying for my stock broker exam. As I straightened my right arm to reach for a paper, I felt a shooting pain in my elbow. Like anything you would call a pain, it hurt, but it was very familiar. More familiar than anything on the stock broker exam. There was at least a little bit of pain about 90 percent of the time. But when it was going to rain, the pain was sharper, and tonight I wouldn't need to catch the weatherman on the eleven o'clock news.

I was twelve years old at camp in Maine. I was a strong swimmer, and doing the crawl about a hundred yards out to the dock in the middle of the lake was no big deal. But as I pulled myself up, I felt something pop. I looked at my right elbow, and there was a problem. I didn't really understand it. It looked like I had two separate elbows where one was supposed to be. And one of the two elbows was sticking out, almost pushing through the skin.

I didn't remember much of what happened next. But as I woke up,

I saw two very white nuns, which is not your everyday vision for a Jewish girl. I felt like I was floating around the room, but this wasn't exactly what our rabbi told us heaven would be like. After a little while, though, I realized I was in a Catholic hospital. I had been operated on, and my right arm was in a cast.

The next couple of years were rough as far as my right arm was concerned. The elbow healed, but slowly, and not all the way. For a while, I wore a half-cast and an ACE bandage to hold the bones in place. At night, I would put a heat lamp on it to manage the pain. As I regained my flexibility, I went back to playing tennis, swimming, and diving at the Philmont Country Club in Huntington Valley, where our parents took us. I could still hit a good forehand and backhand with my right arm, but the serve—with the full extension it required—was a casualty. So I served with my left and played with my right.

I never gave up on anything I loved. Instead, I adapted. After a few months, I had a decent left-handed serve. If anyone asked how and why I became ambidextrous, I told them all about the dock, the nuns, and floating around the room. Most people seemed to think the adjustment was great.

I kept swimming and diving, too. The girls all wore a tank suit in those days, and when we dove, the guys were usually staring for the reasons that guys stare. But I was self-conscious and thought that rather than some other protruding body part, they might be staring at my elbow. It was always a little crooked, and because of it, the splash I made was never really even. Still, I was a good diver, first on the team until in eleventh grade I hit my head on the board. That was it for diving. I didn't have another head to switch to.

Years later, I went to see Dr. John Royal Moore at Temple and Shriners Hospital in Philadelphia. Dr. Moore was a world renowned orthopedist who had seen me as a kid for just about the most mundane reason in the world—my flat feet. My feet were so flat as a young girl, when I stepped out of the swimming pool onto the deck, all you would see were wet squares. Dr. Moore fitted me with steel arches, and they worked. Kind of. Eventually, those wet squares shrank to wet rectangles.

What Dr. Moore had to tell me as a young adult was a little more serious. I had a deformed radial head and ulna. It wasn't a result of a mishap on a dock in Maine. I was born with it. Without an operation, what happened on the dock could happen all over again, to the point where I would be severely deformed and the arm would become useless.

With the operation, there was a fifty-fifty chance my arm could be paralyzed. I didn't like those odds. But as it turned out, it was a very small world. Dr. Moore's own daughter had the exact same condition. I had to ask if she had the operation and if she had, if she was paralyzed. She had had the operation, and it was successful. I liked those odds a lot better.

But this was not a snap decision for either of us. Dr. Moore explained this operation could only be performed once my bones had reached full growth, when I became twenty-one. That was almost a year off. I was already engaged to marry Lewis B. Sharp and old enough to know I wanted this operation. But the most important thing for me at that moment was that my parents not find out what a roll of the dice the procedure was. I didn't want them worried, so I made Dr. Moore promise me he wouldn't tell them.

As my day of reckoning drew near, I thought about what it might be like to loose the use of my right arm, and I decided I'd have to be prepared for anything. So with six months to go, I started practicing writing with my left hand. I read about what the operation entailed—nerves would be arranged, bone fragments would be removed. And if it didn't go according to plan, I'd be using my left hand to write Mom and Dad a letter about why I had sheltered them from the facts.

The operation lasted four-and-a-half hours. As far as I was concerned, it could have been a month. I was on Demerol for the pain, in la-la land, but I understood one thing—I wasn't going to be paralyzed. In my room, directly across from my bed, there was a large clock on the wall with a big sweeping second hand. My next shot of Demerol came every hour on the hour. The shot lasted about a half hour. During that half hour, I was giddy. I felt like the hostess at a cocktail party. During the following half hour, the party was over. I was in pain and watching that second hand till the party would start again.

On my third day of recovery, Dr. Moore walked into the room with his entourage of residents and interns right behind him. The doctor had a nickname among this crew, and that nickname was "God." He was very strict with his students in the hope they would one day wind up more like God. But this happened to be the hostess-at-the-cocktail-party half-hour. So I flew out of bed in my blue babydoll nightgown and gave God a hug.

*　*　*

Now, at the kitchen table in Fort Washington, the clock on the wall hit eleven-thirty. My daydreaming—and my night dreaming—had worn off. It dawned on me that I really needed to be studying for a different exam.

The next day, I found Zach Clayton's phone number and called him at his office. I asked him to send me a copy of the state rules and regulations book for boxing. He was only too happy to do so. And he told me to study hard. Not only did he expect accurate scores on the rounds of each fight I saw, but he would be asking me questions at any given moment, some out of the rule book and some not. Like the boxers I would be scoring, I would have to be fast on my feet.

"Judges should not be swayed by blood or the swelling of a boxer. There is no question that some boxers cut more easily than others. Just because a boxer is cut does not necessarily mean he is losing the round."

So read the *Pennsylvania State Athletic Commission Judge's Manual*. I had learned that one without even trying, but I had a feeling if I was going to stick with this thing, I would have to relearn it at least a few times. Not far below was another guideline.

"Everyone in boxing knows there is no one infallible method of scoring. In fact, no two rounds of a boxing contest are precisely the same, even though they may appear to be to the novice observer. Judging is not an exact science."

This was a concept I had also more or less grasped on my own. But I didn't know if seeing it in print should bring me relief or distress. On one hand, or glove, I wanted the freedom to see action in the ring—or anywhere else in life, for that matter—as I honestly saw it. On the other hand, I wanted the security of being right. With that security came the satisfaction of doing a good job.

But who was setting the standard here, when the very rulebook I was relying on stated outright that there was no such standard? I knew the answer in my gut. The standard was the other judges. At the moment, the only other judge in my world was Zach Clayton. But maybe, just maybe one day, the standard would be a whole slew of other judges. And every last one of those judges was a man. Was this, then, the point of the whole exercise? To see things as a bunch of men did? If that was the case, then maybe by succeeding I would be failing. If, however, what I developed was truly my own perspective, then perhaps by failing I would be succeeding.

The Arena, located on Market Street not far from the University of Pennsylvania, had been the home to countless high-profile and local fights in the Philadelphia for the better part of the Twentieth Century. When you saw it from the outside, you were less than impressed. It had the look of an oversized concrete block pool hall or a garage dominating a treeless corner with overhead electric poles standing not quite vertically, like many of the fighters inside. I couldn't imagine what would have brought me there prior to marrying Bob. But now I was thrilled to be there, and excited someone cared exactly what I knew.

"Where do you focus?" Zach Clayton was asking me a question, and right now I was definitely focused on him. "Come on, lady, I'm asking you, where do you focus when you're watching a fight?"

"A judge," I said, quoting from the good book, "should always focus at a point directly between the two boxers so that he can observe the actions of both boxers. Never allow yourself to get lulled into looking at just one boxer."

"Not bad, lady. Not bad." The commissioner had a twinkle in his eye again. "Now make sure when you're actually watching, that's what you're doing. Don't drift off. Don't get conned by the guy throwing fancy punches all over the place. Remember, you may be watching the loser."

"I didn't memorize the book so I could forget it during the bout," I said.

"Well," Clayton said, "I hope you didn't memorize all the wrestling rules. You're not responsible for that."

"Don't worry," I said.

The commissioner's comment was a reference to the fact that the book I had, as of late, been married to as much as to my own husband also included the state's wrestling rules. I had enough to wrestle with without learning how to judge that, too. I walked back to my seat in the third row. I had on a straightforward dark pants suit with a white collared shirt. After all, "Judges should dress professionally in a coat and tie, in a business-like manner." I skipped the tie. If I was going to succeed at this or at least have a shot, I would have to interpret and adapt, right down to the attire.

That included my demeanor. As I settled in, I recalled another line from the book: "Judges should conduct themselves in a 'professional' manner at all times. This includes never talking or commenting about the work of other ringside officials." My approach to life, at least prior to now, had been easygoing. I was comfortable in my own skin and could trade funny comments whether I had to or not. Holding in your feelings and opinions as a busy mom or an aspiring whatever wasn't going to do you much good. In fact, it was going to give you an ulcer.

But the code of conduct here in the Arena—or for that matter, in any other arena I hoped to succeed—seemed to be different. I took a quick glance at the people seated near me and reminded myself not to fraternize with them. That included even my own husband.

Zach Clayton didn't seem to have that conflict. He seemed to be himself at all times, jokes and everything else. If he was particularly bored at a meeting, he would have an aid come get him with an "emergency" phone call. I envied Clayton a bit, because I wanted the best of both worlds—not just to be successful, but to be successful *as myself.*

Then I caught myself being less than fair. Clayton had come a long, long way. And it didn't all happen ringside. The truth was, making a full living in or around the ring was next to impossible. Clayton had been a Philadelphia fireman for thirty years and was a lieutenant by the time he retired. That was three decades of running into burning buildings and hoping to come out alive. It made the ring seem tame.

During those years, Zach Clayton made an effort to talk to and work with underprivileged youth in Philadelphia, particularly kids in gangs. That cause survived beyond the firehouse, and just a few weeks earlier, December 19, 1972 to be exact, Clayton had been appointed by Mayor Frank Rizzo as chief gang control coordinator for the City of Philadelphia. He had an office on the 16th floor of the Municipal Services Building. Most days revolved around reaching out to many of the more than 5,000 gang members in 100 different gangs around the city and giving these guys some sort of alternative—whether they took it or not.

And yet, Zach Clayton was far from finished proving himself. I had just read an in-depth article in the *Temple News* discussing whether Clayton was part of a "celebrity syndrome," where fame in one walk of life opened doors in other walks, regardless of merit. The article went on to dissect whether it was possible for anyone to really make a dent in the gang situation. Worse still, it conjectured whether the man some had called an "Uncle Tom" was the right man for the job.

So in truth, even Zach Clayton, with all the feathers in his cap, was not done being accepted as himself by the public. Maybe no one was ever done. If you were a black man, that particular struggle was likely to outlive your time on Earth. If you were a woman trying to do anything out of the ordinary, it was usually the same raw deal. Perhaps, I thought, that was part of what motivated Commissioner Zach Clayton when it came to me. He was more than my mentor. He was my advocate.

It was intermission at the Spectrum. I had turned in all my cards for the first three bouts. Zach Clayton was making his way over to where I sat in the fourth row. The final two or three rounds of the last fight could have gone either way. One of them I scored a draw. That was a no-no, and no doubt the commissioner was going to give me a demerit.

"Lady," he said, "I've got good news and bad news for you."

"Give me the bad news first," I said. "I always like to get that over with."

"Okay," he said. "The bad news is, you and Bob have to drive to Harrisburg Thursday."

"Well," I said, "Harrisburg's not so bad from Fort Washington. Only two hours. There are worse cities. What's the good news?"

"The good news, lady, is Thursday, you're going to be appointed the first lady professional boxing judge in the country."

Two words came out of my mouth unfiltered: "Right on!"

CHAPTER THREE

IN THIS CORNER, AT FIVE-FOOT-ONE...

I knew Governor Milton Jerrold Shapp saw the future. After serving in the U.S. Army Signal Corps in North Africa and Europe during World War II, he took out a $500 loan backed by the G.I. Bill and started a business. While thousands of returning veterans did the same thing, Shapp's loan wasn't for a dry goods store, a butcher shop, or a garage.

At a time when commercial television itself was in its infancy, Shapp's new company would provide TV via coaxial cable. While American families in 1948 would be thrilled to be able to afford a TV and get any sort of signal, Shapp knew certain parts of the country would receive only weak signals from a transmitter due to land formations or distance. The Allentown region of Shapp's adopted state of Pennsylvania was a prime example. The area known as the Lehigh Valley was surrounded by mountains that would block almost any TV signal, cutting off the home of Bethlehem Steel and tens of thousands of middle class families from the new and promising medium.

So at the very same time another Milton—Milton Berle—was winning millions of fans with his new show *Texaco Star Theater*, Shapp set up shop and made the Lehigh Valley one of his first customer bases. By 1967, when Milton Shapp sold his interest in Jerrold Electronics to the General Instrument Company, he was a very rich man.

But in the 1960s, Shapp's maverick streak was really just beginning. After working on the campaign to elect John F. Kennedy president, Shapp immersed himself in politics. He spent millions of his own dollars fighting the merger of the Pennsylvania Railroad with the New York Central and made a lot of powerful enemies along the way. He lost his first bid for governor of Pennsylvania in 1966 due in part to those same enemies. And when he won the statehouse the next time around, in 1970, Governor

Milton J. Shapp was a maverick who hit the ground running.

His agenda was progressive by any standard. It included welfare reform, consumer rights legislation, and a flat no-deductions state income tax. His insurance reform included making Pennsylvania one of the first no-fault states in the country. He created the Pennsylvania State Lottery to help fund infrastructure improvements and pay for other things the taxpayers were reluctant to do. And as the Watergate crisis started heating up, Shapp was way out in front, proposing a Sunshine Law as thorough as anything any state had ever seen.

And now, I was part of that future. As Bob and I rode along Route 76 toward Harrisburg, the phrase still rang in my head like the bell at the end of a round: *First woman professional boxing judge in the country.* I was excited. I was numb. I tried to figure out exactly where I fit in during this tumultuous time, when equal rights and equal pay for women was debated publicly on a daily basis. I hadn't tried to strike a blow on behalf of women. The blow I was striking was really on behalf of myself. I needed to get out of the house, and if nothing else, I had already succeeded wildly at that.

Then I recalled a few other things about Governor Shapp. He was Jewish, born in Cleveland to Mr. and Mrs. Aaron Shapiro. Milton Shapiro changed his name to Shapp to avoid some of the stigma that still went along with being Jewish in America, even in the first half of the Twentieth Century. But he remained a practicing Jew in every way. Faith would come in handy. Shapp went through the Great Depression finding no employment luck even with a degree in electrical engineering and took a job as a coal truck driver.

Shapp was tested again in just his second year in office. In June of 1972, only a matter of months before my trip to Harrisburg, Hurricane Agnes swept through Pennsylvania and wreaked havoc. So much rain fell in the Scranton/Wilkes-Barre area that graveyards were destroyed and coffins floated down the streets. Forty-eight people in the state died, thousands were left homeless, and the damage was put at over two billion dollars. When the Susquehanna River overflowed, Shapp and his wife had to be rescued from the governor's mansion. Pennsylvania faced a massive recovery effort, and Governor Shapp took it on like he did everything else, boldly and aggressively.

With this as his past, I decided that I really did fit in to the future. I was a survivor, too. I had always put a hundred and ten percent into everything I did. And this endeavor, professional boxing judge, was not going to be any different, except that maybe this time I'd go for a hundred and twenty percent. Whatever happened and whatever anyone thought about why I was doing what I was doing and how it might fit in, I was going to be damned good at it. No matter what the women's libbers or their detractors might assume. *That*, as I saw it, was the *future*.

As Bob and I walked up the stairs of the Capitol Building, I caught a reflection of myself in a window. I had on a colorful print dress with all sorts of flowers all over it. Why not? It was a colorful era. I was a big fan of the miniskirt, but Bob had nixed that, and I didn't argue. He was insistent that once I got the chance to judge a real fight, a conservative pants suit was the way to go. He was probably right, but this wasn't a fight. It was my big day, and the print dress represented a compromise of sorts. Plus it was just a little short, and I had decent legs.

Governor Shapp's office was very austere, far more so than my short, colorful print dress. The only colors standing out were on the various flags hanging. But that was only true of the office itself. Crammed into the office were at least a dozen members of the press, radio reporters, and TV crews. It was a spectacle, and as they swarmed I realized I was at the center of it.

Zach Clayton stood near the governor. The commissioner asked me if I was "ready for round one, lady."

"You bet," I said.

Both Clayton and Shapp gleamed. Governor Shapp was a friendly looking man about halfway between my height and Bob's. Shapp shook hands with both of us and congratulated me. Someone handed me a big pair of boxing gloves. I got the idea before it was even explained. I was supposed to mug for the camera while pretending to take a swing at the governor. It sounded like the most clichéd gimmick some overworked staffer could think of at the moment. I thought this would be the first of dozens of photo-ops like it—that is, if I was lucky to last that long.

So I put the gloves on because, after all, this was only round one. But I didn't want to take a jab at the governor, not even in jest. That wasn't the idea here, not even close. I was the governor's creation, his and the commissioner's. I wanted to make them proud and never regret the day they stuck their necks out for me. The three of us had something in common, and it wasn't precisely boxing.

I reached my left glove out gently—my right arm unable to straighten completely. But I didn't quite straighten out my left arm either. Governor Shapp held up his right palm to block my fictitious punch, and the cameras flashed. Then I let out my real jab. I smiled at the governor and said, "Local Jewish girl makes good." He broke out laughing. The cameras kept flashing. Shapp was hysterical, and I laughed with him. He got it. I connected.

After I was sworn in, the questions came flying at me and answers came flying back out. Joe McMahon of the *Philadelphia Bulletin* asked me about my approach to judging. "One good punch is as good as ten jabs," I said. "I will look for aggressiveness, defensive skill, and clean hitting."

Speaking of defense, Zach Clayton came right to mine. "While preparing, Carol has done exceptionally well," Clayton said. "Especially on some unusual fights that were hard to judge." Bob was next into the ring: "She'll be fine. It's actually harder to judge a fight sitting in the audience than it is being isolated, sitting on a stool at ringside."

McMahon wanted to know where I stood on women's rights. "I'm for them," I said. "Of course I am. I'm a woman. But I'm not a women's libber. I'm not in it for that reason. I just want to get enjoyment out of it. I will be just like the other judges. I won't smoke a cigar, but I might wear a turtleneck." Next, McMahon wanted to know how my kids felt about my new career. I had to stop and think a second. I knew what they thought about practically everything, but I only had a hint of what they really thought about this strange development. It was so new.

"Margie and Carol Paula are really excited," I said. "My sons Jimmy and Kenny are 12 and 10, and they're excited too, but they're also a little annoyed. And I think that's because they feel their mother knows something better than they do. They're boys. They should know a little more than Mom about fighting, don't you think?"

Connie Bramson of the *Harrisburg Patriot-News* stepped up and asked if I was an athlete myself, and I told her all about my father, Solo Blank, the New York State tennis champion during his NYU days. Then about my mother, Dorothy, the horseback rider. Then about my brother Arthur, the golfer, and my sister the tennis player. As for me, I did a little bit of everything. Bramson's next question seemed logical—whether the athlete in me had any desire to take my abilities into the ring, not as a fighter but as a referee. I looked over at Bob quickly and considered some of the feats I had seen him pull off over the past eighteen months.

"That's carrying it too far," I said. "That takes great physical strength. Sometimes the referee has to push the two bodies apart. Have you seen the size of those heavyweights?"

Bramson wanted to know what I would consider to be the pinnacle of my career. I surprised myself with a quick answer: "To someday judge a heavyweight title fight. And also to someday judge a title fight in Europe." These thoughts hadn't crystallized for me until they passed through my lips. But they made sense. What woman with any ambition didn't want to go as high as she could? And what woman didn't want a trip to Europe? A reporter named Stan Hochman took the conversation down another road entirely—what might happen if the husband is refereeing a given fight and the wife is judging? What would breakfast be like the next morning? "We'd probably put on the gloves ourselves," I said. "Actually, Bob is so flamboyant, he'd like the idea of us working the same fight. You know, it might make things more exciting at home."

"Actually," Bob said, "they're already exciting enough."

"So when is this fight?" Hochman asked. "You know, Carol's first fight."

Yes, there was that little matter—judging a real fight with real consequences. That was an unknown. I explained that had been one of the topics of conversation on the ride over to Harrisburg on this very morning. The next fight card was at the Spectrum on the 19th of February, less than three weeks away. Neither of us had received a call, but a call could come any day. And so as bleak as the weather was in the Northeast and as much as we thought about going to Florida for a little vacation, we decided to stay home in Fort Washington and make ourselves available.

It was time to go, and I didn't want to. I took one last look around the room and thought, *Wow, this is the way Marilyn Monroe must have felt*. And I liked it.

I was still a little numb on the ride home, but as Bob drove I had some reading material to keep me occupied. On my way out of the governor's office, I had been handed a copy of a press release. "Carol Polis," it read, "has landed a solid blow against male supremacy in an arena where women have never before been able to enter. Governor Shapp is delighted that the challenger is a Pennsylvanian and that the victory was achieved in the Commonwealth."

If there had been any doubt left about where the governor's heart lay, it was now gone. But a little farther down, what jumped off the page was something I had evidently said. "Mrs. Polis, who describes herself as a 'very, very bored housewife,' developed her eagle eye for the nuances of the ring from the close observation of professional fights refereed by her husband and from years of arbitrating amateur encounters among her sons, aged ten and twelve, and her daughters, aged six and eight." I thought the extra "very"—their add, not mine—was gratuitous. And I considered how in the future I'd need to consider how far my quips and exaggerations might travel.

Most importantly, I doubted I'd ever be bored again. As we pulled up in front of our house at 1301 Highland Avenue, we saw reporters waiting for us on the front porch and on the lawn. I thought back to how I hadn't wanted my press conference in the governor's office to end. And then I thought, *Be careful what you wish for*. Tomorrow was February 2,

Groundhog Day. But there was already a long shadow over me, an intense mixture of excitement and dread.

It didn't take long to get an assignment. I thought it would take a month or two and be for a minor card at the Blue Horizon or some comparable mid-size venue somewhere in eastern Pennsylvania. Instead, it took less than two weeks and was for a major card at the Spectrum. It was now February 14, Valentine's Day, and the fight would be February 19. It was a good thing we didn't go to Florida.

My first question to Bob was why the Athletic Commission waited until the event was so close to assign me? Bob's answer was not to take it personally one way or the other. From seeing what he went through, I knew he was right. Given the history of gambling and related corruption in the sport of boxing, the less notice the better. Knowing who would be refereeing and judging a particular fight well in advance gave the dark forces ample time to get to or influence an official. Even if there were no such dark forces, public perception of the fight game was better when officials were not open targets for very long.

The opening hours of my public assignment to a card contained no shady characters, only more reporters. The only dark forces were in my head. Yet I was probably happier than anyone else for the short notice. I couldn't have waited weeks in this condition.

Was I really going to be judging a fight between Ernie Shavers and Jimmy Young? I certainly knew who they were, and I was learning more every minute. Ernie "Black Destroyer" Shavers was a top contender for the heavyweight crown. He was originally from Alabama and had turned pro in 1969. In only four years since, he had compiled an almost unimaginable record of 43 wins and 2 losses.

Simply having that many bouts in a period of four years was amazing in itself. It meant fighting once a month or so with little or no recuperation before training for the next fight. Of course, winning all but two of those bouts was a feat. But how Shavers won most of those fights was the real story. Of 43 victories, 42 were by knockouts. These were knockouts, not merely knockdowns.

Ernie Shavers was known as the hardest puncher around, and in an era of super strong, lightning quick heavyweights, that was certainly saying something. He was aggressive from the opening bell. He had an overhand right punch that was described alternately as a thing of beauty and an instrument of death. He came at you swinging, looking for a place to land that killer right, and far more often than not he found it. The television and radio ads for the upcoming fight announced: "Ernie Shavers causes blackouts."

Shavers' one serious liability was his tender jaw. He wasn't the best at taking a punch there. And while he swung away, he often tired himself out, possibly leaving himself vulnerable. So to win the fight, Shavers had to get his work done early, which he almost always did.

Jimmy Young was what his name said. At twenty-four, he was three years younger than Shavers. Young had turned pro the same year Shavers had but in that span fought only nine times, bringing in a record of six wins and three losses. Jimmy Young was known as a good defender and counter-puncher. He was agile in the ring, moving, bobbing, weaving, and hopefully wearing out his opponent by making him miss a lot. Young was considered a less powerful, less talented version of Muhammad Ali. Boxing experts generally considered the Shavers-Young bout to be a mismatch arranged opportunistically by Young's management for the primary purpose of a quick payday.

But Jimmy Young had something else going for him. He was a product of Philadelphia. Aside from New York, the City of Brotherly Love was the American capital of boxing. Its ambassador and king throughout the '60s and into the '70s was its most notable hometown product, Joe Frazier. Frazier was the man who inspired Jimmy Young to fight, and Young even trained in Frazier's famous Broad Street gym. It would go almost without saying that Jimmy Young's fondest hope was to have the torch passed to him.

But if that torch was going to be passed to him, it wasn't going to come directly from his idol, Joe Frazier. Just a few weeks earlier, on January 22, Joe Frazier had lost his heavyweight crown to George Foreman. In a bout called the "Sunshine Showdown", Frazier and contender Foreman met in Jamaica. This was a championship bout hyped to the hilt. Millions of Americans saw the fight courtesy of the new cable company, Home Box Office, or HBO, which for the very first time was carrying a championship bout. Milton Shapp, father of cable, must have been watching somewhere in Harrisburg and smiling.

The fight was short but did not disappoint. Foreman came out swinging. In only two rounds, he knocked Frazier down a total of six times. After the first knockdown, Frazier wasn't his normal alert self. Foreman's reach was incredibly long, several inches longer than Frazier's. If he was going to do any harm to Foreman, Frazier was going to have to get close, and that was going to be very hard. By the middle of the first round, Foreman was taking uppercuts. The uppercut was mostly a throwback to another era and a luxury in a fight this competitive. But Foreman's uppercuts were landing, and Frazier looked disoriented. Each time the champion fell, Howard Cosell yelled from ringside: "Down goes Frazier! Down goes Frazier!" It was what they called an instant classic.

The last knockdown was more of a knock-up. Foreman's blow appeared to lift Joe Frazier off his feet, shocking fans at ringside and around the world. When you took a closer look at it, Frazier's feet were still planted immediately after Foreman's final uppercut and didn't actually hop off the canvas until a split second later, probably the result of Frazier's own physical reaction to being hit so hard. Still, the visual effect at first glance was overwhelming. Amazingly, Frazier got up before the count of ten, but the referee waved his arms, mercifully ending the fight.

Foreman and Frazier had both gone into the fight undefeated—Frazier at 29-0 with 25 knockouts, Foreman at 37-0 with 34 knockouts. But Frazier was beginning to age, and Foreman was coming into his prime. George Foreman had been a wild man, often street fighting and getting into trouble with the law while growing up in Texas in the 1960s. When that energy got funneled into boxing, he won a gold medal for the United States in Mexico City at the 1968 Olympics. Foreman took criticism from many black Americans for proudly displaying the flag while others held their fists up in protest of racism in the U.S. But Foreman was no Uncle Tom. He was just grateful for the opportunity.

Now the deck was shuffled. For almost two years, a Frazier-Ali title fight rematch was being dangled in front of the public's eyes. But now George Foreman was the one to chase, for Ali and everyone else. Ernie Shavers was in a very small handful of top heavyweight prize fighters in the running for that chance. Every fight along the way meant either a big step closer or possibly the end of the dream. Shavers could be likened to Foreman in approach, Jimmy Young to Ali. Shavers and Young provided a contrast in styles with each other and a glimpse of the future of heavyweight boxing.

So Philadelphia, reeling from the defeat of its heavyweight champion and favorite son, had another big reason to root for its up-and-coming son, Jimmy Young. And squarely in the middle of the entire scenario, weighing in at 115 lbs., was yours truly. I wasn't sure I wanted to do it. It was too early in the game—way too early—to possibly change the course of boxing history one way or the other. I didn't want to rely on beginner's luck. I wanted my start in obscurity somewhere in a little hole where a mistake was simply a learning experience.

Only a few days earlier, a radio talk show host in Philadelphia had asked me what my greatest fear was. It wasn't an earthquake, fire, an explosion, or anything like that. It was a centipede. Just the thought of a hundred little legs crawling on me, up my arm, up my shoulder, moving slowly up my neck, was enough to send me screaming out into the street. But I had a new centipede now—Shavers vs. Young.

The Spectrum in Philadelphia seated eighteen thousand people. On this night, February 19, 1973, every last one of them seemed to be screaming their head off, and the fights hadn't even started yet. I had been here before, of course, but this night was different. My neck was on the line now.

Back in March of 1968, during hockey season, a piece of the Spectrum's roof had blown off during high winds. As a result, the building was closed for a while until repairs could be made. The Philadelphia Flyers had to relocate their home base to Quebec City. But as I looked up at the large circular roof of the building, it appeared solid, and I knew I would be staying right here in Philadelphia on this night.

Bob marched me down the aisle proudly, but at the end of the aisle was no altar. I was not wearing white but rather a white blouse with wide lapels beneath a sleeveless blue velvet vest. I had on a matching skirt. Bob wore a blue blazer over an open collared polo shirt and towered over me. People sitting to either side of us stood and watched. Flashbulbs went off, blinding us for an instant. Perhaps we made an attractive couple and that explained the attention. But more likely, the folks at ringside had some idea that a little bit of history was being made on this night and they were looking at the woman about to make it. That's how knowledgeable Philadelphia fight fans were.

They were more than just knowledgeable. While fight fans had a reputation for appearing disheveled and reeking of tobacco and alcohol, things had been changing the last few years. Many of the fans were dressed "snappily," as Bob put it. There were tailored suits, mink stoles, flashy jewelry, Rolex watches, two-hundred-dollar wing-tipped shoes. Boxing was where it was at. Ali, Frazier, Foreman, and the others were celebrities, and people around celebrities sort of became celebrities themselves, at least for a few rounds.

The moment came. Bob had to walk back up toward his seat and leave me at mine, ringside. His last words were, "This is your night, not mine." I felt like a kid left at sleep-away camp for the first time. The smile left my face. That was a good thing, because as the manual said, this was a serious endeavor. But the absence of my smile was no act.

Briefly, I said hello to the other judge. I was not going to say much. The more I said, the more inexperience I might reveal. The metal chair reserved for fight judge Carol Polis, as for any judge, was a bare Spartan hardback metal chair. I sat down literally at the ring, with the ring platform at chest level. Sitting back in the chair was awkward. The chair back was angled too far rearward. The last thing I wanted to appear to be was comfortable. Now that would have been an act. So I leaned forward, keeping my back as rigid as possible.

In front of me, the apron of the canvas was tied to the ring itself with a series of thick, taut ropes. I didn't think I ought to be touching the canvas in any way—not during the fight and not now. But I gave it one quick feel, because it was there and it relaxed me a bit. I could feel the crowd getting louder and louder, though I couldn't say I was actually hearing it. Just beyond the ropes, Ernie Shavers in his corner and Jimmy Young in his, looked much larger than fighters did when I was a spectator sitting several rows back. They were huge. I thought about what I would do if either of them sailed out of the ring on my side and decided I would panic. I was halfway there now.

I received a small temporary reprieve as we all stood for the National Anthem. This was a story in itself. The Supremes belted out the *Star Spangled Banner* in stupendous Motown fashion. But it was Jean Terrell singing lead, not Diana Ross. Terrell had replaced Ross three years earlier when Ross went solo. The Supremes were doing a show not far away in Cherry Hill, New Jersey, but convenience wasn't what brought them to the fight. Jean Terrell was the younger sister of Ernie Terrell, who was fighting in the third bout on tonight's card.

At six-foot-six, Ernie Terrell was one of the tallest heavyweight fighters ever to step in the ring. Like so many great fighters, he was from Chicago. Terrell had been a contender for a few years when a fluke of an opportunity occurred. On June 19, 1964, the World Boxing Association stripped Muhammad Ali of his heavyweight crown because of his association with the Nation of Islam. The country was split on this ruling and so was boxing itself. The World Boxing Council continued to recognize Ali as champ. Ernie Terrell was picked by the WBA to fight Eddie Machen for the vacated crown. When Terrell emerged victorious from that fight on March 5, 1965, he effectively held half of Ali's crown. Millions of boxing fans didn't like it, and neither did Ali.

Terrell had held his half of the crown for almost two years when on February 6, 1967 a unification bout was held. Animosities ran beyond professional pride. In the days leading up to the fight, Ernie Terrell refused to call Ali by his chosen name, calling him instead by his birth name, Cassius Clay. Ali announced to Terrell and to the world that he would do to this pretender what he had done a few years earlier to Floyd Patterson for committing the same offense. Ali would punish his opponent for as many rounds as possible without mercifully putting him on the canvas.

When it was Terrell's turn that night, Ali made good on his promise. For fifteen long rounds, Ali battered Terrell's nose and eyes till he could barely see from behind the swelling and blood. In between flurries, Ali taunted Terrell by screaming, "What's my name, Uncle Tom?" Terrell refused to utter it and went down in a lopsided decision which came too late for all but the most blood-thirsty onlookers.

The National Anthem—rockets, red glare, and all—was bloodless, and my reprieve was over. And then I got another one. Zach Clayton was suddenly a foot from me. He was like Moses at that moment, coming down from whatever mountain he came. I wanted him to take me to the promised land, which was life after this fight was over, my reputation as a sound judge having been firmly established. Neither he nor anyone else could do that for me, but Commissioner Zachary Clayton gave me the next best thing.

"Lady," he said, "don't worry. It'll be over in the third round."

"Thank God!" I said.

I didn't know how he knew, and I didn't want to know. I guessed he had been around the fight game so long, talked to managers, trainers, fighters, and understood who was up and who was down before the fighters themselves did. I also guessed Clayton understood me. I wondered how stone cold scared I looked. *Shavers is in the black trunks*, I thought. Just remember that. *The black trunks*.

The bell rang and the fighters rushed to the center of the ring. Shavers came out like a mad man on a mission swinging for the head. Young was weaving and bobbing. But here and there Shavers was connecting a glancing blow, and Young wasn't quite connecting with the counterpunch.

I thought it was strange the crowd had settled down so much with the action so fast and furious. Then I realized something. I couldn't hear a thing. I had lost my hearing. The noise, wherever it was, had gone past my threshold. I was in shock. In my own zone of fear. Ernie Shavers really did cause blackouts. The blows continued and I had to focus. Focus. But where? *A judge should always focus at a point directly between the two boxers so that he can observe the actions of both boxers.*

Shavers connected over the top with a right and Young's legs folded. He dropped to the canvas. The referee backed Shavers away and then began the count. It was as the commissioner said, but even earlier. I was out of the woods. Free and clear. Untested and grateful. I had some thoughts on the round, but they no longer mattered to anyone but me. Or so I thought. Jimmy Young rose from the canvas. The referee's count stopped at eight, and he brought the fighters back to the center of the ring. It was initiation all over again. And I still couldn't hear a thing.

A minute can be a long time when it's between rounds of your first fight. Even longer when you can't discuss it. With my right arm aching, I wrote down the score using my left hand. It turned out my left hand could shake as well as my right. And there it was, round one 5-3 for Shavers. This wasn't the back of a program. It wasn't for the commissioner's amusement. Playtime was over.

As round two began, I could see Jimmy Young had pulled himself together. He was focused again and counterpunching more effectively without taking solid blows. That was good for Young, bad for me. With the fight settling down this way, it could go on and on. And once it passed the fifth or sixth round, it would probably go all the way and I'd be on the hook. Another flurry of blows went by and strangely, I heard a lone male voice cut through the deafening silence: "Carol, did you know that was a low blow?" Whether it was my guardian angel or just some guy in the crowd being a smart alec, he was right. Score one for Young.

A cut had opened up around Jimmy Young's nose. I thought this might be my out. But I thought again. *Judges should not be swayed by blood or the swelling of a boxer.* Just because a boxer is cut does not necessarily mean he is losing the round. Another voice sliced through the crowd, a male voice, not the same as the one before: "Carol, I think I love you!" *I love you too, wherever you are.* Round two was ending and Jimmy Young was holding his own. Five to four for Young.

Round three began as round one had, in a fury. Shavers threw lightning combinations and Young was defensive, trying to minimize the damage. The fighters drifted over to my side of the ring, then precisely over to my position. Shavers' black trunks were against the ropes and towered directly over my head and strained neck. His black shoes were level with my eyes. I checked to make sure my hands were nowhere near the apron of the canvas.

I couldn't see Jimmy Young's face clearly when Shavers connected with a right over the top. His face was obscured by Shavers' shoulder. But I saw the aftermath—the spray. Jimmy Young was down and the referee was into his dance again. Young was dazed and bleeding. It was Hart versus Moyer all over again. Someone needed to stop this fight. But Young was now on his feet again and my heart was back in my throat. This was round three. Didn't anyone else hear what the commissioner said before the fight!

Shavers followed Young around the ring like a predator tiger on the television show *Wild Kingdom*. Young had his gloves up, and Shavers landed body punches that would have made a thud had I heard them. When Young lowered a glove, Shavers was there with a right-left-right. The fighters were now on the opposite side of the ring, potentially sparing me from a fall through the ropes. Round three was, mercifully or not, almost over, and I had it 5-3 for Shavers. Or maybe 5-2. Or maybe . . . .

The fight was over. The time was 2:59 into round three. The referee had thrown up his hands and called a TKO, a technical knockout. Young couldn't see and he was like a walking dead man. I was happy for Young he would live to see another day. I was happy for Shavers. Most of all, I was happy for myself. I could hear again. Like Rocky Graziano once said, "Somebody up there likes me."

Every face seemed relieved, maybe reflections of my own face. Bob was suddenly towering over me. "Well, Carol," he said, "you were saved, but not by the bell."

"You got that right," I said, looking up from my superfluous scorecard. Suddenly I felt disappointed, perhaps in myself. I didn't want to be saved. Not by the bell or by anything other than my own ability. The fight had been an initiation into battle, but for me not into victory or even defeat. I had limped through on crutches, one of prayer, the other of luck. That had to end sooner or later, and for me the sooner the better.

The second fight began. The opening bell and all other sounds rang clear. The bout was a ten rounder between heavyweights Richie Kates and Billy Freeman. I was zeroed in, focused, and relatively calm. For the crowd at the Spectrum, the bout was sort of a lull between the fight they had just seen and the next fight, the headline bout between ex-champion Terrell and Bill Drover. But I was sure this fight was everything to Kates and Freeman and sure it was everything for Carol Polis.

I was back to my training days, observing carefully, making mental notes, not getting wowed by fancy moves or dramatics. My back was straight, my hands off the apron, and my eyes almost unblinking. There was no reprieve here, no easy out, and I didn't want one.

I had it Kates over Freeman in ten rounds, 47-43. I handed in my scorecard feeling a little like a freshman at the University of Wisconsin knowing she had just passed a biology exam with flying colors. More importantly, like the fighter I needed to be, I was still standing.

CHAPTER FOUR
THE SMALLER THEY ARE, THE HARDER THEY FALL

When the phone rang at 6:50 AM, I knew from the ring it was my father. There were people who claimed that was impossible, that a ring was a ring no matter who was calling. But they didn't know my father. My father was a good guy and a great tennis player, but very strict and self-disciplined. My brother, sister, and I were supposed to make honor roll every time, and if there was a B mixed in with the A's, Dad wanted to know what the B was all about.

Dad was originally from New York and had come to Philadelphia to open a store with his brother. They named the store Consolidated Home Furnishings, but my mother, the easygoing one, nicknamed it Constipated Home Furnishings. Judging from how well the store did, however, it couldn't have been too constipated. TVs, dish sets, dining room sets, linens, and anything you could think of for the home came in and went out. My father was the first retailer in the area to sell things on an installment plan. He sent his men out every day to make the rounds and collect the weekly payments.

My brother and sister and I didn't know much about the business, though, other than the fact that it provided us with a pretty good lifestyle. And that it made us famous. Dad named a mattress for each of us. My brother's was dubbed the "King Arthur." Mine was the "Queen Carol." Our little sister, born five days after the attack on Pearl Harbor in December 1941, got the "Princess Nancy." People all over the Delaware Valley were sleeping on us, and we felt like royalty.

On this cold morning in February with the sun not quite up, the man of the house already on a commuter train, and the woman of the house scurrying around to make sure four kids were matched with the correct lunchbox, my father was calling from sunny Florida sounding relaxed but concerned.

"Your mother and I were watching *The Today Show*, and they did a piece on our daughter."

"Oh, that," I said. "I taped that yesterday."

"I wish you had called us," he said.

"Well," I said, "that's just how busy it's been. It's funny, I was going to call you today as a matter of fact."

"How on Earth did you get to be a professional boxing judge, Carol? How did this all happen? Last we heard you were getting your stock broker license."

"This is really Bob's thing," I said. "You know, he's been a referee for so long, and he kind of got me involved. And we thought it was a good idea to give us something to talk about. Something in common. It's really no big deal."

"Boxing's a rough sport."

"Well, I won't be in the ring, Dad. I can promise you that. They couldn't pay me enough to jump in there for a second!"

"Well, that's my point," he said. "Don't try to make any money out of this."

"I wish I could," I said. "The problem is, I honestly don't know how. But if you have any ideas, I'm all ears."

I played the whole thing down as much as possible, painting my newfound profession as a hobby and myself as an appendage to my husband. My father's fears seemed allayed, at least enough for him to put my mother on the phone. My mother could light up the room, even electronically from a thousand miles away. She was the peacemaker in the family. And even when she took a potshot here and there, it never sounded that bad. She saw things her way.

Her maiden name was Groskin. Her side of the family immigrated from Germany, and according to my mother the German Jews had all the education. Behind them flowed in the Russian Jews, who she said were still catching up. But there wasn't a mean bone in her body. She liked everybody. Everybody, that is, except Nixon. She hadn't joined the anti-Nixon chorus with everyone else in the past few months. My mother started her own chorus back in the '50s. And it wasn't about politics, which was discussed fairly infrequently around our house. My mother's opinion was based primarily on her own physical reaction.

According to my mother, whenever Nixon appeared on the TV screen, the hairs on the back of her neck stood up. She became generally uncomfortable and told us he was a liar. I remembered as a young lady watching him sweat bullets during the debate with handsome, young John F. Kennedy and feeling kind of sorry for Nixon. I couldn't dislike him, because he was a Quaker, and I had gone to a Quaker school. The meetings I had attended were so simple and beautiful. It was hard for me to believe that Richard Nixon didn't embody at least a small piece of that beauty.

But my mother was evidently on to something. What had started out as a slightly noteworthy break-in at the Democratic National Headquarters in June, had been linked to the Committee to Reelect the President. The FBI, prosecutors, and reporters were in a race to find out just how high up this conspiracy went and exactly who ordered a cover-up. What was now known as Watergate was beginning to dominate the nightly news and coming closer and closer each week to validating what my apolitical mother was saying back in the days of Elvis and Eisenhower.

I was a combination of these two wonderful people, my parents. Like my father, I could be focused and even stern when I needed to be, as I was sitting at ringside. Like my mother I was a conversationalist, caregiver, humorist, and an occasional shoulder to lean on. Somewhere in between I was a heck of a pragmatist, and that was the part of me that invited my mother and father to come to a boxing event with me whenever they visited from Florida.

What I learned from both of my parents over many years was what you refrained from saying was as much a part of being a lady—or, for that matter, a human being—as what you did say. As they wrestled with the notion of their daughter the professional boxing judge, there was plenty they didn't need to hear.

I felt sorry for my husband. He worked hard to pay our bills and his ex-wife's bills. She called our house several times a day, and that was a ring I could tell just as easily as my father's. Her main goal in life was to get her ex-husband on the phone and sling as much Jewish guilt as the line would hold. Bob was competent when it came to keeping two heavyweights in the ring from hitting each other below the belt, but his skills on the phone, at least with his ex-wife and current wife, were horrible. He was particularly nasty and sarcastic and, whether he knew it or not, propelling her to the next unpleasant call.

Bob's upset carried over well beyond the phone conversation and onto my kids. Kenny was very hyper, and Bob would tear into him. "Why don't you quit bouncing off the walls? Or better yet, why don't you try shutting up for a minute?" My instinct as a mother was to give it right back to him. My instinct as my parents' oldest daughter was to recognize the strain Bob was under and just let it go. In the end, what I sometimes found myself doing was worse than either of those two options—starting in on his kids.

Then there were the phone calls that lit up my world. They came from newspapers, radio stations, and TV stations looking for a piece of the story on America's first female boxing judge. I was champing at the bit, but I tried to answer every last call with the same gracious, polite "Hello, Carol Polis speaking." One of those calls came from veteran Philadelphia sportscaster Al Meltzer. Another, right behind it, came from Joe Pellegrino, who was the sports reporter at Philadelphia's ABC network affiliate, WPVI Channel 6. Everybody in the City of Brotherly Love, however, knew Joe not by the station call letters but by the name of the news broadcast—*Action News.*

Action News discontinued the practice of having a staid newscaster sit behind a desk for a half hour and read the day's events. *Action News* sent reporters and even anchormen out to where the stories were happening and kept the news segments brief, lively, and chock full of footage. In the three short years since taking its name, Philadelphia's Action New had been cloned all over the country.

Along with Larry Kane and Jim O'Brien, Joe Pellegrino was a

household name in Philadelphia. Pellegrino had been a top college athlete himself. The questions he asked me were ones that for the most part I was already used to answering: What I thought of the violence in boxing, what my kids thought of my new job, whether I thought women should get into the ring, and what advice I had for young women looking to get into the world of sports.

Like Frankie Valli, Joe had a real ease on camera and classic Italian good looks, More than that—he had an audience. After my appearance on *Action News*, our phone rang off the hook just from friends and neighbors who had seen it. What constituted fame in the eyes of most people was a visit to their own private celebrity corner, and with *Action News*, that's where I was for this particular fifteen minutes.

Bob, however, thought I was burning the candle of fame at both ends and let me know it from time to time. When I received an interview request from Lester Bromberg, the boxing writer, Bob told me I should turn it down. "Lester Bromberg," he said, "was covering boxing before you were born."

That was true. Bromberg, who for the past several years wrote for the *New York Post*, covered boxing for the *New York World Telegram* from 1931 to 1966, scrutinizing action in the ring while the action outside the ring changed the planet several times over. In 1962, Bromberg's book, *Boxing's Unforgettable Fights*, was published and soon became as much of a classic as the bouts it described. Each feather in Bromberg's cap was a reason in Bob's eyes for me to decline and a reason in my eyes to jump at the chance.

"Why does it matter what he did before I was born?"

"When it comes to boxing," Bob said, "you were born yesterday. You've judged exactly one card. You're not ready for this. You're not ready for Lester Bromberg. He's a walking history book of the entire sport of boxing. You're a novice. A promising novice, but a novice. I just don't see why you would want to go around advertising that fact."

"I think that fact is already well established," I said. "Who cares?"

"What if he asks you about the Louis-Marciano fight in 1951? Do you remember that fight? Did you even see it or listen to it? You can't really talk boxing with the likes of a Lester Bromberg unless you have what's called a lexicon. There are dozens of fights you would just be expected to know all about before the conversation can even begin."

"Bob," I said, "this is an interview, not the Spanish Inquisition. Did it ever cross your mind that he might just be fascinated with the idea of a woman in the ultimate man's world? Did it ever occur to you that having done thousands of boxing stories, he might want to do one that's a little different?"

"And what would make you think that?" Bob asked.

"Because that's what he told me," I said. "On the phone, when we spoke."

I wound up doing the interview. Not only wasn't it the Spanish Inquisition, Lester Bromberg thought it was vital for the sport to change with the times. A woman judge was, in his view, a good example of what needed to be done. In fact, he thought the sport probably needed a few more women. Bromberg's wife sat in on part of the interview and was very gracious. Given her husband's first-class demeanor, I wasn't at all surprised.

But pressure is a formless entity. Going against my husband's wishes in one instance meant complying in another. I found myself turning down requests for interviews and appearances selectively for good measure. Doing so somehow relieved me of the gnawing feeling that I was stealing Bob's show. It also made me angry.

Zach Clayton called on a Thursday to let me know I'd been selected to judge the next Monday night fight card at the Spectrum. That meant literally the next Monday, four days away. And this time I wouldn't be told till the day of the fight which bouts I'd be working. This was an additional precaution the Commission often took to reduce the odds of a fix. At the moment, I wasn't even sure I knew enough to fix a fight if I wanted to.

There was one immediately noticeable difference at the Spectrum on Monday, March 26 when Bob and I walked in as compared to the last time. An immense, thick curtain hung from the ceiling literally cutting the arena in half, blocking the south side from view. Bob had explained to me a while back that Monday night fights without a major bout on the card were unlikely to come close to packing the Spectrum. The sight of thousands of empty seats wasn't favorable for the venue, the crowd, the fighters, or the sport itself. So the empty seats were cordoned off— out of sight, out of mind—with a more realistic eight thousand or so seats remaining.

There was another difference on this night, this difference solely regarding me. Gone was the white blouse, now replaced with a dark brown one. And gone were the colorful vest and skirt, also replaced by darker versions. When I had arrived home from my "initiation" back in February, I noticed a few tiny dark red dots on my sleeve. Then a few more, then a whole lot more on the other sleeve and still more along the front buttons. It dawned on me that these were blood stains.

They certainly weren't the kind of blood stains I was used to. As a mom, I got blood out of my kids' clothing all the time, but those were big blotches from scraped knees, skimmed elbows, and an occasional bloody nose. I was more worried about drying up the tears than removing the blood from shirts and pants, which just took a little presoak with Tide. But these numerous tiny dots were foreign to me and even a little chilling. The idea that the air was so diffuse with blood that you couldn't see it coming was kind of macabre.

The solution, at least near the ring, was simple—wear dark clothes. The darker the better. Yes, the blood would still be there, but like the empty seats behind the curtain wouldn't be seen. Then at home, all fight clothes would go immediately into the wash. The other judges all wore dark clothes as well, and it wasn't for style points.

The third and final difference tonight wasn't about the arena or me. It was Bob. Whereas in February he escorted me down the aisle so proudly, tonight he was preoccupied. One way that showed was in the warnings he issued me every few seconds about not talking to this official or that spectator. It bordered on paranoid. Whatever was driving him, the message to me was clear—I lacked judgment, the one thing I was being paid, however little, to have.

As we filed into our seats, we couldn't avoid talking to Jerry Green. Green was known around Philadelphia as the King of Mirrors. He owned a chain of stores specializing in mirrors for the walls, the ceiling, the bathroom, and anywhere else one might care to see oneself engaging in some of life's most private or mundane activities. He was a celebrity in the sense that if you bought up enough local air time during soap operas, professional wrestling, and game shows and had the chutzpah to do every last commercial yourself while shouting at the top of your lungs in a showroom, you were a celebrity.

Jerry Green was currently under investigation by the Department of Consumer Affairs. Were he to look in one of his many mirrors, he would have seen a middle-aged man dressed as billed, in all green. His jacket, slacks, and shirt were green. His tie had green stripes, and his socks were green with a hint of aqua. His toupee was brown, but the night was young. He had on more jewelry than I owned, but as far as I was concerned, the King of Mirrors didn't have a thing over Queen Carol. After a few pleasantries between local celebrities, it was to our seats, where my husband could continue to explain to me just how green I was.

My thoughts drifted to our babysitter, who might have been in for more bouts this evening than I was. That it was a Monday was bad enough. It was also one of those days where the preliminaries at home were building up to the main event, which I sensed was scheduled for sometime after Mommy and Daddy were out of the house. The way it worked out was the babysitter would be refereeing for the kids, Mommy would be judging for the adults, and Daddy would be refereeing no one on this particular evening.

That had to be part of the problem as far as I was concerned. Bob felt a little left out. He hadn't gotten an assignment in a while, and here I was after two months in the limelight showing him up just by showing up. I had to accept his disappointment. My mantra as of late had been, "Please, God, just give me one problem a day." So although I had a sulking husband on my hands, at least I wasn't home refereeing, and I had to consider myself even.

I had some time to settle in. My first bout was the third scheduled bout of the night—Paul Kallai versus Leroy Krienbrook. It was a flyweight bout. There was heavyweight, light heavyweight, middleweight, welterweight, lightweight, featherweight, bantamweight, and flyweight. The only thing lighter than flyweight was my weight. On a good day. Krienbrook and Kallai were both listed at 112 pounds. That was generally not a weight you associated with a boxer, but rather one you associated with a jockey. Funny thing, Paul Kallai *was* a jockey.

Kallai was well known locally from races at Garden State Park in Cherry Hill, New Jersey and other nearby venues. But there was a time when he was a genuine international star. Kallai was originally from Hungary. In the 1950s he was considered by many to be the top jockey in both his home country and neighboring Austria. But during the 1950s in Hungary, you couldn't enjoy the freedom off the racetrack that you enjoyed on it.

After World War II, the remaining great powers of the planet were determined not to have a third world war and in particular not to allow Germany to start it. Europe was effectively divided up between the United States and the Soviet Union, and the Cold War was on. The U.S. formed NATO freely with Great Britain, France, Italy, Portugal, the Netherlands, and several other countries; while the Soviet Union compelled Hungary, Poland, Czechoslovakia, Bulgaria, Romania, and Albania to join the Warsaw Pact. Like the other countries in the Eastern Block, Hungary's only crime was its geography—that it lay between the Soviet Union and what was left of Germany.

Following World War II, Hungary was controlled by the Communist Party, which was in turn controlled by the Soviets. The specter of Joseph Stalin pervaded the country's affairs, and when a reformer such as Imre Nagy tried to liberalize the government, he was promptly removed from office. The Magyars had been an inventive, freedom-loving people for a thousand years, and a major conflict with the Soviets at some point was inevitable.

In 1956, students, workers, and citizens from all walks of life revolted against Hungarian Communist rule by taking to the streets and shutting down day to day affairs. For a few weeks, the rebels had the sympathy of the entire free world and most of the non-free world. The Hungarian police showed up at the scene, took one look at the protesters, and decided not just to join them but to help arm them.

But crushing popular revolts was a Soviet specialty, and when the Kremlin sent tanks rolling into Hungary in November 1956, hope turned to horror. The Soviet generals ordered tanks to drive straight over men, women, and children occupying the streets in Budapest. The penalty for not following such orders was immediate execution. Leaders of the Hungarian revolt begged the U.S. to intervene, but America had a containment policy that accepted the Soviet right to dominate its satellite nations.

Like many thousands of ambitious young men and women, the famous Hungarian jockey Paul Kallai immigrated to the United States after the failed revolt. He carried with him a name that was very famous to Hungarians. Gyula Kallai, perhaps a distant cousin, served as prime minister after the 1956 revolt. Jailed in the early 1950s by the Communists for straying too far from hard line communism, Gyula Kallai was "rehabilitated," which consisted mostly of recanting a series of controversial statements.

But Paul Kallai wasn't interested in being rehabilitated. He was interested in riding. He was a very young man and had his best years ahead of him. There were plenty of racetracks in the United States, and horse racing was a universal language. In 1962, he rode Accordant in the Fall Highweight Handicap at Aqueduct in Queens, New York and weighed in at only 109 pounds. The horses were booked to carry 124 pounds. The usual means of making up the difference was to strap lead pads under the saddle. Instead, Kallai wore a leather belt filled with 15 pounds of sand. He claimed the belt method was easier on the horse.

There was no making up the difference in a boxing ring and no thought of anyone's comfort other than perhaps your own. Why a successful horse jockey in his late 30s felt compelled to get between the ropes and expose his compact features to the kind of punishment normally reserved for a dirt track was a bit of a mystery. According to one newspaper, Kallai had boxed as an amateur back in Hungary and as of late had been mixing it up for fun with some of his peers. I supposed tonight represented a sort of jockey's midlife crisis.

Before it was time to take my seat at ringside, I was propositioned. And the proposition involved jewelry. One of the owners of Bailey Banks & Biddle happened to be sitting behind us and struck up a conversation between rounds. Fortunately, Bob was busy having his own conversation. Bailey Banks & Biddle was the oldest jewelry store in the country, dating back to 1832, when they were established right here on Chestnut Street in Philadelphia. Their customers included presidents, senators, and ambassadors. They minted coins for both the Union and the Confederacy. And now they wanted to do a commemorative piece for Carol Polis.

It wasn't going to be a diamond necklace or a silver dollar, just a dog tag. Over the past couple of years, dog tags had become a fad with young people. What started back in the Civil War as a way to identify a soldier's body was now also a way of paying homage to a hero, a celebrity, or a loved one. Young women wore dog tags with the name of their boyfriend fighting in Vietnam. Kids wore dog tags with the name of their favorite band.

And now the man from Bailey Banks & Biddle wanted my permission for his company to issue a commemorative Carol Polis, First Woman Professional Boxing Judge dog tag. Gold plated. To appear in a print advertisement. The idea that wearing my name on an identification tag might inspire some young lady was a nice ego boost, especially moments before my fight as I was beginning to feel my nerves. It took about a second and a half to consider it, and I said yes on one condition—that he send me a Carol Polis commemorative dog tag for each of my kids.

I settled in the best I could in my stiff metal ringside chair. Right off the bat, I was relieved. This was no Shavers-Young fight. At 112 pounds a piece, neither fighter could do that much harm by landing on me. While of course I knew their weights going in, seeing was believing. The very next thing I noticed was how cute Paul Kallai was. His opponent, Larry

Krienbrook, was a good looking man of 25, but Kallai reminded me of a combination of Gilligan and Ringo, with the added attraction that he was in tremendous shape. There was literally not an ounce of fat on his body.

The fight began in a fury. Kallai and Krienbrook came right at each other swinging. Their exchanges were almost too fast to follow. Whatever the heavyweights had over them in raw power, these little guys—whose weights just about added up to one heavyweight—made up for easily in speed. It almost looked like a different sport, like kids fighting frantically in a sandbox. Like regular boxing in fast forward.

Except it wasn't quite regular boxing. Krienbrook was a pro. Between flurries of punches, he moved his head around looking for an opening. When he threw punches, most of them landed. Some were body blows and some landed on the side of Kallai's boyish face. Kallai was fearless. Fast as they were, no barrage of jabs and hooks from another flyweight could compare with the prospect of being trampled underfoot by a 1,600-pound thoroughbred, or a 40-ton Soviet tank.

The scrappy jockey, it turned out, could really give it back. But Kallai's blows missed far more often than Krienbrook's. The jockey ended up off balance again and again. But just like he never fell off his horse, he never slipped up completely in the ring. He recovered a moment later and took a few more blows. He connected a few times, too.

Then Kallai went down. Krienbrook had waited and delivered a solid right to the jockey's jaw. I could hear the sounds all around me this time. The crowd was screaming for Kallai to get back up, and he did. He practically bounced back up. For a moment I wasn't sure whether to count it as a knockdown, but the referee indicated it was. The round was over, and I reluctantly scored it 5-4 for Krienbrook.

Round two was more of the same. Between the small stature of the fighters and the fact that this was only a four-round bout, there was no reason for the fighters to hold back. I found myself losing track of the blows. One flurry was almost inseparable from the next. The crowd was yelling for the jockey. The fighters danced, tangled, and spun to my side, and I could see a cut had opened up under Kallai's right eye.

And then he scored. Kallai landed a left-right-left combination, and Krienbrook stumbled backwards before hitting the canvas. The place went wild. The noise was so loud I thought I heard booming cheers from both sides of the curtain at the Spectrum. If there had been any doubt before, it was clear now that this was the jockey's crowd. Philadelphia liked an underdog. And so did I. My height, my weight, about my age, and trying something new against all odds. What wasn't to like?

Krienbrook now bounded back up as quick or quicker than Kallai had in the first round. He threw combinations at the jockey as if there had been no interruption. But I was relieved. The pressure was off this round. I had it 5-3 for the Hungarian and could coast for the remainder of the round. Or so I thought. Krienbrook's discipline and skill paid off as he caught the jockey lunging and made him pay with a vicious left uppercut. It seemed to come out of nowhere. Kallai was dazed and down, then up again. I kept hoping the referee wouldn't give credit for the knockdown, but he did, and the deck of cards in my brain was shuffled. I had the round 5-4 for Kallai, and I wasn't sure exactly why.

They didn't have instant replays at the Spectrum, but round three was as close to one as you could get. Krienbrook went down first, then Kallai next. This undercard bout would be an impossible act to follow. I tried not to have "rabbit ears," which meant paying too much attention to what was being said around you. But everyone was yelling at the jockey to duck and swing, because he looked so swift doing it. Even Krienbrook was fooled a couple of times. The jockey seemed to hear the crowd and follow directions. The last 30 seconds of the round were his most effective, so I gave it to Kallai 5-4.

The crowd was on their feet for round four. Luckily I had the best seat in the house. Between rounds, while Kallai's corner guy stanched the bleeding under the jockey's eye, I could hear his manager shouting. The manager, who looked like another jockey, was telling the Hungarian to watch out for sucker punches. And that's what Kallai was doing. He was clearly doing a better job of biding his time and protecting himself in this round than in the first three. Krienbrook was still landing more blows, but neither fighter went down. The bell rang with both fighters holding their own. The shouting was deafening. There was something to be said for learning on the job. I definitely knew what that was like, so I gave the round to Kallai 5-4.

The crowd remained on their feet and then took it to the next level. They started throwing coins at the ring. I had heard of "nobbins," old English slang for throwing coins in appreciation of a good contest, but had never actually seen it. Now I saw it and almost felt it. Those coins were coming at me from all directions, and like a good flyweight, I ducked. Better still, I hit the ground. Even better, I gathered up a handful of quarters and dimes and put them in my purse. But it wasn't my purse in the end. This was to pay the referee at home, the babysitter.

Upright now like most Homo sapiens, I thought about hitting the floor again before my score was read off by the ring announcer. The referee had it four rounds to none for Krienbrook. The other judge had it three rounds to one the same way. So the fight was a decision for the experienced fighter no matter what the novice judge had to say. And I wished to heaven they would just leave it that way. The excitement had left me, leaving only embarrassment over a job not well done.

But the ring announcer proceeded, his tuxedo making him look like a mortician. "And Mrs. Carol Polis scored it 19 to 17 for Kallai." A split decision, and all I could think about was splitting. The boos at the Spectrum turned to cheers. These were cheers I did not want, not one of them. To me they were sarcastic, each one cutting like a knife. If I could have given the coins back, I would have.

There was silence in the car on the way back home. I had encountered this silence before during rides back from losing Little League efforts in which a son struck out with the bases loaded. But this was my silence now, and it seemed more deafening. Inconsolable. Bob broke it.

"I don't know how you could have done that. I don't know how you could have given a decision to that little runt."

"Which little runt do you mean?" I said.

"The little runt who got his ass kicked," Bob said. "That little runt.

I don't know, Carol, maybe you give extra points for getting back up off the canvas."

"I guess I called it wrong," I said. "Is that what you're trying to say in between insults?"

"I wouldn't worry about it too much," Bob said. "Live and learn, right? It can't all be beginner's luck."

Bob actually didn't seem that upset. And that upset me. It was as if my obvious lapse was a feather in his cap. The silence was back again. The honeymoon was over. This could never happen again. *I could never allow it to happen again.* If I had to put myself in complete mental isolation for every fight I would ever call, then that's what I would do. If it was going to be no fun at all, then so be it. This gig was worth absolutely nothing to anyone unless I was damn good at it and willing to pay the price.

A voice spoke to me. Whether it was my own or Zach Clayton's or a combination of the two wasn't clear. But the words were quite clear: "A judge should always focus at a point directly between the two boxers so that he can observe the actions of both boxers. Never allow yourself to get lulled into looking at just one boxer."

I watched as another light pole on the Turnpike flew by. *Put a dog tag on me*, I thought. Tuesday was practically here. It would feel just like a Monday but with less sleep. I had a mildly amused husband doubting me while I doubted myself and while a bunch of grizzled Philadelphia sportswriters were probably busy clicking away at their typewriters undoing a decade's worth of women's liberation at my expense. I definitely had more than one problem today.

CHAPTER FIVE
HERE COMES THE JUDGE!

I loved my cigarette first thing in the morning. Or perhaps I needed my cigarette first thing in the morning. Maybe it was a little of both. My brand was Virginia Slims. Lately I had gone from about a pack a day to more like a pack and a half. It seemed like the most natural thing in the world to me. When I was little, my parents held a weekly bridge game in our home. Their friends included the likes of Rona Bronfman, heir to the Seagram fortune. Though my father stuck to cigars rather than cigarettes, everyone there smoked. I considered smoking and bridge a birthright, although in those days, I didn't play much bridge.

The non-menthol fumes cleared my head and woke me up to the task at hand. I had a few minutes to thumb through my copy of the *Pennsylvania State Athletic Commission Rules and Regulations* before everyone else in the house stirred. There were five hundred and thirty-six rules and regulations in all, ranging from the most useful to the most mundane, and I was going to memorize every last one of them. Here was one of the more useful ones: "One method employed by many of the better judges throughout the country is the effective use of boxing zones. The zones are established by splitting the upper torso of a boxer with an imaginary line, down through the head and shoulders to the waistline."

I studied the accompanying diagram, which reminded me a little of an instruction kit for an autopsy. Meanwhile, I was busy conducting my own postmortem of the night before. The result each time I made an incision was the same. I needed to go back to the drawing board. Or, as the saying went, to get right back in the ring. Then I heard a couple of light footsteps down the hall and realized I already was back in the ring.

By 10 AM, I had gathered the big three newspapers—the *Inquirer*, the *Daily News*, and the *Bulletin*—and combed each for stories about the

Kallai fight. I found them, read every word at least twice, and exhaled. There were various accounts of the novelty aspect of the fight and the number of times the jockey hit the canvas, but no direct mention of how the fledgling woman judge who got her appointment through her husband completely blew her second assignment due to a silly schoolgirl crush.

I would live to judge another fight. So I lit another cigarette. The Virginia Slims brand was aimed at young, ambitious women who could identify with a smarter, not-so-fat cigarette. The slogan was, "You've come a long way, baby." This morning, I really didn't think so.

Bob had a sensitive side. When my brother Arthur told me about a 1970 Alfa Romeo up for sale, price negotiable, my heart leapt at it, and Bob didn't get in the way. My brother was into fast cars and was friends with a fellow named Giuseppe Di Nardo, who had bought the Alfa from an Argentine race care driver. Di Nardo needed the cash, and one of my dreams had always been to drive a little lipstick red convertible with a black top. This Alfa was exactly that. The asking price was a little over two million lira. We certainly weren't millionaires, but in dollars it came to about $4,000. That we had.

For many years, the Alfa Romeo was the car to beat in the Grand Prix. The one delivered to me on that wonderful spring afternoon was a Duetto, also called a Spider, and was everything a bored housewife could possibly want in a race car. It was a two-door, compact, and low to the ground. It had 109 horsepower under the hood. Next to the big "Alfa Romeo" insignia on the rear hood, in smaller letters, was the word "Iniezione." That was Italian for fuel injection.

Domestic creature that I was, this was not the bulky black Alfa the Sicilian Mafia blew up, killing Michael Corleone's fiancée. Although *The Godfather* was about the best movie I had seen in the last ten years, this Alfa was more or less the one Dustin Hoffman drove like a mad man in *The Graduate* to rescue his beautiful bride, Katherine Ross, from the clutches of Anne Bancroft. Talk about bored housewives.

But this Alfa Romeo had something over Dustin Hoffman's, Al Pacino's, and all the other Alfa Romeos in the world. It was customized for

Carol Polis. We ordered custom plates from the Pennsylvania Department of Transportation that read: "HERE COMES THE JUDGE." The phrase was popularized by Flip Wilson and Sammy Davis, Jr. in the recurring skit on *Rowan & Martin's Laugh-In*. But Pennsylvania only provided a plate for the rear of the car. So to be more accurate, the plate should have read: "THERE GOES THE JUDGE."

And I went. I would pack the four kids in the car—one in the front, three just barely in the back—and speed off to the next stop sign. The kids were thrilled. It wasn't that I was exceeding any speed limit. What the kids experienced was what anybody did—the power, the acceleration. And every time we went out for a spin, like clockwork some joker in a Corvette or a Mustang pulled up alongside me and wanted to drag race. I would think about it for a moment. I had a good feel for the gear shift. I had sixty years of Italian race car engineering under the hood. I could have left them in the dust like Dustin. But I had an example to set. So I just smiled, grabbed the stick, and dreamt.

Most Philadelphia suburban families on a Sunday afternoon in the spring might play Frisbee in the yard, go to a ball game, or catch a matinee. We did those things like anyone else. But on this particular day, our family went to see boxers train. The Alfa Romeo was not going to do the trick unless we pushed the front seat back for Bob's long legs and put the kids in the trunk. So we piled into the station wagon, our 1972 Chrysler Town and Country. Our destination was more town than country.

There was a lot of time between the fights I was assigned to. Memorizing the rule book could only take me so far. In between, if I was going to approach my potential, I needed to live and breathe boxing. There was probably no better place in the world to live and breathe boxing than Joe Frazier's Gym on North Broad Street in Philadelphia.

Frazier was the eleventh of twelve children growing up in Laurel Bay, a poor area of South Carolina. His parents were sharecroppers and by default so were the kids. Joe's father, Rubin, had a side business bootlegging white lightning. As an amateur boxer, Joe Frazier was black lightning. In 1960 as a sixteen-year-old, he took a Greyhound bus north to Philadelphia.

He found work in a kosher slaughterhouse, where during odd moments he sparred with hanging carcasses that doubled as heavy bags.

Frazier found more formal training at the 23rd Police Athletic League boxing gym. His intense routine included a daily run through the streets of Philadelphia, highlighted by an ascent to the top step of the Philadelphia Art Museum. In 1964, Frazier won an Olympic gold medal in Tokyo in the heavyweight division.

Frazier turned pro the next year and didn't lose a fight the rest of the decade. In 1969, he bought the building at 2917 North Broad Street and opened a gym where young boxers could perhaps catch the same kind of break Frazier himself had caught almost a decade earlier at the PAL gym.

Or maybe a break of a different sort. Not everyone was destined to become a Joe Frazier or a Muhammad Ali. The doors at Frazier's Gym were open to anyone, especially kids with nowhere else to go. In the 22nd District, burglary, arson, assault, and auto theft were everywhere and on the rise. Membership at Frazier's Gym was twenty-five dollars, but if you didn't have it, you could work it off skipping rope and hitting a speed bag. If you were willing to undergo the rigors of training, you might develop overall self-discipline. More importantly, you might absorb the notion that someone actually cared what happened to you, whether you became an accomplished fighter or not.

Route 611 in Pennsylvania followed the Delaware River down from the small city of Easton, then wound its way through the suburbs of Doylestown and Willow Grove. By the time you crossed over the borderline into north Philadelphia, the road was called Broad Street. The surroundings changed, first subtly, then not so subtly. There were fewer trees, more graffiti, more broken windows, and a bit of an industrial feel. Another three miles or so south along North Broad and you arrived dead center at City Hall. As close as it was, most people who lived and worked in this neighborhood would never quite get there.

When our station wagon pulled up, there was a limousine parked in front of the gym, so we assumed Joe Frazier would be upstairs in his office. The overpass and platform for the North Philadelphia train station was right near the building, adding a final accent to the gritty urban ambiance. The building itself was a four-story brick structure with tall, narrow windows and simple concrete façade work. Engraved in the concrete above the first floor in large, block letters were the words "JOE FRAZIER'S GYM."

With my family in tow and Bob a step ahead, I walked into the gym and into another world. The smell of sweat was instant and intense. It wasn't a stale smell like a commuter train. This was the smell of fighters hard at work, and there were dozens of them. A row of fighters were hitting the speed bags, which were light teardrop shaped leather sacks, each hanging from a metal rack. You could see the fists but barely see the bags, which moved so fast the image was blurred. The rhythm was steady and hypnotizing. It was like tap dancing for the fists, with a single motion somehow making multiple sounds.

A little further down was another row of fighters hitting heavy bags, each one a large cylinder filled with sand. The punches landed like thuds, the bag swinging grudgingly like the carcasses Joe Frazier once hit in the slaughterhouse. Some of the bags were being held by a trainer, who used the bag as a shield and in the process took a portion of each blow. The proximity and punishment seemed to give the trainer the right to shout instructions at the top of his lungs. The fighters needed to shift their weight more efficiently from back foot to front, or to recover faster after delivering the blow, or not to leave themselves so exposed.

One trainer was breaking down the mechanics of a jab. A left jab started from the lead shoulder and thrust out quickly, without warning. The fist started in an upright position and rotated clockwise, so that upon impact the knuckles were horizontal. The rotation was not simply a physical necessity. It added to the effectiveness of the blow.

Still more boxers were skipping rope, some forward, some backward, some crossing over, some not. All skipped at a furious pace. Ropes cut through the air like whips cracking, skimming the wooden floorboards like buffers, rarely making a full smack. To walk through would mean being cut to shreds, or at least it seemed that way. And if once in a while a boxer tripped up, the correction was made so quickly it appeared almost part of the drill.

Most of the action was going on toward one side of the gym floor. The reason was the other side was all mirrors, an entire wall's worth. As in ballet, form was all-important. Grace was not so much beauty as it was the absence of waste. If you flailed around out there, it was going to come back to haunt you in the ring. As a fighter you needed an awareness of everything you did. The mirrors helped develop that awareness, but in the end it was ingrained.

Self-absorption by the fighters and their dedicated trainers meant little or no attention to the lady who came in off the street with her underage entourage. My motley crew was split clearly into two camps. The girls saw the place as the inside of a nuthouse and hung close to Mommy. The boys, kids in a candy store, ventured off. Kenny was the first among us to break through. I recognized the fighter he was talking to as Richie Kates, a young light heavyweight from New Jersey who had fought on one of my cards at the Spectrum.

Kates was showing Kenny how to bob and weave, where you avoided a punch by moving your body to the side, down, and back up again. That was a form of defense Joe Frazier himself was still perfecting under the guidance of his trainer, Eddie Futch. He could have used a lifetime supply against George Foreman. As for Kenny, he was going to need the bob and weave too, because not far away his brother Jimmy was learning to throw a cross.

Way out in front of me and my entourage was Bob the veteran referee, who was schmoozing with some of the older trainers and fighters. They had a common lexicon that went back twenty years. Maybe a hundred years. Bob was in his element. He was making headway, and before long I knew it would lead to a visit upstairs. Overhead, a few men in Joe Frazier's inner circle leaned casually over the second floor railing and gazed out over what must have looked like the Roman Coliseum between events.

On the walls not covered with mirrors were dozens of framed photographs. A closer look revealed that many of them were taken during

Joe Frazier's bouts. The one a few inches from my nose showed Smokin' Joe and Jerry Quarry in the ring at Madison Square Garden in New York, June 23, 1969. In the shot, Quarry was staggering backwards into the corner after a left hook from Frazier. Quarry looked disoriented but still determined as blood clearly drips from his right cheek.

As part of my ongoing "education," I had seen a rebroadcast of this very fight on ABC. In the long wake of the Ali disqualification, the heavyweight title was at the time split between Frazier, who held the World Boxing Council belt, and Jimmy Ellis, who held the World Boxing Association belt. Facing Frazier that night was Quarry, the latest and possibly greatest "White Hope." His corner men wore robes that read "Irish Jerry Quarry" on the back, even though Quarry was from Bakersfield, California. His fans were known for being obsessive and sometimes even disruptive.

I knew automatically that the picture on Joe Frazier's wall was not from an early round. Quarry won the first two rounds with flurries of alternating left and right hooks. Frazier returned them but took more blows than he landed. The two fighters had similar styles, and half the time their heads were locked like bulls without the horns. But by the fifth round or so, Quarry fell off the pace, and Frazier began to dominate. Quarry could take a punch better than just about any man alive, but he had a tendency to bleed. In round seven, the referee stopped the fight. Smokin' Joe retained the WBC crown, and Jerry Quarry wound up on Joe Frazier's wall.

What pulled me out of my greatest hits daydream was a bizarre sight I associated more with the *Jack LaLanne Show* than with a boxing gym. A muscular fighter probably in his early twenties lay back on an exercise mat while an older fellow dropped a medicine ball on his stomach. The ball was probably twenty pounds or so, the drop about a foot. The fighter tensed up his abdomen—and in the process his face—to receive the blow. The winner was the fighter, on points. The fighter's stomach gave just a little, while the medicine ball bounced a bit and rolled off. The trainer lifted the ball back up and began round two.

Toward the back of the room was a standard size boxing ring with a worn blue canvas. As I neared, fighters were in various states of either preparation or recovery from sparring. Hands were being wrapped with tape, not because they were injured but to prevent injury. Even with a large boxing glove over it, an untaped hand could fracture. With the tape the impact was distributed across the fist, reducing the chances of dislocating or breaking the numerous bones inside. For the trainers, wrapping a hand was practically artwork. The loops overlapped perfectly, forming a tailored glove that when complete looked a lot like a sculptor's mold.

In the ring, the fighters wore head gear while sparring. It wasn't simply a custom, it was a requirement. In amateur fights, it was required during the real thing as well. The trainer, however, now stopped the imaginary round to show his fighter the slip. Slipping was a subtle defensive move, but a very effective one if you were quick. The defender turned his hip and shoulders hard and fast so that the punch just missed. Ali was the master at slipping, and sometimes almost seemed to clown it up as a right or a left nearly grazed him and provided a little chin music.

Here in Frazier's Gym, the trainer was issuing a warning to his fighter that a turn of the shoulders without a turn of the hip was a good way to take a turn on the canvas. The trainer showed the right way a couple of times, and the fighter did his best to mimic his mentor. Other clients of the gym milled around and made cracks, anxious to see if the lesson was going to stick once sparring resumed. Minus the cracks, I was interested, too. But I wasn't going to get the chance to see more this time. An employee tapped me on the shoulder and told me it was time to go up and meet Mr. Joe Frazier, Philadelphia's toughest.

There were black leather sofas all around Joe Frazier's second floor office. One of Frazier's assistants introduced him to Bob, who already knew Smokin' Joe "from the neighborhood." When I was introduced next, I got a warm, casual hello from Frazier. He nodded his head during the part about the first woman boxing judge, so apparently he kept up with current events.

"Maybe you'll be ringside when I get Foreman again," Frazier said with a quick smile.

"Or maybe my husband will be in the ring," I said. Everyone laughed, and we carried on a polite conversation, with my kids—well, at least two of them—looking up in absolute awe.

Joe wasn't huge for a heavyweight. He usually weighed in at just over 200 pounds. His height was usually listed at six feet, and now that I saw him standing next to Bob, I thought the six feet probably included the shoes. But Frazier more than made up for a couple of inches and a couple dozen pounds with the hardness that showed on his face and a physique that was almost superhuman. In the ring, his thighs looked like cement slabs, and you could still see the outline of those slabs through his street clothes.

Frazier didn't need to see us, but he clearly made the best of it. He seemed a little preoccupied, and anyone who cared could easily understand why. He had certainly healed physically from the Foreman fight, but perhaps not as completely mentally. If you knew anything at all about Joe Frazier, you knew he wanted to get back in the ring for a rematch with Foreman while they were unwrapping his hands in the training room that night.

But the fight game didn't work that way. At the moment, Frazier's management was working out the details for a summer fight with heavyweight contender Joe Bugner. The same fight that was supposed to be a title defense was now probably a distraction for Joe Frazier, but a deal's a deal, and a purse is a purse. At some point, Frazier would try to lock horns with Foreman again, but Frazier was already in competition with Muhammad Ali for that opportunity. The ever resourceful, headline dwelling promoter Don King was busy trying to put together the biggest purse in history for a showdown between current champion Foreman and former champion Ali. That left Frazier out in the cold for the moment, chasing both Foreman and Ali. Frazier deserved better.

Frazier was a complex man. When eight top heavyweights were chosen to compete in 1967 for Ali's vacated title, Joe Frazier wanted no part of it, nobly viewing Ali as still the legit champ. Frazier wanted Ali one on one. Ali wanted the same thing. But Ali no longer had a boxing license. So Joe Frazier lobbied for it starting at the top—with the President of the United States. When Smokin' Joe was a guest in 1969 of President Richard Nixon, the champ put in his two cents for Ali. Nixon's authority in the matter of a state boxing license was debatable, but as the country was soon to find out, executive privilege was on the rise. Nixon's only response, however, was to ask whether Frazier thought he could take Ali, and Joe said he had Ali in his back pocket.

In the months following, Joe Frazier lobbied for his rival's boxing license with the proper authorities, such as the Pennsylvania State Athletic Commission. He also lent Ali money, as the ex-champ had mouths to feed, business expenses, and no substantial income. Away from the cameras and microphones, Ali treated Frazier as what he was, a friend. But when the cameras and microphones reappeared, Ali's outsized stage ego reappeared just as quickly. While Frazier understood the value of hype to a fight—whether or not that fight ever materialized—he was taken aback by Ali's frequent gearshifts to the point of distrust and resentment.

That ill will peaked one hot summer day in 1969. Ali had relocated to Philadelphia, Smokin' Joe's hometown, almost as a wolf hunting its prey. He walked up and down Broad Street, Walnut Street, Market Street rapping to anyone who would listen about how he would take apart the hometown boy in the ring given the chance. Appearing on a local radio show, Ali called Frazier a coward and an Uncle Tom. A couple of miles away, Frazier was listening closely. Then Ali took the next verbal swing. He challenged Joe Frazier to a fist fight at the PAL gym. Ali finished the segment and headed down to the gym to see if Uncle Tom would show.

Joe Frazier, smokin' from the ears, got into a car and drove toward his old stomping grounds. Here was the impoverished ex-champ, on Frazier's dime, calling Frazier every name in the book and using as a platform not simply Frazier's city but Frazier's cradle as a fighter. While Frazier was in no rush to make Ali pay back the loans, for this he would have to pay.

When Joe Frazier got out of the car across the street from the PAL gym, the scene on Columbia Avenue was like a ring, but after a bout, not before. There were about a thousand people in the street, every one of them with a free ticket to the impromptu fight of the century. As he pushed his way toward Ali, Frazier ripped off his shirt. Though there was no S on his chest, Frazier was pumped up, yelling and pointing at Ali, who was doing the same. But the throngs between them never got thinner than a half dozen deep, and a heavyweight street fight was narrowly avoided. Later on, according to Frazier, the next time he saw his rival in private, it was for Ali as if nothing ever happened. As if the charade was understood. When it came to his pride and honor, however, Frazier did not understand.

But when it came to kids, Joe Frazier really did understand. He made sure each of my kids got a personally autographed photo. Even my two girls had loosened up by now in the champ's presence. As for my boys, they weren't simply upstairs, they were in heaven. So was their mom. I wasn't going to leave there without a Smokin' Joe autograph of my own. When I saw up close his hand signing the 8x10, I was amazed at just how large it really was. You could have fit three of mine in it.

I took a last look at the gym on our way out, and it dawned on me just why I appreciated the scene so much. I was in training too. I didn't use mirrors, but I reflected constantly. I didn't get in the ring, but I got as close to it as possible without actually getting in. I didn't have a formal trainer. Maybe Bob. Maybe Zach Clayton. But in reality, all of the guys in this gymnasium were my trainers. I tried to learn something from watching everyone.

More than that, I had a special responsibility to these fighters. It was only by spending a few hours in a place like this that you came to understand just how many hours, weeks, months, years of unsung hard work went into stepping in the ring for just one round. Some of these guys would never make it that far. And of those who did, only a small group had even the smallest chance of making it as far as Joe Frazier's wall of fame.

Somehow, through circumstance and fortune, with really not a lot of time invested, I had leapfrogged over so many of these young men on my way to the ring. I couldn't really explain it or justify it. And I knew one wrong move by me could send their whole career into a tailspin, negating thousands of hours of grueling labor put forth in a gym like this one. I couldn't ever let that happen. I owed it to myself. But even more importantly, I owed it to them. I took another look and another breath. And I knew—I'd be back.

* * *

For months now I had been speaking for my kids when the press asked me how they felt about their mother's "brand new bag." Then one day it dawned on me that they might like the opportunity to speak for themselves. So I sat them down and had each one prepare a "press release." Each one got a sheet of loose leaf paper and the assignment to discuss their mom's profession and what it meant to them. It wasn't really for the press. I didn't plan to "release" it to anyone. But I got more than I bargained for. My oldest, Jimmy, 13, had this to say:

> *"When I first heard that my mother was appointed boxing judge I thought it was a joke. Since I thought that my mother was scared at the sight of blood and even 1,000 leggers. But when it all blew over, my Mom came out well. She got a lot of nice publicity and pictures just because she was a woman not because she was a good judge. She beat out many men who tried then finally people started to notice the good job she did. It's kind of tough to be a mother of four and a boxing judge. It might sound funny but most of the referring goes between the kids not the fighters. It's just to bad that boxing isn't doing well in Philly but my mom's doing well enough and she's not a woman's libber." --Jim*

I didn't believe for a second that I was anywhere near as good a judge as Jimmy thought, but now I had an even greater expectation to live up to than my own. Kenny, my eleven-year-old, provided the other half of my boys' one-two combination:

> *"My reaction was good ("bad" erased). I think mom should have a little excitement in her life. If she likes it fine, I only want my mom to do a job so she will be happy. And we*

> *get a reward too, like Joe Frazier autographs. I like what*
> *she does cause I enjoy boxing too. It's fun to watch her*
> *on television. My boxing hero is Richie Kates." --by Kenny*

Margie, my adorable nine-year-old, was faster to the punch:

> *"I like what she does. I like when she is on TV. And I like when*
> *she judges fights. My mother is the first women boxing judge in*
> *the whole world." --by Margie*

Her handwriting was better than both her older brothers'. And her mom's. Batting cleanup was my youngest and sweetest, Carol Paula:

> *"My mom is the first women boxing judge in the world. I like to*
> *watch her on TV. I like to go with her to see her on television.*
> *I like to see Bowling for DOLLARS and I like to go to the*
> *boxing matches and I wish I could go every time."*

I wished they could, too.

* * *

Zach Clayton had me judging five of the six fights on the card at the Spectrum on April 16. I would be doing more rounds than any of the fighters. It was a Monday night, and I knew the drill. I was focused, at times almost motionless. Gazing at the imaginary mirror in my private fight judge gymnasium, I looked a little like a guard at Buckingham Palace. A lot shorter but just as grim. My clothes, of course, were a lot darker too. But that didn't keep tiny red drops of blood from appearing on my white scorecard.

From time to time I had to remind myself not to have rabbit ears. My world had to be limited to the action in the ring. I couldn't pay attention to anything being said behind me. And there was a lot being said. One of the fighters apparently had a busload of friends and relatives at the fight, and the whole gang was parked in the rows immediately behind me. The moment any comment about "Ray" or "our boy" or any utterance to that effect even halfway penetrated my little fortress, I made sure to shut the door harder. At one point, security took away a male spectator who was hanging over my shoulder. The fact that I barely even recalled who it was, who he was for, or what he was saying was my own personal victory. I had come a long way, baby.

The main bout was a ten-rounder between Sammy Goss and Jorge Ramos, both super flyweights who weighted in around 129 pounds. Goss was from Trenton, New Jersey and had fought for the U.S. in the 1968 Olympics at Mexico City. Ramos was a veteran fighter originally from Argentina. They fought furiously, but I judged furiously, too. It was as if by intense concentration, I could slow the punches down.

There was slipping, bobbing, and weaving, blocking, covering up, ducks, and clinches. The actual names of these moves didn't really register consciously much more than what the partisan folks behind me were screaming. But I didn't need names, just a swift, accurate gut reaction. I *understood* what was happening, and at times I even anticipated it.

After giving Ramos the fifth and sixth rounds, I had the final four rounds for Sammy Goss. It was a unanimous decision for Goss. I wasn't holding my breath for the scoring of the other officials. I had left it all in the ring, as they say, and I couldn't hold my breath if I wanted to. I relaxed a little, knowing I had gone from a mommy to a mummy and would eventually go back again. And with my guard down just a bit, I noticed I had a headache purely from having concentrated so hard. This wasn't the kind of headache some women had on occasion to avoid intimacy with their husbands. This was an occupational hazard. This was real. I earned it.

CHAPTER SIX
WHAT'S MY LINE?

"Your group doesn't want just any speaker. What your audience wants is a knockout! How many times have you put tremendous time and effort into a corporate, social, fraternal or sales meeting only to lay the proverbial egg? What you thought would be stimulating, merely bored your audience. Your group needs to hear someone who's truly unique— to enjoy a refreshing presentation. That's why you should know Carol Polis. Carol Polis, the first woman professional boxing judge in America, is someone who isn't just surviving in a man's world. She's put male chauvinism down on the canvas for the ten-count."

I wished I had the budget for a four-color marquee poster with Ann-Margaret portraying me and a couple of boxers played by Paul Newman and Burt Lancaster. But what I printed were 8-1/2 by 11 inch flyers with basic block lettering. No need to overdo it, at least in the production values. Life was a continual attempt to get out of the house for a few hours and maybe even make a little extra money. The flyers said what they needed to say. Now I just needed a few of the right people to read them.

I began where a thousand public speakers began every day—local organizations. I worked the contacts I had and didn't demand outrageous fees, outrageous meaning anything beyond carfare. One such contact was Nick LaSorsa, who managed the Sheraton-Pennpike Motor Inn, not far from our home in Fort Washington. Nick knew several organizations that booked speakers and rooms, whether at his facility or other hotels and restaurants in the area.

In early May, Nick called with some good news. He had booked me to speak to the Rotary Club at the Forest Inn the following month. There was no fee involved, but I'd get some speaking experience under my belt, lunch was supposed to be great, and I would be presented with a nice looking paperweight. With any luck at all, I'd be able to parlay this into a gig at the Lions Club.

I wasn't thinking about speaking engagements when the phone rang a couple of days later. I had six loads of laundry to do. But a moment or two into the conversation, I dropped a basket of cotton washables. It was Helen Marcus, an assistant producer calling from New York. Someone in her office had caught wind of my story and thought it would be perfect for their show—*What's My Line?*

There was no second thought or checking with Bob. When game show royalty called, you answered. A confirmation letter came in the mail on May 11. On May 17 at 2:15 PM, I was to arrive at NBC Studios at 30 Rockefeller Plaza, Studio 8H. "PLEASE BE PROMPT," the letter read. There would be a brief rehearsal, followed by the taping of the show, and we would be done by 4:30. And there would be a reservation at the famous Waldorf Hotel. A check for $40 would be waiting for me at the studio to pay the room charge. There would also be $25 to cover transportation and another $35 for food and other expenses. I had graduated from paperweights before even getting one.

The one sentence in the letter that stood out in my mind and remained a while after I clipped it to the bulletin board read: "Please do not discuss your appearance on the program with anyone prior to the taping." That was going to be even harder than sitting expressionless and judging a prizefight. *What's My Line?* was the king of game shows and even transcended the format itself. When the show began airing in 1950, my family had just gotten a television. Through the '50s, Sunday nights would wind down with everyone watching the show. Four panelists tried to guess the occupation of the contestant. With the help of the host, newsman John Daly, the contestant answered mostly with a yes or a no. Ten no's and the contestant had stumped the panel.

The panelists were tops. Fred Allen was a radio legend. Arlene Francis was everything from a Broadway actress to a film actress to a socialite. Bennett Cerf had founded the publishing giant, Random House. Steve Allen left after a couple of years to take the reigns of *The Tonight*

Show. Before his stint on *What's My Line?* was over, he had popularized the question "Is it bigger than a breadbox?"

The breadbox question was now in the American lexicon, and so was *What's My Line?* There was a definite sophistication about the show. The panelists all dressed formally, the men often with black suits and bow ties, the women with gowns and sometimes gloves. Everyone was articulate, thoughtful, and accomplished. The panelists weren't up there taking wild guesses generally, but rather applying the breadth of their knowledge to whittling down the possibilities for someone's vocation, or "line" of work. There was always an odd twist to the job. At the same time, jokes would often fly. The remarks were spontaneous and clever, and because most of the panelists had occupied their seats for multiple seasons, there was usually a great on-air repartee.

By the time the original version of the show on CBS had broadcast its final episode in 1967, America had changed drastically and I was the mother of four. But like so many great people and institutions, the show violated F. Scott Fitzgerald's quote about there not being any second acts. *What's My Line?*'s second act began in 1968 when the producers, Mark Goodson and Bill Todman, put the show into national syndication.

What's My Line?, version two, aired weekday afternoons around the country on numerous stations affiliated with various networks according to their particular needs. The show was now less formal, with colorful clothing, a new host and a changing panel. Arlene Francis, however, was still on. Twenty-three years on the same show and running. I thought about where my own career might be in twenty-three years. Or my marriage. The first twenty-three months or so had been no honeymoon.

May 17 was a sunny Thursday. Bob took the day off so we could drive up to New York together. As we headed north on the New Jersey Turnpike in the station wagon, the sun disappeared for a while behind billows of industrial smoke. Newark was to our left and Jersey City to our right, but we could barely make them out. The fumes were overwhelming, like sticking your head in a kerosene drum but with more variety. I was actually getting a little dizzy, and not just from nervousness.

Somewhere up ahead, though we couldn't quite make it out, was the New York City skyline, and somewhere within was the RCA Building, where I would show up in a few hours pretending not to be a wreck. Four days earlier, on Mother's Day, fifty-five year old tennis hustler Bobby Riggs had beaten thirty year old current women's tennis star Margaret Court in a match preceded by all sorts of arrogance and bragging by Riggs. He was already looking for his next victim, and I didn't want to be that woman, even very indirectly.

We checked into our room at the Waldorf-Astoria, on Park Avenue. Only a few hotels ever had ever inspired a famous expression. For the Waldorf, it was "Meet me at the hyphen." Movie stars and heads of state had stayed here since its opening in 1931. Franklin Delano Roosevelt used to arrive at the Waldorf-Astoria by rail at Grand Central Terminal below in a modified train car big enough for his automobile. The hotel had built an elevator also large enough for the President's car so that FDR, on the way to his room upstairs, would never have to be seen wearing leg braces.

I looked around briefly at my own room with its plush drapes and mahogany furniture and knew this was about as presidential as it would ever get for me. But I also knew I was too preoccupied with what was coming later on to soak it all in like I probably should have. It was as if I was still downstairs in the car, too.

Bob and I walked around for a short while looking for a suitable restaurant to have brunch. For Bob, "suitable" meant a restaurant he had a coupon for. I tried to explain that a match between his coupon book and any of the eateries on or near Park Avenue was about as likely as my making the leap from professional judge to prizefighter. But Bob was a thrill seeker when it came to this sort of thing. The thrill of being able to pocket most of the thirty-five dollar meal allowance from the show was just too great to resist. Finally however, from hunger and tired feet, we ducked into a Horn & Hardart and got a booth.

I had to admit, though, Bob was in a pretty good mood. The biting comments were at a minimum, and he seemed genuinely excited about the taping. I took this to mean my own enthusiasm was contagious and hoped the intestinal knots inside were not. But I lost my outer glow when the flask came out. Bob usually carried around a flask filled with Scotch. At a restaurant, he would sneak a swig by pouring a shot into an available glass when the waitress wasn't looking. Unfortunately at the moment, she wasn't. I put my mental preparation for the show on hold for a moment and thought, *How cheap can one human being be?*

The ideal antidote for stage fright and marital conflict happened to be a few blocks away. My father's older sister, my amazing Aunt Janet, and her husband Bernie lived in a beautiful apartment on Park Avenue. When I was growing up, Aunt Janet and her first husband, Sol Batt, lived with my paternal grandparents at their house in Brooklyn at 934 East 18th Street. When we visited, I loved going upstairs to the hothouse, where they grew orchids on the roof. While winter winds whipped across Flatbush, upstairs azaleas and roses bloomed like it was late spring. Nearby was the Midwood movie theater and a bagel shop. The bagels out of the oven were so good, they practically melted in your mouth.

Janet's husband Sol would have terrible migraine headaches all the time. One day, like so many other days, he took a walk to the drugstore a few blocks away. An hour went by. Then another hour. Then a day. He never came back. The police looked into it but didn't come up with any leads. Sol was gone without a trace, as they say.

This happened before the war, so as the years went on, I didn't have a clear memory of my Uncle Sol. Aunt Janet remarried my Uncle Bernie, who was an attorney. Uncle Bernie was in the army infantry during the war and was among the first troops to liberate a German concentration camp. He didn't talk about it much.

When Aunt Janet, Uncle Bernie, and my cousin Clifford from Aunt Janet's first marriage moved to the apartment on Park Avenue, it was like a homecoming for Aunt Janet. She was what you might call vain, dripping in jewelry even at breakfast, but no one ever seemed to mind because her personality sparkled even more than the diamonds. She was glad to see us and showed it openly. Aunt Janet not only belonged to every art museum and philanthropy within twenty blocks, she was also the head of it at one time or another. There was no bagel store, but my new thrill was getting a look at Aunt Janet's closet. There must have been fifty hats and a hundred pairs of shoes in there! None of which were strictly for show. I recalled seeing Aunt Janet wearing most of them.

Things were as they always were in Aunt Janet and Uncle Bernie's apartment except for one thing. A TV was blaring in the living room, and the Senate hearings on Watergate were on. I remembered hearing that they would be on one network or another every day, starting today. New names in the scandal were popping up all the time, and people we had heard of once in a while—John Dean, Howard Baker, Archibald Cox—were now getting to be household names.

As I glanced at Aunt Janet's coffin-sized Zenith color TV, I suddenly realized I had been seeing bits and pieces of the hearings all day—in the hotel lobby and shops, at little diners and bodegas Bob and I had walked by. It was like Muzak in the elevator of life. You knew it was there, but there was no immediate need to acknowledge it. With not much time before my own national television debut, I felt like I was in some sort of dream.

I coaxed Bob into squandering a piece of our expense money on a cab. As we got out and walked the last block or so along the Avenue of the Americas, a pang of the dull sensation I had since the moment we stepped into New York crystallized. The city was becoming a dangerous place. No, it had already become one. The streets had the look and feel of having been cleaned but not that thoroughly and not by people who wanted to clean them.

Isolated flyers, candy wrappers, and newspaper sheets darted up here and there. Between them, people walked by. Some of them were on a mission of some sort, like Bob and me, and had a bit of a gleam in their eye. They were the executives, transplants, visitors, guests, tourists. But there was an undercurrent of people, many of whom were not walking but were just drifting or even stagnant. They were casualties of Mayor Lindsay, strikes, budget problems, economic downturn, white flight, racial strife, and who knew what else. There was an air of imminent crime, and you were never quite sure whether you were looking at the victims or the perpetrators.

It was hard to make any eye contact with these people. First of all, you didn't really want to. Second, they didn't want to either. They looked at you like you were Cellophane—right through you. But once in a while you were approached and someone at least pretended to look at you. There were pamphlets and tin cups and cardboard boxes and explanations of things about which you had never asked a question. By the time you responded even once, you knew you were already in too deep. There were deals going on—some out loud, some silent—in front of you, behind you, at either side and across the street. There were about twelve different experiences you could have per block, and none of them were good.

We walked past the granite base of 30 Rockefeller Center, beneath the marquee with the famous NBC Studios sign, and the ominous world of declining New York was gone. The art deco theme inside was oblivious to the Depression era which gave birth to the building or to whatever might have been coming next. This was TV land.

On the eighth floor was the famous Studio 8H. When we walked in, it was a little surprising how small the place was. This was where Arturo Toscanini had for many years conducted the NBC Symphony Orchestra. But it was hard to see how you could get much more than a string section in here, at least in the stage area. The studio audience was filing in. It consisted of maybe eighty or a hundred folks off the street. They were cleaner cut than the teeming masses we had just sifted through. Still, they were a motley crew of mop-tops, sideburns, crew cuts, comb-overs, bouffants, perms, cotton, polyester, and the occasional horn-rimmed glasses. Whenever I had seen this same Studio 8H audience from my living room, it appeared vast. The difference was probably in the wide angle lens and the general magic of television.

Unlike on the street below, I was welcome here with open arms. Helen Marcus greeted Bob and me and explained the drill. The stars were in their dressing rooms, hidden away until the show. That left contestants like me using couches and chairs more or less strewn about the hallway.

Still, we weren't neglected. An attractive young woman, an assistant producer, walked over and handed me a script and let me know she'd be back if I had any questions. The makeup lady went over my face with some foundation like a crop duster over a wheat field. Beneath was the makeup I had carefully applied for a half hour back at the hotel room.

Someone else asked me how I liked my coffee. The assistant producer returned in a frenzy and explained that my segment would be the second of three. A designer of men's clothing was the first guest, and the mystery guest would follow me. The stage manager took me down the hallway toward the stage. On the way, I caught a glimpse of another TV with the Watergate hearings on.

In the studio, director Lloyd Gross was delivering droll commands over the PA system to camera men and lighting personnel. Grips and best boys were rolling cameras and holding onto cables as they went. Sitting in the host's chair was someone who was definitely not the host. Sitting across from him in the four panelist seats were four people who were definitely not the panelists. The stand-ins seemed to be any employee who wanted a break for a few minutes while the rest of the staff worked out the kinks. There were smart remarks from the crew. The stage manager showed me my mark, the piece of tape on the floor I would need to walk up to before signing in. Sure I was nervous, but God help me if I couldn't figure out on my own how far to stand from a blackboard.

I got another quick look at the set before being led away again. The main backdrop was a velvet gold curtain. The panel was a split-level blue and gray table with its own backdrop—an array of two-foot square panels, each with a symbol corresponding to one line of work or another—a plate and utensils, a camera with flash attachment, a telescope, a military eagle. No boxing glove with a pretty ribbon on it that I could see anywhere. In the same way the studio audience looked surprisingly small, the set looked naked and a bit amateurish when standing alone not framed neatly by the edges of a TV screen.

Back at the couch I now called home, I took a look at the script. It was all of one page long. My name, Carol Polis, was at the top. There were a few words from the host, Larry Blyden. "Will our next challenger enter and sign in please? Where are you from?" In parentheses was my response: (Fort Washington, PA). Then more words from Blyden: "As far as we know, panel, Carol Polis is the only women in the country licensed to perform her job. Now let's show the audience what her line is."

From there, the script skipped to a brief notation: "(End of game) She's a professional boxing judge!" Wild cheers. Hoopla. Book deals. Movie offers. A recording contract. Maybe even a few parting gifts and the home version of *What's My Line?* The important thing here, however, was that there was no script for the game itself. Unlike *The $64000 Question* back in the '50s, the fix was definitely not in. With prize money comparable to a bingo game, what would be the point? This was more like a boxing match in that you had no idea what was going to happen, hopefully.

At the bottom of the page were a series of questions I could expect to be asked at the conclusion, along with suggested answers. "Carol, how did this happen?" (Tells how her husband, a stock broker but also a referee, taught her.) "What was the most exciting bout you judged?" (My first, it was a KO.) "And the fighters, what is their reaction?" (Well, one winked at me.) I wasn't sure exactly who that might have been, or if it was just a boxer trying to get the blood out of his eye. And there were several more questions not printed on the sheet that ran through my mind, such as: "Carol, are you nervous?" (Yes. Still very, very nervous.)

My mood lightened instantly as I looked up and saw myself surrounded by four young men. They weren't just good looking, they were absolutely gorgeous. They had names like Gene, Bruce, Michael, and Arthur. They fluttered about me like angels. I stood up so I could at least look them in the shoulder. They explained in beautiful four-part harmony that they were here with the first guest, a well known men's fashion designer who had just put out a line of caftans for men. I wanted to know exactly which designer they worked for, but before I got to the end of my sentence, the Fab Four had fluttered over to Bob.

Bob wasn't as good looking as they were, but he cut a fairly dashing figure in a leisure suit. They looked him up and down, and suddenly I understood what all the fluttering was about. There were few straight men in the world that handsome, and even fewer wearing caftans. Now with a full view, I took a better look at the stripes and various Middle Eastern patterns on their long outer gowns. Then I looked down quickly at my own short, aquamarine ribbed knit dress. It was certainly nothing splashy, just a simple conservative choice that brought out my eyes and showed off a little calf. I found a trace of my nervousness returning, and along with it a small sigh of defeat. The Fab Four were not only prettier than I was. They were better dressed.

While Bob's fan club continued to swamp him, I thought about the other Fab Four in the studio, the names of whom I had seen a little while earlier atop the panel. Those same names were now on the lips of studio personnel, who were relaying any last minute requests or complaints. Arlene Francis was the show's matron, but she was hardly matronly. My fondest hope was to look half as elegant as she did when it was my turn to push seventy years of age.

Where elegance was concerned, Soupy Sales was somewhere near the other end of the spectrum. Soupy was a comedian and DJ who eventually found his niche as the host of the *Soupy Sales Show*, a variety show for children and the infantile at heart. The show had a good run in syndication out of New York in the '60s. There were always half-visible, make-believe monster-sized animals appearing, with names like White Fang and Black Tooth. Soupy got hit with a pie at least once a show, sometimes even two or three. He bragged that he had been hit with over twenty-five thousand pies during his storied career, a dubious record that would probably outlast Joe DiMaggio's fifty-six game hitting streak. Over time, Sales's goofy show took on a certain hipness, attracting guests as celebrated as Frank Sinatra, Sammy Davis, Jr., and the Supremes.

Soupy pushed the envelope a little too far on New Years Day 1965 when he was upset at having to work on a holiday. To get even with Screen Gems, the syndicator, he asked the kids at home to go into their mommy's and daddy's dressers and pants pockets and remove those funny green pieces of paper with the pictures of the presidents on them. Then send the pieces of paper to Soupy Sales at the studio, and he'd send you a postcard from Puerto Rico.

A few days later, batches of ones, fives, tens, and twenties started arriving by U.S. Mail at Metromedia studios, addressed to Soupy Sales. The parents, well out of pie-throwing range, made angry calls to the station, and Soupy was suspended for two weeks. But his tiny, embezzling fans protested, and Soupy was quickly reinstated with an apology. The funny pieces of paper were donated to charity. There was no trip to San Juan.

The two lesser known panelists were Marcia Rodd, a successful Broadway actress in her early thirties, and Leonard Harris, the movie critic for the local CBS affiliate. The host, Larry Blyden, was a former actor himself. His more famous endeavors included starring roles in Broadway plays such as *Mister Roberts* and *A Funny Thing Happened on the Way to the Forum*. Blyden would also show up from time to time on reruns of classic TV shows like *The Twilight Zone*. He was witty and dapper, but really informal—ideal for the new look of *What's My Line?*

I spoke briefly with Alexander Shields, the headmaster—or headmistress as it were—of the Fab Four. Shields was more like a half-mystery guest, if there was such a thing. He was a well known designer. The mystery was his new line of caftans. Shields was an old money jet-setter—not at all pompous, but with his fine breeding it was impossible not to wear it on the sleeve of his friends' caftans.

The real mystery guest was no longer a mystery to me, though I would have preferred to keep him that way. When Ed McMahon played Johnny Carson's sidekick on *The Tonight Show*, he seemed the most likable, agreeable, if somewhat loutish guy in the world. A few minutes in the Studio 8H hallway with him demonstrated, if nothing else, his latent acting ability. He came off as arrogant, barking orders and seeking attention. All hail Johnny's second fiddle!

McMahon didn't seem drunk as he reportedly was so much of his waking life. Maybe if he were drunk I would have liked him a little better. But as he eyed me once up and down, I needed a stiff drink myself.

The Tonight Show had been shot for many years, right up until 1972, in this very studio until they moved it to Burbank, California. That was no excuse, but in any case, Ed McMahon had returned acting like he still owned the place. As far I was concerned, he was the mystery pest.

The show began, and so did the countdown to my own plunge. I watched on the monitor and hoped it was going to be a long, long round in which no panelist came within a mile of guessing caftans for men. The panelists introduced each other, as was the custom, each introduction cornier than the one before it. Announcer Chet Gould called Soupy Sales *"What's My Line?"*'s champagne man. He popped his cork!" *Ugh.* Soupy marched in with his huge head of black, Brillo Pad-like hair and tried to calm his screaming studio audience groupies—both of them. There was no pie in the face. Things got just a little obscene when critic Leonard Harris introduced Arlene Francis as "someone who follows me, but not as closely as I'd like her to." I gave it two stars.

Arlene asked if the item in question was for the beach and got an unconvincing no from Shields and Blyden. Arlene wasn't buying it, demonstrating the uncanny intuition one acquired during twenty-three consecutive years in the same seat. Soupy threw a few verbal pies their way after a negative response regarding whether the item was worn primarily around the house. Marcia and Leonard were wrapped up in a bunch of above- the-waist, below-the-waist questions, neither one inquiring whether it was bigger than a breadbox. So far, so good.

But then things started going downhill. When I heard Arlene Francis use the word "loungewear," I knew it was as good as over. She then drew a negative for inquiring whether the item functioned as pajamas, but the damage was done. It was like when a fighter drew first blood and prepared to go in for the kill.

Soupy inquired whether the item was originally intended for women and drew a negative. But Leonard Harris picked up roughly where Arlene had left off with a line of questions about exotic things from Asia. By the time the ensuing geography lesson was over, Harris had incorrectly guessed kimono. Before the last syllable of kimono had rung and before the camera could catch up to Arlene's brain, she blurted out "caftan," not so much as a guess but as a solution. There were cheers. Three questions were left up on the board. A KO in seven rounds.

After Shields educated Soupy on the male, rather than female origin of caftans, the designer explained how he first came up with the idea. It was definitely years ago when he was traveling around the world on his family's steamship in Casablanca. And what family, when you came right down to it, didn't own a steamship?

Then it was on to the fashion show. The Fab Four, pried away from my husband with a crowbar, showed off everything from a caftan with "brilliant Mogador stripes on French cotton" to a "Persian paisley hand screen print on yellow gold silk." The young men wore adorable self-absorbed grins. With their long gowns, they looked like Joseph from the Bible might have a minute before his jealous brothers threw him and his coat of many colors into a pit.

After a short commercial break, an assistant pulled me out of my own hole and placed me like a prop on my first mark, behind the curtain. There were a few words from Larry Blyden about how the panel on the show never got too mechanical and really wanted to get it. Then a throwaway line from Soupy about how Larry Blyden was going to get it. Before my heart could leap clearly out of my throat, Blyden announced it was time to meet the next challenger, and I received a polite but firm shove off the plank.

I walked through the curtain as the canned trumpet-laden jingle played, and I hit my mark in front of the blackboard. I picked up the chalk and scrawled the most graceful, rounded cursive letters I could manage under the circumstances. Whether he could read my handwriting or not, Larry Blyden carefully pronounced the name, "Carol Polis." The audience applauded loudly. There was something about applause that erased not only self-doubt but even short-term memory of self-doubt. Of course, the applause was mandatory, but that didn't matter. I felt at home, somehow, though only I knew what a feat it was to sign in with my right hand.

Blyden stood to shake my hand. His first question was where I was from. When I answered, "Fort Washington, Pennsylvania," there was exactly one person in the audience clapping, and the sound died of loneliness quickly. So much for home field advantage. Blyden explained that as far as they knew, Carol Polis was the only woman in the country licensed to do her job. Somewhere, the audience viewed the words "Professional boxing judge." My exhale morphed into a laugh, and we were off to the races.

Soupy asked if I performed my duties where I lived, in Pennsylvania. "Yes." But Soupy's next question was in regard to a uniform, and it was on to Marcia Rodd, who wanted to know if there were a number of people who did what I did without a license. "No." Not unless you counted all the people in the crowd who thought they could do it better.

Beginning with the words, "What you are licensed to do," which after repetition took on an almost comedic refrain, Leonard Harris asked a question meant to clear the air. Were men licensed to do this as a rule? Yes. Then the second part of the old comedic one-two: "Was it something that requires . . . a license?" The laughter was about as robust as the clapping earlier from my Fort Washington guy. Harris's next line of questioning never got going. Did it involve strength beyond that which a woman was customarily thought to have? No, and onto Arlene.

Did I do it on the ground? Yes, with a gentle nod from the challenger. *In fact, I was closer to the ground than most.* "Does it have anything to do with construction . . . or destruction?" Arlene wanted to know. As I began to smile and think of some of the professional beatings I had seen administered in the ring, I could see from the corner of my eye Larry Blyden's parallel smile and personal reflections on some of the fights he might have seen. Ironic laughter rose from the audience, and a no for Arlene.

After a mandatory quip, Soupy wanted to know if my license was issued by the government. Yes, I replied—the state government. But Soupy fell into the trap of asking whether I worked for the government. "Not exactly." No one, it seemed, was able to get on a roll, including

Marcia Rodd, who was curious whether I repaired something mechanically or electrically. The panel was fishing for the gender gap factor but was surprisingly nowhere near that huge chasm called professional sports. As a result, I was now halfway to a hundred dollars and a lifetime supply of Turtle Wax.

After a long bout of mildly entertaining clarification, critic Leonard Harris wanted to know if I laid hands on the person with whom I was dealing. No. *That was Bob's job.* Arlene looked pensive, almost confused. And she was their heavyweight. A half-hearted question bubbled to the surface. Did I work for a non-profit organization? My face must have been just as pensive. As referee, Larry Blyden stepped in and broke up what was beginning to look like a clinch. Arlene recovered and led with a right. Did I have anything to do with an exchange of money? I suppressed my own smile. *Not so far.* Blyden spoke for himself, for me, and for the Pennsylvania State Athletic Commission when he replied, "Hopefully not."

With the panel on the ropes and, more importantly, a commercial break coming up, Blyden called a TKO. He gave the panel a chance to guess wildly. "Inspector?" "Something to do with prisons?"

"No. She is a professional boxing judge." Applause. I had stumped the band! From thereon, I followed the script pretty much to the letter, never tripping once over my own words, or those of the writers. Harris the critic remarked that judging a knockout was easier than a decision. Blyden noted that the fictional wink from that fictional boxer was probably his last of the bout. I ad-libbed a laugh, and we were done. Cue canned music. Meet panel and exit stage left. It was all smiles at the panel as we shook hands. The women sat and the men stood—a hint of the disappearing formality of both the old *What's My Line?* and the old world, period.

Bob and the Fab Four waited for me backstage with open arms. I needed a drink, and the water fountain in the studio hallway would have to do. On the monitor, Ed McMahon was giving impish yes's and no's to disguise the voice only hermits without network television wouldn't recognize. The panel zeroed in like a laser anyway, Soupy drawing out the pain just a little longer with a question about the mystery guest's best-selling book and a reputation for tying one on. McMahon explained the origin of his book, *Slimming Down*, which had all begun a while back on the set of this very game show. Arlene Francis had patted McMahon's stomach and told him, "Better watch that." Now McMahon stood up, opened his suit jacket, and proved to the world you could, in fact, drink your way to a slimmer, trimmer you.

Downstairs, the streets of New York were just as we had left them a couple of hours earlier but somehow a little kinder now that I had a show "in the can." There would be a bonus at some point, and not just the free Samsonite luggage and St. Mary's towels that would be arriving at the house. People all over the country would see me as a professional boxing judge, and who knew what would happen as a result?

I reminded myself, however, the actual airing of the show was a while off. In the meantime, I thought about the menu I posted on the refrigerator every Sunday. It mapped out a week's worth of meals. I used the kitchen as a breezeway. I didn't want to linger there, and the better organized I was, the faster I could breeze through. But I still had a few menus to work through before my next fight. So until then, I was a wife and a mom. That was my line.

CHAPTER SEVEN
BATTLE OF THE SEXES

I felt safe in Frank Rizzo's arms. When the Mayor of Philadelphia gave me a hug, I knew he meant it. Rizzo was six-foot-two, two hundred and fifty pounds, and if he meant it any more he might have crushed me. The hug wasn't for the cameras, even though Bob and I were there at the mayor's request. This was Rizzo's personal gesture. When he let go and my feet returned fully to the floor, he told me he was a big fan of mine. In much the same way I wasn't supposed to be a boxing judge, I wasn't supposed to be a fan of Rizzo's.

Frank Rizzo was a heavyweight if ever there was one. He grew up Italian in Philadelphia and rose through the ranks of the city's police department in the 1940s and '50s. He was appointed Police Commissioner in 1967 by Mayor James Tate. The way some people saw it, the timing couldn't have been worse, though others thought the timing couldn't have been better. There was civil unrest in every racially mixed city in the country in 1967, and things only got more tense in 1968 when Dr. Martin Luther King, Jr. was assassinated. But unlike Los Angeles and Detroit, Philadelphia didn't see all-out riots, looting, or torching. One reason was Commissioner Rizzo. As a beat cop, he had no problem getting into the thick of it and using his hands. He ran the police force the same way.

In the late summer of '70, Rizzo's force raided the offices of the Philadelphia Black Panthers. It was not a pretty sight. Officers strip-searched Panthers with news cameras rolling. But just a few weeks earlier, the Black Panthers' national office had declared war, literally, on the country's police officers. Rizzo's preemptive strike was seen by many as not only legitimate, but absolutely necessary.

Rizzo was gruff. His speech was full of "dees", "dems" and "dose." On occasion his speech was outright incendiary, even by the forgiving standards of his supporters. It was Commissioner Rizzo who bragged famously when talking about his plans for a group of anti-police demonstrators, "When I'm finished with them, I'll make Attila the Hun look like a fag."

Rizzo's bite was bad, but some of the bark was just for effect. When he was Deputy Commissioner, he helped institute a policy that put one white and one black officer in each patrol car in racially sensitive neighborhoods. Under Commissioner Rizzo, twenty percent of the force was black, which was the highest of any major American city. When Rizzo ran for mayor in 1971, his campaign slogan was, "Firm but fair." Fifty-three percent of the city agreed, as Frank Rizzo beat out Republican blue blood, Princeton graduate, Chamber of Commerce President W. Thacher Longstreth.

Not long after taking office, Mayor Rizzo endorsed President Nixon for reelection. Most Philadelphians who supported Rizzo were not too happy about the endorsement, with my mother certainly among them. But Nixon, of course, was elated. Rizzo was a prototype of the kind of "hard hat Democrat" the President wanted to pull into the Republican party. Rizzo promised the City of Brotherly Love his support of the President was not simply idealogical. The city, Mayor Rizzo said, would reap all sorts of favors as a result.

But at the moment, it was Nixon who needed the favors. During the Watergate hearings which were now, in the summer of '73, like a daily campfire, it had come out that there was a taping system in the Oval Office that recorded virtually every meeting. Archibald Cox subpoenaed the tapes, and Nixon refused to hand them over. There was a national potboiler going on, and Rizzo seemed to be on the wrong side of it.

For better or for worse, Mayor Rizzo had enough of his own political problems to keep the city's attention off of the Nixon endorsement most of the time. Rizzo had gotten surprisingly good treatment from the local media during his campaign. It seemed less surprising once he was elected and then appointed more than twenty favorably disposed members of the press to good City positions. Meanwhile, the mayor was accused of doling out dozens of patronage jobs in exchange for the chance to handpick the district attorney and comptroller. Naturally, Mayor Rizzo looked to the media to help him out, but ironically most of his supporters in those ranks no longer had a column or a TV news segment.

As far as I was concerned, though, Rizzo had delivered on his central promise. He kept the city relatively safe in times that were far from safe. As the mother of four and even as a ring judge, that was priority number one for me. Besides, he was adorable, kind of like a big, cuddly teddy bear. He had a nice, friendly smile and was genuinely happy to see me. To the surprise of absolutely no one, he was a boxing fan. To the surprise of some, he thought what I was doing was great for the city, for the sport, and for women.

The pose for the press photographers was more formal. Rizzo shook my extended right hand, swallowing it up like a ping-pong ball in a catcher's mitt. I had on a short-sleeve cotton collared polo shirt and felt a little sorry for the Mayor, who had to wear a suit and tie in the sweltering July heat. When the flashbulbs died down, he asked me if more women were going to the fights these days. Yes and no, I told him. Most women were "fight fans" early on in the relationship. Once they had that wedding ring, life took over. As for me, it was working in just the opposite way. I had a fight coming up, and the more boxing took over, the better.

A promise was a promise in my family, and I had promised Mom and Dad to take them to a fight I was judging. The most important thing about the fight card on August 6 at the Spectrum was that it wasn't at the Blue Horizon. I loved judging at the Blue Horizon, a mid-sized venue on North Broad Street. Most bouts there were between hungry boxers working their way up and sometimes road-weary fighters winding their way down. It was small, exciting, a little seedy, and definitely not for Mom and Dad.

To be truthful, Mom might have liked it anyway. She was cavalier and good-humored enough to appreciate all sorts of variety. She didn't want to spend her life cooking and didn't try to cover for it. She cooked when she had to, hired good help, and played bridge. I inherited my own impatience for the kitchen directly from Mom, and neither of us were embarrassed about it. She liked nice things. Mom and Dad had a running joke. She would put on a new dress. He would ask, "Is that new, Dorothy?" She would reply, "Of course not. I've had it for months."

There was plenty of room for irony with Mom, and that meant some slack for her oldest child. She was curious, and the story that stuck in my mind was the one about when she was a little girl and tried to teach a chicken to walk a tightrope. I don't think she or the chicken had much luck, but the point was at least she tried. Tonight, I felt like I was the chicken on the tightrope.

There was less slack where Dad was concerned. He usually didn't appreciate our antics at the dinning room table. Dinner was fairly formal, like something out of *Father Knows Best*. That formality could easily be ruined by the fake buckteeth I fashioned out of corn niblets. I hated my peas, so I got them down my throat like vitamins—one at a time with a big gulp of milk. That kind of stuff got us sent to the kitchen to finish our meal where we couldn't be seen or heard, though usually we were still heard. Years later, when I was out on a date, Dad was the one who worried and stayed up till I came home. Mom was out like a light.

Tonight at the Spectrum, I had a date with a half-dozen fighters looking to take each other's heads off. Mom and Dad were wide awake in the fourteenth row, especially Dad. Bob was the chaperone, but his mind was elsewhere. He wanted to be in the ring tonight, but he wasn't selected. This was becoming a chronic problem. As I put more and more notches on my boxing bedpost, Bob slowly boiled. Tonight was probably worse than usual for him, but because his mother-and father-in-law were there, he had to keep his lid on a little tighter.

Not everyone, however, kept his lid on. As my parents took their seats, a few rows over a middle-aged black gentleman looked at them, smiled, and politely tipped his toupee. Beneath the rug was a darker version of Mr. Clean's head. I had never seen this particular gesture before from anyone of any color and laughed. Mom followed, and then Bob. Dad looked like he had seen a crazy person on the street. A few rows up, my eyes caught a joint being passed from spectator to spectator to spectator. I knew it wouldn't be long before that joint or another one just like it made its way over toward where my parents were. The smoke was already well on its way. And with that, it was time for me to take my judge's seat.

The second fight of the night was my first—Eugene "Cyclone" Hart versus Doc Holliday. It was a ten-round bout between a couple of young middleweights, only one of whom would leave the ring tonight with a decent shot at a title fight. Middleweights were my favorite to watch. They were not little guys by any stretch of the imagination. Many, like Cyclone Hart, were just shy of six feet tall. If they weighed 160 pounds, there was at most a pound or two that wasn't sculpted for the purpose of leveling an opponent. The middleweights—the really good ones, anyway—combined the power of a heavyweight with the incredible quickness of the lighter divisions.

Cyclone Hart was as fast as his nickname implied, though the source of the nickname was a little different. After winning something like seventy fights as an amateur, Cyclone began his pro career in 1969 at the Blue Horizon with a knockout. The next one ended the same way. In fact, his first ten fights, all at the Blue Horizon, ended with knockouts. When his manager, Jim Jacobs, and trainer Cus D'Amato, took him to greater "horizons"—including the Arena and the Spectrum—the streak continued. Overall, Hart's knockout streak out of the gate went eighteen professional fights. Most of the KOs occurred in the first, second, or third round. When you looked at the sheet with his fight-by-fight record printed on it, you thought it was an ad for KO-pectate.

I didn't root for anyone as a judge. I had learned that lesson for the first and final time in the Kallai fight. But as a onetime philosophy major at the University of Wisconsin, I was able to think abstractly with some of the best of them. If ever there was a reason to root for anyone, it was Eugene Hart. Some fighters passed through Philadelphia on their way to bigger purses in New York. Others came here, remained, and called it home. Others, like Hart, were born here and stayed. Cyclone *was* the City of Brotherly Love.

His birthplace on North 24th Street was the kind of working class neighborhood that stamped Philadelphia into your DNA. His father skipped to New York in the first year of his life, and Eugene was raised by his mother. In the early 1950s, Drs. Jonas Salk and Albert Sabin were working hard on polio vaccines, but children all over America and the world were still contracting polio.

Eugene Hart was one of those kids. For all those kids, the vaccine, however wonderful, represented the barn door closing after the horse got away. Or, as Eugene Hart might see it later, being hit just before the bell. The dreaded disease paralyzed and atrophied major muscles, and if it ran its course you might easily wind up in a wheelchair for life. How Hart was not only able to walk again but able to fight, was a miracle he never fully explained to the public except to say his mother did an amazing job raising her son.

At Eugene Hart's middle school at 24th and Jefferson in the early 1960s, gangs were rampant. Gang members basically gave you two choices—join the gang or get beaten up repeatedly. Eugene's mom did what she could to keep her son away from this element, but she couldn't do it all. Eugene learned to fight with his hands, and the gangs quickly learned trying to have Hart as a gang member wasn't worth the price of admission. The kid could have stopped there, but instead he protected the other, weaker kids from bullies and gang recruitment programs. No one had more heart than Hart.

Having dropped out of school not long after his twelfth birthday, Eugene Hart, like so many other kids, found a home away from home at the Police Athletic League recreation center on Columbia Avenue. There he met other kids looking for a better way, including promising young fighters like George Watts and his brother Bobby. Eventually, it was on to Joe Frazier's gym, where Hart solidified his style and made the leap to professional.

As a fighter, there were elements of Cyclone Hart that did not stand out right away. His stance was conventional. He would stand straight up with his forearms vertical in front of him, his gloves not far below his chin. He bounced a lot in the ring like many fighters, always in a rhythm, just about never flatfooted. His combinations were lively and effective. Sometimes the left-right combination would come from the sides, giving the opponent a bit more of a warning than Hart may have wanted.

But then there was the left. If Cyclone Hart hit you squarely with his straight-ahead left or the hook variation of the same, you were probably on your way out. It was a heavyweight's left attached to a middleweight's body but with flyweight speed. When you slowed down a standard 16 mm movie of it, the left was usually caught only by two frames—the one before and the one after. It was the left that kept Eugene out of the gangs and later made him "Cyclone."

Unfortunately for his opponents, the left had some cousins—a series of baby left jabs Hart threw at times to bait the other fighter. While lots of fighters had that same gun in their arsenal, Hart's was more like a machine gun. The left would fire six, seven, eight times. You couldn't really call them jabs and look yourself in the mirror. They were shots from a jackhammer, just longer. And if one caught the other fighter, a second and third probably followed even before the shock set in.

But Hart had had his problems as of late. First the streak of knockouts ended with a first-round technical knockout of Kitten Hayward, but why quibble over technicalities? Not long after, Hart won an exhausting ten round decision over Don Fullmer. Perhaps the streak really ended in Hart's bout with WBC/WBA light middleweight champion Denny Moyer. The fight was not for the title but rather an interesting match-up of top fighters in neighboring weight divisions.

The bout, however, got more interesting than anyone in the Spectrum that night had ever anticipated when in the sixth round, Hart threw his deadly left. Moyer avoided it, sort of, but the fighters wound up in a clinch. The momentum from Hart's left carried both fighters through the ropes and clear out of the ring. Moyer twisted his ankle. Hart blacked out. The fight was declared "no contest." The referee was Bob Polis. And one of the spectators gasping was yours truly.

Yes, here I was, Carol Polis, mom, wife, daughter, boxing judge having traveled in a few short years from appalled audience member to seasoned arbiter of professional pugilism, ready to take even the most gruesome matters into my own hands if necessary. In fact, I had my own audience with me now that included the folks who brought me into the world and the man who brought me into the boxing world, now grudgingly reduced to a spectator himself.

Once he regained consciousness that night, Hart declared a moral victory, but any pretension to the throne was eradicated shortly after by two consecutive losses. Both were by late round knockouts, one in the eighth round to Nate Collins and one in the ninth to Jose Gonzalez. With the Cyclone streak of early knockouts long over and his undefeated streak over as well, Hart's brain trust kept their fighter at arm's length. The word was that Hart's worst bout ever—the one with polio as a child—had limited his stamina.

Playground fights never went more than a round, if that, but professional fights could go ten or twelve. In looking ahead at the fighters who stood between him and a middleweight belt, Hart and his team were looking at knowledgeable opposing camps that would do whatever it took to keep Cyclone blowing long and hard till he was winded. So Jacobs and D'Amato took Hart up to their training facility in the Catskills and made sure he could go the distance if he had to. Workouts consisted of more than extra legwork and longer sparring matches. Cus D'Amato let Cyclone Hart have a full dose of his unique philosophy on boxing and life. According to Hart, at one point, "Cus held up a blade of grass and gave me a twenty minute theory on it."

Even if he got by Doc Holliday tonight, and no matter how many pebbles he managed to snatch from his master's open palm, if Cyclone Hart wanted to advance toward a World Middleweight title, he would have to move up the ladder in Philadelphia. And if he was to do that, he would have to go through several local fighters, including his old PAL gym mate, Bobby "Boogaloo" Watts.

Watts was born in Sumpter, South Carolina but moved north to Philadelphia with his family when he was ten. Bobby's cousin, future heavyweight contender Jimmy Young, pulled Watts off the basketball courts, into the gym and the ring. A year or so earlier, a group of bullies had taken Young's transistor radio, and Jimmy was determined to win the rematch.

During an amateur championship bout in Richie Kates' hometown, Vineland, New Jersey, the ring announcer introduced Watts' opponent as Johnny "Shing-A-Ling" Jones. As his nickname suggested, Shing-A-Ling danced up the aisle and into the ring. When Watts did his own dance up the aisle, he got the name "Boogaloo," and it stuck. Boogaloo kept dancing over the next few years. Of his first twenty-five professional fights, he lost only two. Watts hadn't accumulated so many knockouts as his friend, Cyclone Hart, but when you danced like that you didn't have to. Boogaloo was tall for a middleweight and had a dark, intense, dead-on stare. He stood straight and square in the ring and bounced through just about every round.

Boogaloo used a "peekaboo" stance, where he held his gloves up near his face and peered through briefly every once in a while. Opponents thought they could sneak a quick blow to Boogaloo's body, but they were almost always wrong. Booglaoo was one step ahead. He was rangy with a good reach. He would often swing from the side, his lean body turning with the punch and making his opponent's target virtually disappear. Then he made his opponent disappear.

Boogaloo Watts had already been compared to Sugar Ray Robinson, the greatest middleweight and possibly the greatest prizefighter of all time. But serious critics of the ring knew Boogaloo was still many steps away from the biggest dance of them all—the one that goes on in the mind of the critics themselves, where the standouts of the day stood toe to toe with the ghosts of the past. Robinson had everything a boxer could have and then some.

According to boxing analyst Bert Sugar, a legend in his own right, "Robinson could deliver a knockout going backward." According to *Time* magazine, "Robinson's repertoire, thrown with equal speed and power by either hand, includes every standard punch from a bolo to a hook—and a few he makes up on the spur of the moment." Boogaloo had Sugar Ray's speed, perhaps, but not his power, and it was an open secret that Boogaloo couldn't take a punch with the absolute best of them. Still in his mid-twenties, however, there was time for Boogaloo to close the gap between himself and the ghosts.

Like Hart, however, Watts would first have to deal with the cream of the Philadelphia crop, and that included Willie "The Worm" Monroe. Willie grew up and fought his amateur fights in Buffalo. He won forty-three of them in a row. When as a young man he visited friends in Philadelphia, he was so taken by the wealth of world class boxing talent, he decided to stay a while. When he married a Philly girl, the decision was final—Willie wouldn't be shuffling back to Buffalo.

Willie Monroe trained with Joe Frazier's team, and Frazier's manager Yank Durham crowned him "The Worm." Willie was tall and lanky with a big afro. Like Boogaloo, he bounced a lot, but Willie held his gloves down at his chest. Where Boogaloo baited you to take a shot at his body, Monroe baited you to take a swing at his head. Few fighters managed to hit either one solidly. Willie was always wiggling, wriggling, moving from side to side. When a punch was coming, it caught the outer skin of Monroe's twisting body. He was truly as hard to get a hold of as a worm.

Cyclone, Boogaloo, and the Worm would each have had their hands full having to go through the other two to get their title shot. Unfortunately for all three of them, they would probably have to go through Bad Bennie Briscoe, too. Briscoe was five or six years older than the up-and-coming coterie of Philadelphia middleweights and had spent those years in Spartan style. He wasn't bad in the sense of lacking skills. He had those to the hilt. Briscoe was bad in the new sense of the word. He was bad like Shaft. He was bad like Jim Brown. But he didn't look the part. Briscoe was just about the first fighter to shave his head bald, and only very lately were a few other fighters following suit.

In spite of having fought around the world and having met dignitaries like Princess Grace, Bennie Briscoe kept his day job. If a contender were lucky—or perhaps unlucky as he might see it—he could fight maybe a half dozen worthy opponents a year, and likely fewer. Some purses were only a few thousand dollars. So eleven months out of the year, Bad Bennie Briscoe could be found on his sanitation route. Briscoe was usually not the guy hanging off the back of the truck waiting for the next pickup. Briscoe was more often chasing the truck, making jabs and hooks in the air, killing two birds with one stone as he trained for his next fight. Residents of North Philadelphia, Briscoe's birthplace, looked forward to garbage pickup day, where for the price of a Hefty bag they got to see a hometown contender in a simulated fight.

They hoped one day to see Bad Bennie become champion, even if it meant no more exciting garbage days. Briscoe's odyssey as a professional had started back in 1962. Though he fought other first rate middleweights who would go on to become champion, it took a decade to garner a title fight of his own. Briscoe lost that one in Buenos Aires to Carlos Monzon in a grueling fifteen round decision. Even more recently, Briscoe had won the North American middleweight title against Art Hernandez and defended it successfully against Billy Douglas, both bouts occurring at the Spectrum. Bad Bennie now had plans to take another crack at the world title in Monte Carlo and say hello again to Princess Grace.

Whenever Hart, Watts, or Monroe was to have the displeasure of facing Bennie Briscoe, they would experience a style very different from either their own or that of their peers. Briscoe's body was compact. He usually stood flat and punched from his heels. He leaned his head directly toward his opponent. The head would often bob and weave in reaction to oncoming blows. Other times, however, the head would go forward and down, the blow usually missing over the top. This move gave Briscoe the appearance of a charging bull, which was an apt description of his style and character. He wasn't running from anybody. If you gave him some trouble, he wanted to see for himself exactly what you had.

People thought Bennie was Jewish. He wore a large embroidered Star of David on his robe and another, smaller one, on the front right leg of his boxing trunks. The same symbol had led the Judean tribes into battle thousands of years before against Assyrian and Phoenician armies of superior size. So the star was a fitting symbol for the proud and dangerous underdog image Briscoe had cultivated in the city of underdogs, Philadelphia. But unlike Max Baer, the former heavyweight champion who fought in the '30s, Briscoe was not born Jewish, and unlike Sammy Davis, Jr., he had apparently not converted. Bad Bennie claimed he simply found the symbol to be a powerful one. Outside the ring, he was a Baptist. For sure, he had Baptized many a young middleweight.

As I settled into my judge's chair, Cyclone Hart and Doc Holliday were in their respective corners getting ready for their fight. I could hear their trainers and cut men dishing out all sorts of advice on strategy and all sorts of dirt on the other fighter and his team. I was happy to be relaxed enough to take all this in. It was truly entertaining, like listening to a Redd Foxx routine, only with multiple Redd Foxxes.

But with the first round bell moments away and the distant memory of the brutal Hart-Moyer bout suddenly fresh in my mind, a different sort of reality took over. I looked around at the timekeeper and the writers near me and said, "Just so you know, if either one of those fighters goes through the ropes on this side, I'm going under that table." That got a big laugh. But I was dead serious.

Doc Holliday had flown all over the world. In recent months, he had been to Halifax, Nova Scotia; Sao Paolo, Brazil; Buenos Aires, Argentina; and Monte Carlo, Monaco. The problem was, he had lost all four fights. Hart had been no place more glamorous than upstate New York, but he was home now and prepared. When the bell sounded, Cyclone came out swinging. There was no left, right, left. It was left, left, left, left, with an occasional right. This was a sure sign Hart was in no mood to test his post-polio, D'Amato-driven stamina. When the first round was over, Hart looked like he wanted more, and Holliday looked like he wanted less. Five-four for Hart.

About a minute into round two, with the action on my side and straining my neck, Hart found an opening. One thing among many I had learned in my fist year of professional judging was how quickly the nature of a bout changed when one fighter smelled blood. Once a truly effective blow was landed and the opponent lost his orientation even for a few seconds, the window of opportunity was open. The crowd knew it as well as the fighter. The noise level rose dramatically. People stood, and there was mass anticipation as in a bull fight.

The fighter on the offensive picked it up not by a notch, but by a quantum leap. He threw ten punches where just a few seconds earlier he would have been content to throw two. He chased his dazed opponent around the ring if he had to, into safe corners that were suddenly no longer safe. He didn't want to hang around all night and maybe become prey for the same hunt. He didn't want to put his fate in the hands of a judge. He wanted to go home, now.

No one was more suited to this particular task—finishing a stunned opponent—than Eugene Cyclone Hart. His lefts to Holliday's head were piston-like, followed by a ridiculously hard right-left combination that left Doc needing a doctor. Holliday went down hard, thankfully not on my side and not beyond the confines of the ring. The ten count was inevitable, but largely a formality. Holliday was awake but in no condition to resume the match. Sitting and leaning back on his hands was a moral victory, and you could see from his facial expression that's where it would end.

As I handed in my card for the round—an utter formality—I glanced back at my entourage. Dad seemed least impressed, even distant. Impressing Dad, of course, was never easy. He was at one time president of Big Brothers of America, which had its national headquarters in Philadelphia. In appreciation for all his work helping to mentor young men who needed a male figure to look up to, Dad was invited to meet President John F. Kennedy in 1962.

Whenever I closed my eyes, I could see that black and white photo from the Oval Office picturing a group of gentlemen in suits and ties apparently conferring about America's youth or some other such topic of great importance. One of those men was the President, another my father. If they were discussing me right now, maybe they'd be saying I'd be more suited to a golf tournament or maybe badminton. Something a little less violent and more ladylike. "Mr. President," I'd say. " . . . Dad. I'm having a blast."

"The Battle of the Sexes," as it was called, was fought on a tennis court on September 20, 1973. In the Astrodome in Houston, Texas, women's champion Billy Jean King was brought out like Cleopatra on a chair held aloft by a bunch of bare-chested, well toned men posing as Egyptian slaves. The great old white male hope, Bobby Riggs, was carted out on a rickshaw by a bunch of female models. The event was hyped as the last word on which gender was superior, but for about an hour we all watched a middle-aged man try to catch his breath while chasing balls sprayed all over the court by a young woman. The young woman won in two sets, 6-2 and 6-1. It was fun to watch, but very little was settled.

A different battle of the sexes was being fought in my own home, and even less was settled there. Bob had been getting very few assignments, while I had been getting quite a few. The publicity for me kept coming. Bob seemed to think he had created a monster. For me, the monster was Bob's fragile ego. The more I catered to it, the more it wanted. The image I had of myself was a lot different, more like a horse champing at the bit, with a jealous, king-sized jockey holding me back.

Our battle of the sexes was fought not with lobs and volleys but with reverse psychology and taking one for the team. A case in point was the phone call I was making this very evening to Commissioner Zach Clayton. I asked Kenny to make sure no one picked up the extension in the kitchen, and I cupped my free hand over the mouthpiece.

"Zach," I said, "what I'm asking for is simple. Just give Bob more assignments than me."

"I understand what you're saying," Clayton said, "and I absolutely can't help you."

"Why not?" I asked.

"Let me he explain it to you this way," he said. "If I need an attorney and I know a husband and wife who are both attorneys, and the woman is the better attorney, I'm going to go to the woman."

"Well, we're not attorneys," I said.

"But I do believe I've made my case," Clayton said.

"Yes you have," I said. "You're also making a lot of trouble for me at home. I want you to know that."

"I'm sure you'll work that out."

In the months that followed, we did make an attempt. Since they wouldn't put us together working a fight, Bob had the idea to put us together on a stage of sorts. We started to do speaking engagements together at men's groups. Our shtick was fairly straightforward. Bob was the opening act and would talk a little about boxing and what it was like to be a ring official. That would include a few words on how subjective the fight judging process really was. Then the lights would go out and the projector on. We would show a round from a classic fight, stop the projector, and turn the lights back on. Then Bob would ask the audience members who thought fighter "A" won to raise their hand. Then fighter "B." That led to an interesting discussion of who really won the round and why.

Then came the main event, which was me. I usually felt like I was going to vomit when I got ready to speak in public, but I had learned to hide it well. For me public speaking was like having blood taken from my veins, a sensation I hated so much that I always had the nurse take it from my hand, a much more painful process. But once I got going in front of the audience, I was basically okay. It was like learning not to look at the blood going up the tube. A friendly whistle once in a while didn't hurt, either.

Aside from appreciating a spontaneous show of affection, I continued to learn perhaps the most important lesson you can learn from appearing in public—be yourself. Among other things, that meant not faking it. If you didn't know the answer to a question, you had to say so. Maybe you had a hunch or an educated guess, but you needed to be frank about it. If Bob and I were in a Y or a synagogue or wherever else, there might easily be ten men in the audience, if not ten times ten, who for all practical purposes were boxing history buffs. Fudging it would sink me, whether I was caught immediately or not.

So if I didn't know, I said openly I wasn't an expert, and I'd get back to them. I actually meant that. I took notes and made follow-up calls. Some of these men might have thought that, as I was the one person in ten thousand who really did follow up, I was either out of my mind or fishing for a date. Neither, of course, was true. Sometimes Bob let me hang there a bit before stepping in himself to answer. Sometimes even he didn't know the answer. But these gigs seemed to be an answer for us, at least for a couple of hours. It was a paid date. There was plenty of adulation to go around, and no arguing between us about who won a given round. The fights we showed on the screen were ancient history, as I hoped our own fighting would become.

CHAPTER EIGHT
THE BLUE HORIZON

By the time I appeared on *To Tell the Truth* on February 12, 1974, I had judged thirty-five professional bouts. In the same way that I got judging assignments, I got offers to make media appearances. I was in the mix. There was little mystery as to how I got the call for *To Tell the Truth*. The show was produced by Goodson-Todman, the same producers as for *What's My Line?* I must have been on a Rolodex or short list of some kind. I wanted to know how to get my husband on the same list, because to tell the truth, he was a little ticked off at having to drive me into New York.

To a degree, I knew the drill. The city was the same and so was 30 Rockefeller Center, although the studio was 6-A instead of 8-H. The big difference in this case was having to go in a couple days early to train my imposters. The show, another American classic originating in the 1950s, featured a host, four celebrity panelists, and three players, each of whom claimed to be the person of interest. That person typically did something a little offbeat, just as in *What's My Line?*

But here, the panelists asked detailed questions far exceeding the yes-no fare of *What's My Line?* After a few minutes of sleuthing and probing, the panelists wrote down a 1, 2, or 3 on a card, indicating which contestant they thought was the real deal. The more wrong answers, the more money the contestants got. The climax was the moment at the end of the round when the host asked the real whoever to stand up. The fakes and feints were a cheap but clean thrill. When executed correctly, it looked something like a bunch of bus riders not sure if they were getting off at the right stop.

My imposters were both great gals. Ginger Folmer was a homemaker and executive secretary from New York. She was tall, slim, pretty, and had about the worst hairdo I had ever seen. It looked like

Dolley Madison's wig after going through a carwash. Ursula Byrne was a pioneer in her own right, both a teacher and a lawyer. She stood about three inches shorter than I was, so if any panelists were going for irony, she was probably first in line.

My imposters had only a few hours and some time overnight to become Carol Polis, and I was only too willing to help. We met with a couple of the assistant producers in a small conference room, where I gave my life story and discussed everything from the difference between a hook and a jab to how heavy was a featherweight. It felt good to convey some of my boxing knowledge to other women, even if they were interested on only the most expedient level.

As we sparred, I wondered whether either of these imposters might want to continue on and play the real Carol Polis for a few more weeks in the "home version" of the show. I needed a break. I would be willing to show them how to pull chewing gum wrappers out from between the sofa cushions while telling your husband over the phone no one called for him. While I caught some sun and shopped, they could even judge a fight or two if it wasn't a major card.

The set of *To Tell the Truth* was all blue panel and gold carpet, with steps leading up to the panelist's booth at the left side and the contestant's booth on the right. Along the back wall were three oversized cartoonish stick-figures with their fingers crossed, like mine. I had used an eyebrow pencil to paint a small fake beauty mark on my right cheek, and I hoped it reminded people more of Marilyn Monroe than Bela Lugosi. Front and center stood the host, Garry Moore, a friendly TV gameshow veteran. Nipsey Russell, Kitty Carlyle, Bill Cullen, and Peggy Cass were well groomed and raring to go.

The first guest wrote a book on psychic phenomena entitled *Psycho-Kinesis: Moving Matter with the Mind.* Two large men on the ends and a petite woman in the middle all claimed to be the author, Adrian Clark. Garry Moore's synopsis of the book described one woman who could make a slice of bread jump across the table into her mouth and another who could knock down any man who came near her just by willing it. You knew right away the panel was going to have fun with that one.

Nipsey Russell was about to have some fun all his own. Nipsey first made a name for himself as black cop on the TV show *Car 54, Where Are You?* More recently, he had been a regular on *Rowan & Martin's Laugh-In.* He was known for writing clever poems pertinent to the moment, many of which he composed on the spot. And here in studio 6-A, he had doodled something during a commercial break: "It was in a gypsy tea room, in a fortune telling place, a lovely girl read my mind, then she slapped my face."

My premonition about the woman who knocked down men was correct. The round was full of quips and asides about women who did the same thing with their looks or who at least tried. Kitty Carlyle got serious with a question regarding why all these so-called psychics weren't doing something more useful like looking for oil. Contestant number 3 replied that indeed they were. Peggy Cass wanted to know how many books Edgar Cayce, the Sleeping Prophet, wrote during his life. Contestant 3 replied he didn't write any. But to tell the truth, he dictated dozens.

Amidst talk of sending thoughts to other people and foretelling the future, I tried to envision whether I would still feel so anxious after my own round was over. Normally the same tension that built up before an event was released afterward, with maybe only a headache left over. But I was getting a strange answer at this moment from the beyond. Whatever was tugging at my state of mind had well preceded this taping and would linger long after.

Only Peggy Cass and Bill Cullen tuned into the correct frequency and picked contestant 3. Cullen claimed his selection was the product of automatic writing and held up a card with a "3" on it that looked like it had been written by Edgar Cayce with Parkinson's disease. I had a strange feeling I was next.

I had on the same aquamarine ribbed knit dress as on What's My Line, but I could see right away I should have worn protective gear. This was no amateur fight. The panel came out swinging like they were a men's group at one of the speaking engagements I did with Bob. I knew we were all in trouble when Bill Cullen revealed that his father once managed fighters in Pittsburgh.

Nipsey asked me how many types of parries there were in boxing. I thought a parry was a fencing term and said I didn't know. Nipsey explained to the studio audience that boxing was modeled after fencing and that to parry was to knock aside a blow with your arm, in either sport. I certainly hadn't parried that one. Nipsey kept coming with a question on whether a championship had ever been won or lost with a foul. To my knowledge, one had been lost. But I didn't know which one. Maybe this one right here.

Nipsey made quick work of my crazy-haired executive secretary friend and then yours truly by asking who Hammerin' Hank was in the world of boxing. The game show poet had us on the ropes. If there was a Hammerin' Hank on anyone's mind, it was Henry Aaron, the baseball player. In a few weeks, the season would start, and Aaron needed one more homerun to tie Babe Ruth's all time record and another to surpass it. But Ginger and I whiffed. Then Ursula hit a homerun, or landed with a right as it were, when she said, "Henry Armstrong."

That rang a bell. Armstrong was a star back in the mid-1930s. No one was going to outshine Joe Louis in that era, but Hammerin' Hank came as close as humanly possible without ever laying a glove on Joe. Managed by the likes of celebrities Al Jolson and George Raft, Armstrong took on opponents like he was barnstorming or bar fighting, beating more than twenty in one year. To put an exclamation point on the story, he held three separate world titles simultaneously—featherweight, lightweight, and welterweight. For a moment, I felt like a lightweight myself.

Before I could stop the bleeding, Peggy Cass asked me who fought in the Fight of the Long Count. Apparently girls could play rough, too, especially with other girls. But I ducked and recovered halfway. "That was a long time ago," I said. "That was between Tunney, and I forget who the other one was." Thank you, Carol Polis number 2. Next! Kitty asked Carol Polis number 1 why she wanted to be a boxing judge. Ginger, who really never wanted any such thing, explained that it all started with a bet at a New Year's Eve party. That was rich. As if anyone would remember a bet like that the next morning.

Suddenly, I remembered who the other fighter was in the Long Count. But the bell had rung. Nipsey, Peggy, Bill, and Kitty all picked contestant 3, the diminutive Ursula who had hit one out of the park. Now it was time for the real Carol Polis to stand up, and she did with a fake or two. Fortunately, I was taller standing up than Ginger was sitting down.

As I stood there and received a resounding ovation, I wasn't quite sure whether to be proud or embarrassed. The art of drawing a blank, honed at B'nai B'riths all over the Delaware Valley, had now been perfected on national television. And this time it was good not only for brownie points but a three-way split of a $500 purse, the prize for shutting out the panel. Not to mention another case of Turtle Wax.

More importantly, Jack Dempsey was the other fighter in the Fight of the Long Count. It was 1927 and Dempsey's last fight, an attempt to regain the heavyweight title. After six difficult rounds against the younger, taller Tunney, Dempsey put his opponent down on the canvas. Dempsey then made what might have been a mistake by standing over Gene Tunney. The referee was not allowed to begin the ten count until Dempsey had returned to a neutral corner. This gave the somewhat dazed Tunney about thirteen seconds in all to stand up. He did and then returned to beat Dempsey.

Garry Moore asked the real Carol Polis if she had any plans to venture beyond the respected but limited sphere of Philadelphia boxing and do a title fight, perhaps in a world famous venue like Madison Square Garden in New York. I wasn't sure if the host had read my mind, but I was certain great minds thought alike. I was, as a matter of fact, in the process of applying to New York for an out-of-state boxing license.

If I had won my Turtle Wax by decision, I had won my crown as a self-reflecting psychic by knockout. My premonition was spot on. *To Tell the Truth* was in my rear view mirror, and I still felt anxious. Something wasn't quite right.

Mom went into a coma on February 16. The doctors called it

an atomic coma. Mom's appendix had burst when she was twenty-one. There was no pain at first, so she didn't know it. The operation to remove the appendix was successful except for the fact that adhesions gradually formed from the incisions.

During the healing process, the walls of the intestines joined together at certain places due to the formation of scar tissue. Mom had trouble digesting after that, and she and Dad decided that at age sixty-five, it was time to have the adhesions removed. But it turned out the cure was worse than the disease. She was allergic to the anesthesia, and three days later—four days after *To Tell the Truth*—she went into the coma.

I took a Monday morning flight out of Philadelphia International down to Miami. I wasn't a hundred percent certain it was the right thing to do. Still ringing in my head from earlier in the morning was Bob yelling at Jimmy and Kenny. It was over something ridiculous, like how the phone was put back on the receiver. This while my mother lay in a coma. It was a menacing yell. I could only imagine things getting worse in my absence, not better.

At the hospital, Dad gave me some time to be alone with Mom. I sat by her bed and watched her face for expressions, but there was none. She had been given a tracheotomy, and her breathing through the tube lacked vitality. It was my mother for sure, but she was not quite there somehow, somewhere just beyond sleep. I thought if she could hear my voice, she would want to leap up and start a bridge game. I had nothing at all prepared to say, but stories just came out of my mouth. Like the time when I was five and stuffed the bathroom bowl overflowing with toilet paper. Then threw lit matches into the whole works. Pretty soon I had a bathroom bonfire big enough to cure even King Kong of constipation.

Around the same age, I was standing on the sun porch looking out from a tall window screen at the gardeners. They were planting a rose bush. One gardener was stout, the other tall and lean, both black gentlemen. I called out to them, "Do you make chocolate wee-wee?"

The next thing I felt was a hand, a sort of feminine Vise-Grip on my wrist. Mom had heard my little play on words and was not amused.

Tiles and wallpaper flew by, and the next thing I knew we were in the bathroom. Mom washed my mouth out with soap. People actually did that in 1941.

All that bathroom humor and not a stir from Mom. Maybe she was saving it up for a big breakout belly laugh. But Dad came back in with the doctor, so the next story would have to wait. There were charts to be read and tubes to be adjusted, and I had a few questions of my own about the I.V.

The following day I had a fresh batch of ancient stories for Mom. One of them was bound to work. There was the time I was sixteen and "rented out" my driver's license to my brother, Arthur, who was barely fourteen. He really wanted to try driving and I really needed seventy-five cents for I couldn't remember what. Arthur was still awaiting a growth spurt and put a pillow on the driver's seat. The car seemed to pull out of the driveway by itself. Ten minutes later, it pulled back in followed by a police car. The policeman stopped, got out, and explained he noticed a car driving without a driver.

The next ditty took place in the winter, around 1943. I loved when icicles hung down from the eaves of the garage. Each one was like a sword, some as long as three feet. The object was to take the shovel and knock them down. Sometimes when you were lucky, a really long one fell to the snow intact. A bunch of short icicles coming down in droves wasn't bad either. A few moments after one particularly fruitful swat, I felt a warm liquid pooling over my eye. It was blood. One of the bigger icicles had missed my eye by a tiny fraction of an inch, but somehow in all the celebration I hadn't noticed it till then.

I still had the scar over my eye, and I felt it now in the hospital room. Was I really that mischievous? This was like a Jewish confessional. But the icicle incident wasn't really my fault. It was just a kid being a kid. As I considered the stories I was telling my mother, who was very still, they took on some other pattern of meaning, like a series of dreams where the whole was greater than the sum of the parts. The car without the driver was suddenly me. The bloody eye belonged to a boxer. Or maybe it was a bloody eye belonging to one of my kids.

I got up and wandered the hallways for a while. This was the best I could do. I knew I had to get out of there, fly home, and protect my children. Just as much, I needed to stay with my mother who I loved more than anything in the world. A lifetime of doing two things at once, but there was no way to be two places at once. I felt like I was being physically torn apart.

As I neared my mother's room again, I spotted a man in a white coat. I hadn't met him before but assumed he was one of the doctors checking in on my mother. He had a kind face, and next to a smile from my mother herself, that's what I needed most. So I flagged him down and explained my dilemma—that I just didn't know where my place was at this point. The man in the white coat offered to go inside Mom's room, where Dad was now, and have a talk with him.

A few minutes later, the man in the white coat with the kind face emerged and said he and my father agreed there wasn't much I could do for my mother. My place was with my children. Disappointment and relief arrived together. My Jewish confessional ended with a doctor's note. By the time I had my things gathered up from Mom's room, my father had explained that the man in the white coat was Dr. Fritz, the head of the entire hospital. I was welcome to call him whenever I might need some comfort. I just hoped his staff was half as good as he was.

The phone rang at home in the late afternoon of a chilly day in mid-March. It was definitely Dad's ring. Mom had come out of the coma a few days earlier but was very weak and frail. My father urged me to wait a little while before coming back down, because he said Mom looked like an Auschwitz survivor. The key word, I thought, was "survivor." The terrible dread of answering the phone was now thankfully gone. Either Mom was getting better or was the same as the day before, and I could live with either one.

Dad said he and Mom had watched me on *To Tell the Truth* in the hospital room. Because of her tracheotomy, Mom couldn't say anything, but she recognized me and motioned a few times with her hand.

Dad's reaction to the show was typical Dad. He zeroed in on the fake beauty mark. "Carol," he said. "What was that strange black mark?" You just didn't tell Dad you were trying to look like a movie star to extend your fifteen minutes of fame by a few seconds. So I told him it must have been a piece of dirt or something.

My mother's return to consciousness made it a little easier to go back to the fights. There was always enough to shut out of my mind as it was. Tuesday, March 19 at the Blue Horizon featured an assortment of six fights that held no special significance for anyone other than the fighters themselves and their ring teams. But for me, any night at the Blue Horizon was special.

The Blue Horizon consisted of a pair of four-story brick houses at 1314-16 North Broad Street in Philadelphia. They were built as apartments in 1865 and were Second Empire structures. The label referred to French styled buildings of the period. They were usually squarish masonry buildings with a mansard roof and a lot of ornamentation. One other typical feature ideal for a public exhibition was their high ceilings.

There may have been fighting inside these two buildings in the first century of their existence, but there was no boxing until 1961. That year, new owners Edna and Jimmy Toppi knocked out the first floor ceiling and created a quaint but exciting venue with a balcony. Within a few years, the place was legendary. Cards ranged from run-of-the-mill to title fights, but you were no one in Philadelphia boxing if you hadn't given and taken blows there.

Chairs on the main floor were the folding kind. Up in the balcony, the chairs were anchored to the floor. That was a good thing, because you got the feeling that otherwise they might fly out from time to time. The balcony wasn't like the ones in an old-fashioned movie theater, where couples went to hide from the world. At the Blue Horizon, the balcony was part of the action. It hung down and out over the fight, giving the ring the feel of an observatory during surgery. During quieter moments, you could hear individual comments, catcalls, snide remarks, and belches from upstairs. These sounds resonated along with and equal to every punch.

All told, the capacity was around fifteen hundred. As a ring official, there was nowhere you dreaded having your score read aloud more than at the Blue Horizon. There were as many as fifteen hundred judges in there, and easily five hundred knew more boxing than you did.

The place was maybe two-thirds filled tonight, which would give the running commentary from above a slight echo. I was settled in with my stack of cards. The referee, Frank Cappuccino, was announced to applause. The announcer at the Blue Horizon always emphasized the first syllable for Frank, so when you heard "CAP-a-chino," you knew you were home. "Carol Polis" wasn't quite as resonant, but I seemed to have a few very loud and vociferous fans scattered throughout the building. I had kept my hello to Frank and the rest of the officials brief. We all knew we were under surveillance. We were being filmed along with the fights. A hand gesture here or a protracted conversation there, and you might be up for review.

The second fight was one of those contests where you didn't know whether you were coming or going. When you did back-to-back fights with a short break in between, you sometimes had to remind yourself exactly which fight you were judging. If you got that straight, the next order of business was making sure which fighter was which. That wasn't always as easy as it sounded. Sometimes the bell for round one arrived before the cards for the fight. Sometimes the cards arrived and the names were wrong. Sometimes both fighters wore black trunks, black shoes, white socks, and a green top. Sometimes the fighters looked alike.

But tonight took the cake. Amidst all sorts of other confusion, both fighters were named Tyrone. Tyrone Freeman and Tyrone Taylor, a couple of welterweights from Philadelphia, were meeting in a six round bout. Neither had a very good record. When you're 1 and 4 or 3 and 12 in your pro career, you're helping to provide much better won-loss records for other fighters. But when you're going against another fighter with a similarly sub-par record, you are keenly aware that most likely one of you will not be invited back.

As great as championship caliber fights could be, fights of

desperation were sometimes even better. Tyrone vs. Tyrone was one such fight. For my part, I paid close attention to which Tyrone returned to which corner. When they returned to center ring for the next round, I hung in there with them and didn't let go of my card until they returned to their corners yet again. My headache tonight would be as great or greater than either Tyrone's or Tyrone's. Needless to say, the winner of this bout—a six-round decision—was Tyrone. Tyrone, however, had put up a valiant fight, though it was probably his last one.

A long break between bouts was a chance to eat the dinner you had missed a few hours earlier. And that's when the toughest fight of the night occurred—the one between you and a Blue Horizon hot dog. Usually the hot dog won by decision. They were basically rubber hot dogs, but if you were hungry enough you bought two and finished one-and-a-half.

While gagging, I looked at the program and around the arena, but either way I couldn't locate the skirt boxer. I couldn't remember his name, but I did recall the leopard print pattern on the African kilt that hung from his waist when he did battle. Whenever I saw this guy getting ready to enter the ring, I knew I was getting a break. He was rarely hit solidly, but the breeze of a passing glove always seemed to put him on the canvas in round one or two. He was tall, thin, and landed hard. The skirt boxer didn't really hale from Africa. He was from Brooklyn, and if that's where he was tonight instead of Philadelphia, he was probably better off.

The fifth fight on the card was a contest between lightweight Alfonso Evans with a decent record and lightweight Ken Muse with a lightweight one. Evans was from Philadelphia, but Muse was from Camden, and tonight because of the skirt boxer's absence, was the most exotic fighter on the card. But when all else was mediocre, there was one form of entertainment that never failed—the ring card girls. Before each round, a tall, thin young thing in pumps and hot pants would enter the ring and display a sign showing the round number to each of the four arena sides.

The ring card girl's moment of entry into the ring was unmistakable, the highlight of the round for many a man whose memory of local fights and romantic encounters with his own forlorn bride was a blur stretching back to the 1940s. The ropes caused the ring card girl to bend over precisely, providing a brief view that made a tough act to follow for even the best pugilist. Once in the ring, a card held aloft correctly did more to transfix the grizzled Philadelphia fight fan than a tenth-round knockout or a Wonderbra ever could.

But this time it apparently wasn't enough. It started to my left somewhere and seemed to be drifting around during round 2 of Evans vs. Muse. It was ugliness, like a small hurricane that didn't yet have a name. There was a low growl, the sound of animals preparing to eat their prey. You couldn't see the eye of the hurricane, but the swirl of people at the outer edges told you all you needed to know. There was a fight going on, and it wasn't in the ring.

I called it "the wave." It was as good a name as any. The wave moved around the floor. It ebbed and flowed, picking up momentum here, losing some there. It bounced off of walls and deformed around pillars. It gobbled up some innocent bystanders and spit out some not-so-innocent ones. Maybe it was headed for me. Maybe not. But if it did hit me, the wave would have to knock me out cold and drag me away with its undertow. I had a job to do. I had a fight to watch. Even if it wasn't the best one in the house.

No one likes to be beaten to the punch. Especially on Mother's Day. Especially when your mother was in the hospital. So on this Sunday, May 12, I beat the alarm clock to the punch. I beat my snoring husband and four hungry kids to the punch. As I whipped some pancake batter, I focused in on 6 AM. Somewhere around then I would make the call to Florida and wish my mother a happy Mother's Day long before anyone would do the same for me.

Bob and I took the kids out to dinner, and a few minutes after we got back home, the phone rang. It was a Florida ring, I thought, and when I heard my sister Nancy's voice on the line I knew I was right. She had been down there visiting for a couple of days. Nancy sounded overly sweet, and then there was a pause. Sometimes when you are hit very hard, you don't feel it where you are hit. I felt this in my legs first, which began to buckle. Then I felt it in my stomach. But I was still standing and waiting for it to arrive at my head. Then and only then would it be real. Maybe it would never arrive and this phone call would land on the scrap heap of a thousand disturbing but forgettable dreams.

But I heard the words now, and with every moment it seemed less possible to exit the nightmare. My mother had gone into cardiac arrest overnight and passed away. I got a few details from my sister and said I'd call her back.

I decided to take a little time to gather my thoughts before telling the rest of the household. Somehow, against all odds, I would put things in order. I would call Rabbi Korn and thank him for all he had done. I would find the letter I had written the day before to my mother but had never sent. I would reread the letter with all the loving things I had written and then find a special place for it.

Now, I glanced out the window and noticed the clouds at sunset were in a pattern I had never seen before, something like a ladder to heaven. There would be no putting things in order tonight. So I crawled into the bathtub and sobbed.

CHAPTER NINE
FIASCO AT THE FELT FORUM

My New York State professional boxing judge license was granted on July 17, 1974. The bout I had begun when I applied in February was not one I could fight alone. Much the same way when a high school senior seeks admission into West Point or Annapolis he needs the written recommendation of a congressman, I needed a sponsor from within the higher ranks of the state government. Herb Posner, Secretary of the Select Committee on Environmental Conservation for the State of New York, became that sponsor.

I had never met Herb Posner, and though he had written a concise, complimentary letter of recommendation on my behalf—recommending that New York be "among the first to grant a license to a woman to be a boxing judge"—I still hadn't met him. He was a friend of a friend. I had a lot of friends of friends now. As much as there were people out there who did not wish me well for having punctured the bubble of what had been exclusively a man's world, there were even more who not only wanted a spot on the bandwagon but wanted the chance to drive it around the block a couple of times. I appreciated every last one of them.

I had on a blue skirt, a blue and white houndstooth blouse, and teardrop earrings when Bob and I took the train into Manhattan. When we walked into the downtown offices of State Athletic Commission Chairman Edwyn Dooley, I expected some sort of instant replay of the scene at my Harrisburg induction a year and a half earlier. But this was clearly a new round. While there were reporters and photographers there from the *New York Post*, the *Daily News*, and *UPI*, the fanfare didn't match up well. Pennsylvania Governor Schapp's New York counterpart, Nelson A. Rockefeller, was elsewhere that day. Chairman Dooley was gracious but nowhere nearly as visibly elated as his PA counterpart, Zach Clayton, had been, or for that matter Governor Schapp.

This was no big surprise. I loved New York, and perhaps New York loved me. But I was not their hometown girl. And though as a woman judge I was a first for New York, New York had been beaten to the punch by Pennsylvania and seemed to know it. The good news was Dooley thought I would probably be selected to judge a fight in New York sometime in either August or September. It couldn't come soon enough.

The days since my mother had passed were filled with sad, empty moments that found their way in whenever motion subsided. I had given my well wishes to many other people who had lost their moms, telling each of them I couldn't imagine what it must be like, and it turned out I was right. I literally couldn't bring myself to sprinkle my mother's ashes over the synagogue garden. True comfort was hard to find.

Everything now seemed to be divided into a before and after, with the before being the time I could pick up the phone and share a laugh with Mom and after being the time I could not. The dividing line seemed so arbitrary, cruel, and unfair. There were strange moments, too, when I almost reached for that phone and then quickly remembered which side of the line I was now living on.

I wanted to control those moments. I wanted to think about my mother when I wanted to, but there were unexpected and sinister hair triggers all around me. The most inane of all those triggers was the song *Seasons in the Sun. Seasons in the Sun* by Terry Jacks, to this point a one-hit wonder who could have been a no-hit blunder, played on AM hit radio at least three times an hour while my mother lay dying.

It so happened that *Seasons* was a song about someone dying and bidding farewell to loved ones. The song was number one in the country and number one on my personal hate list. When those first four somber notes chimed in, I knew I was in for another dose of "Goodbye to you my trusted friend" and another losing bout with a box of Kleenex. Now as a half-orphan for a little over two months, AM radio showed me no mercy. We were down to maybe twice an hour, but it still felt like three. I could turn off my clock radio, but *Seasons* continued to intrude in cars, bars, restaurants, supermarkets, and beauty parlors. It was the leitmotif for my own personal hell.

Not that life was entirely predictable. The roller-coaster ride that was Watergate seemed to be approaching the big incline. Indictments of key White House staff for obstructing justice had been handed down, and a few days after my appointment the House Judiciary Committee voted to recommend impeachment of the President. No matter what else was going on, there was really one and only one story that summer. It was compelling and even a little scary at times, but it wasn't good enough. I needed a story of my own. So when I got the call notifying me that I would be judging a card at Madison Square Garden on August 5, a new song started playing in my head.

Bob and I took the train in early in the day on Monday, the 5th. With the oil crisis, the train seemed to be the responsible way to go. There was a nice symmetry to the trip. We left from Penn Station and arrived at Penn Station. Penn Station 30th Street in Philadelphia was a gorgeous Roman structure with a large atrium, travertine walls, and tall Corinthian columns. Penn Station in New York had the same sort of grandeur yet was even bigger. But there was one problem. The Penn Station in New York was no longer there.

When they started tearing down New York's Pennsylvania Station in 1963, protests began almost right away. The objections continued but got drowned out by a hundred and one other protests over the Vietnam War, civil rights, women's rights, and countless related issues. By the time the 1960s ended, it seemed as if no one was happy and there was nothing left to protest. As for Pennsylvania Station, it was now a hole in the ground. Trains still arrived and departed, but above stood a circular steel and glass building known as Madison Square Garden.

The original Madison Square Garden had stood at 26th Street and Madison Avenue, otherwise known as Madison Square. The arena was known more than anything else as a velodrome, which is a venue for indoor bicycle racing. By the time the new Madison Square Garden was erected at 50th Street and Eighth Avenue, it was Madison in name only, and its most prominent events were boxing, hockey, and basketball. The newest one, located over the railroad tracks between 31st and 33rd Streets and Seventh and Eighth Avenues, was finished in 1968. It was large, modernistic, and hated by many.

New Yorkers, especially the educated, saw it as a symbol of destruction. When "air rights" were sold by a railroad and bought by a developer, everybody won except the people who had to look at and pass through the new structure. Probably the most famous quote about the new configuration was made by the architectural historian Vincent Scully, who said that while at one time, "One entered the city like a god, one scuttles in now like a rat."

I scuttled in, not so much as a rat, but as an early bird trying to catch a worm. As a judge, you were supposed to arrive early. As a debuting judge in a city that happened to be the boxing capital of the world, you wanted to arrive extra early. Bob and I made our way up various staircases and escalators toward the light of day like divers emerging from the deep sea looking for air. We found it, but it wasn't entirely fresh air. The swirling debris and faint urine stench down below was more or less the debris and urine above. You weren't entirely sure at first that you were really outside. People walked through the heat and humidity in a kind of harried haze of their own. Either things hadn't gotten any better since my last visit or they had gotten slightly worse.

But what did I care? Rat or early bird, I had made the big time. It reminded me of that old joke where a tourist walks up to an elderly Jewish New Yorker and asks how to get to Carnegie Hall. The answer: "Practice, practice, practice!" Fifty-five professional fights in, and I had made it to boxing's Carnegie Hall—Madison Square Garden.

Only not exactly. The card I was scheduled to judge was not at the main arena but at the smaller venue next door known as the Felt Forum. I had heard the name a thousand times and thought it sounded like a wholesale clothing outlet. In reality, the building had been named after Madison Square Garden president Irving Felt. I thought it was generally more polite to wait until you were dead and have other people name a building after you. On the other hand, the MSG president's original name was probably something more like Feldstein or Feldheim, so it could have turned out worse. Whatever the name, until further questioning, I told people I would be officiating at Madison Square Garden.

The Felt Forum director of public relations, Marvin Kohn, met us outside the arena and took us inside. In spite of our chaperone, the security guard wanted some ID. I was equipped with my Division of State Athletic Commission license card, complete with close-cropped head shot of squinting, smiling yours truly. The strange thing was, the guard wanted Marvin Kohn's ID, too. This after addressing him with a straight face as Mr. Kohn. Either New York was such a major venue that even the most routine personal transactions were subject to official review, or "just doing my job" had been reduced to a state of brain death.

The Forum seated about 4,500 and was still fairly empty. Before I took my own seat, I had a rite of passage to go through known as "first night formalities." I was introduced to perhaps two dozen officials from Madison Square Garden, the Felt Forum, and the State Athletic Commission, each time shaking hands and repeating their name. In a few minutes, I would remember these names like I remembered the posted arrival times of the dozens of trains down below, but it was good to know the people here were really on top of things.

Two Deputy Commissioners, Frank Morris and Joe Scicca, escorted me down toward my ringside seat. I would remember their names because there were only two of them and because Commissioner Dooley wasn't in attendance tonight, leaving these two gentlemen with final authority. Not that I anticipated needing that authority, but the identification was always good once you were on your own, judging a fight.

I received a few stares as I was led toward the ring. That wasn't a bad thing in itself. Some semi-tough guy shouted out, "Look at that, the lady judge!" Either he had seen my photo in the *Post* or *Daily News* recently or he thought I carried myself like a judge. Either was okay with me.

The judge's seat, however, didn't look much like a judge's seat.

It was quite low compared to the ring, and when I sat, most of what I saw was the edge of the apron. A young reporter told me not to worry, because some of the judges "sucked even though they could see everything." I smiled and worried anyway until some clever employee found a nice fluffy seat cushion for me to sit on. I might have been only five-one, but tonight I felt five-five.

There was no visual obstruction in any other direction, so I took a quick look around. The room had the feel of a large theater more than an arena. The ceiling rose maybe twenty to twenty-five feet above the ring. Except for a smattering of seats along two sides of the ring, most of the seats slanted back in one direction. At the rear of the room, the seats were not far from the ceiling.

I had seen red velvet curtains in the lobby, and there were more of them out in the arena—walling off portals, exits, and the big stage behind the ring. The stage was typically used for concerts but was obviously not in use tonight. Someone mentioned to me that the Grateful Dead had played here a few years earlier and that you could still smell the pot. In any case, with all the red velvet curtains, the Felt Forum more or less lived up to its name.

I looked behind and up for my contingent. I spotted Bob about ten rows back but no Dad, Aunt Janet, or Uncle Bernie. I was glad they were coming. Aunt Janet would be her usual radiant self, Uncle Bernie his usual jovial self, but I wouldn't get to enjoy any of it. I was, of course, concerned about Dad so soon after my mother's passing, but you could never exactly gauge his state of mind. He was quiet then and he was quiet now. I hoped he realized what a step this was for me, but for all I knew it might seem to him like a step backwards from the Spectrum. Maybe to him it was all one giant leap backwards. Regardless, the room started to fill up.

Someone pointed out a couple of celebrities in the audience, world lightweight champion Roberto Duran and undefeated heavyweight contender Duane Bobick. This was just the type of celebrity watching I could not and would not be doing. It was time to turn around, look forward, sit up straight, and behave like a judge.

There were at least four fights ahead of me, five if time allowed. If just the four went off, I would be judging a pair of six-round contests, an eight-rounder, and the ten-round main event. Assuming no knockouts, that added up to thirty rounds of professional boxing. It so happened that my pay for the evening was thirty dollars. That was a dollar a round. And if the post-windup fight went on, I'd be into pennies per round. Well, it would still be about a buck a round—if you rounded up.

The undercard fights were basically matches between fighters from the Bronx, Brooklyn, and New Jersey who had not much professional experience. In most cases, the majority of their previous fights had been fought right here at the Felt Forum. The venue was, in many ways, the equivalent of the Spectrum in Philadelphia. The regular weekly fights were Monday nights, and both venues provided a chance for local pros to showcase their arsenal.

The main event was a ten-round bout between two successful featherweights, Domenico Monaco and Eduardo Santiago. Santiago came in at eleven wins, six losses, and a draw, Monaco at thirteen wins and only one loss. Aside from having the better record, Monaco was considered the favorite because of his solid style of fighting as well as having beaten a few contenders on his way up. Monaco had a loyal following who thought their man deserved a title shot next door at the real Garden.

Meanwhile, Santiago's wife had just had a baby a few days earlier, and Daddy was thought to be running low on both training and sleep. But Santiago had taken down a few contenders of his own, like 21-3-3 Walter Sweeny and 16-4-2 Jose Fernandez, both within the past year and both at the Felt Forum. Both Santiago and Monaco had fought the bulk of their professional fights at the Forum but never once fought each other, either here or anywhere else. That made tonight's main event a natural.

Something else also made the fight a natural. There was no getting around the fact that this was a contest of two prominent, loyal, ethnic groups. Santiago was a Puerto Rican who had migrated to Spanish Harlem. Monaco was Neapolitan, an Italian-born fighter who had moved to Brooklyn to seek his fortune in the ring. Either fighter was likely to attract a boisterous entourage of local supporters. Together, they would bring in even more. And though there were couples in New York where one was Puerto Rican, the other Italian, the two groups weren't always on the best of terms. In short, this fight was a promoter's dream.

You couldn't blame either group for their combination of pride and occasional defiance of convention. Both Italians and Puerto Ricans had suffered indignities on their way up. After basically discovering the New World, the Italians—mostly from Sicily and Naples—started coming over to America in droves in the late 1800s. A succession of corrupt Italian governments and accompanying poverty all but pushed them out. They brought over their masonry, carpentry, fishing, and a dozen other trades. They took what work they could find and built enclaves in New York like Little Italy in Manhattan and Sheepshead Bay in Brooklyn.

They were called Wop and Guinea and unfairly identified with the sliver of the group who brought over the nefarious trade of organized crime. And when those in political power in the U.S. thought there were too many Italians—along with too many Jews and Slavs—they created the immigration quota of 1924. The quota pared down the roughly two hundred thousand Italians arriving each year through the terminals at Ellis Island and elsewhere to a paltry four thousand.

The Italians who had already arrived produced baseball legend Joe DiMaggio and New York Mayor Fiorello La Guardia. But when World War II came in 1941, more paranoia came with it. Six hundred thousand Italian-American citizens were forced to carry identity cards labeling them, humiliatingly enough, "resident aliens." Another ten thousand were relocated inland from the West Coast, and some were even detained in military camps for up to two years. At the very same time, well over a million Italian Americans served in the U.S. armed forces to help defeat Italy, Nazi Germany, and Japan. Practical, expedient, and essentially two-faced, the U.S. Federal Government enlisted American Mafioso to help defeat Mussolini.

Natives of the island whose name meant "Port of Riches" had

already been immigrating for decades to the United States—especially to New York—when Puerto Rico became an American possession in 1898, following the Spanish-American War. But until the Shafroth Act of 1917, Puerto Ricans needed a passport to travel to the mainland.

That same year, Puerto Rican boxing star Nero Chen fought a celebrated bout against Panama "Joe Gans" at the Palace Casino in Harlem. Moments of glory, however, did not stop the exploitation of Puerto Ricans as cheap labor. As signs of the Depression revealed themselves in Puerto Rico and in poor neighborhoods on the mainland, Puerto Ricans organized, fought for legal reforms, and in one unfortunate case in 1926, rioted in Harlem.

As bad as things got in Harlem, they became worse in the Port of Riches. During the Depression, the Great Migration of Puerto Ricans to the States began. It picked up steam during World War II, when they arrived and took factory jobs to replace the soldiers who had left them. When air travel became popular, migration became still more so, until during one year alone, 1953, seventy-five thousand Puerto Ricans resettled in New York.

Barrios emerged in Spanish Harlem, the South Bronx, the Lower East Side of Manhattan, and along Atlantic Avenue in Brooklyn. Bodegas by the hundreds sold papayas and guavas, and Tito Puente led his salsa band at the Palladium dance hall. Roberto Clemente redefined the meaning of the word "talent" in baseball, and Oscar Gonzales Suarez, Esq. led the first Puerto Rican Day Parade. At the same time, one could spot cardboard signs in New York City store windows that read: "No dogs or Puerto Ricans allowed."

Puerto Ricans were welcome at the Felt Forum as was just about anybody with a few bucks to spend on a night of boxing. With the first fight minutes away, I refrained from looking back for fear I would turn into a pillar of salt like Lot's wife. My lot was to concentrate on the action ahead of me, at least until I popped a headache. But through both the volume and the energy level, I could literally feel the crowd growing behind me.

The first fight was a six-rounder between lightweights Alphonso

Taylor and Bobby Alexander. You wouldn't have known it was Alexander's first professional fight. Aside from an exchange of knockdowns—Alexander going down in the fifth and Taylor in the second—Alexander simply out-pointed Taylor, whose four years of paid battle in the ring were no match tonight. I scored it five rounds to one for Alexander. The other judge was Columbia University graduate Harold Lederman, whom I had never met before. The referee for the fight was Paul Venti.

I imagined both men scored it similarly for the winner, but the strange thing was I didn't know for sure. Whereas in Pennsylvania they read off the scores of each official, here in New York they had a new rule. The ring announcer declared the winner, and that was it. The intent was clear—to protect the ring officials and keep the peace. The less detail the crowd had to mull over, the thinking went, the better.

I wasn't so sure this thinking was flawless, but I wasn't one to object. I recalled many a night at the Spectrum or Blue Horizon when I cringed at my own scores being read off. No matter how many fights I had done, and no matter how much in the majority my scores fell, every night seemed like an audition. It was probably better to be anonymous and safe than famous and in peril. I didn't have much time to think about it anyway, because the second fight had begun.

They were another pair of lightweights, but in weight only. Jose Resto was as quick as could be expected and had experienced moderate success during two years of professional fighting at such venues as the Singer Bowl and Sunnyside Gardens in Queens, the Steelworkers Hall in Baltimore, and the Catholic Youth Center in good old Scranton, PA. Ricky Ortiz was the apparent favorite, though, coming in at five wins, two losses, and two draws. Three of the five wins were by knockouts. Through the first couple of rounds, it was easy to see the potential for another one. He may have only been 130 pounds or so, but Ricky Ortiz could ring your bell.

When the real bell had rung, however—the final one at the end of the sixth round—both fighters were still on their feet and giving a quick, respectful hug. I had it five rounds to one for Ortiz, the winner, and under

New York's cloak and dagger system I had no reason to believe Venti and Lederman had it much different. Something, however, was different. The crowd had really come alive during the second bout. I was a bit surprised. I was already wondering whether the thirty bucks was going to be this easy all the way through, but from the noise behind me you wouldn't have known the fight was lopsided.

There was a lot of cursing in Spanish. The only word I knew for sure was "maricón," which is, for lack of a more polite word, "faggot." Neither Ortiz nor Resto fought like one, but at least now I had put two and two together. Both fighters lived in New York but were born in Puerto Rico. The crowd as a whole may not have had a favorite, but hundreds of individuals in the audience evidently did.

The semi-windup was an eight-rounder, and I could feel my perennial headache coming out of hiding. The rounds between the two middleweight upstarts were almost all close. Jose Colon, originally from Puerto Rico and now living in the Bronx, had a small advantage over his opponent, Larry Davis of Teaneck, New Jersey. Colon was a little taller. In most of the rounds, Colon was a little more aggressive and effective as well, but Davis did manage to land some solid blows in certain rounds. There was a new referee for this fight, George Coyle, who would also be handling the windup. Coyle seemed to have his hands full as he chased the pair around the ring and issued sporadic warnings.

I totaled up my scores as the noise from the crowd ramped up. I had it 5-3 in favor of Colon. There was always the question of whether the whole equaled the sum of its parts or, put differently, whether the decisions on the individual rounds added up to an overall decision that made sense on a gut level. I felt in this case it did. It seemed that Colon was more in control of the fight than Davis—but honestly not by much. And if just one of the five rounds I had for Colon were ever so slightly different, I would have had it as a draw. It was the razor's edge, and for the fighters maybe the fork in the road they had been on their whole lives.

The crowd cared about this one and let it be known. The cursing, much of it in Spanish, reached a crescendo like a Latin orchestra with no conductor. Worse still, they had no score. Referee Coyle and Deputy Commissioner Morris were now conferring at ringside, Coyle crouched down on the canvas. I heard through interlopers that something Coyle had written on his card wasn't clear. Both men knew what we all knew, that the only thing more dangerous than subjective judgment of a contest was subjective judgment of handwriting.

This hiatus gave me a few moments to take in the mood of the crowd. There were more voices shouting "Colon" than "Davis" or anything else that you could print in a family newspaper. But the most troubling part was the notion—spoken and unspoken—that the decision had better be the "right" one, or else. With each second Coyle and Morris huddled, the communal growl grew more menacing, like an engine left in neutral too long starting to give off a burning smell. I felt I had it right, but I didn't ever want to think of it as "correct." There was a big difference. In fact, all the difference in the world.

The Coyle scorecard matter was cleared up, and the ring announcer gave Colon as the winner. The crowd didn't exactly quiet, but the growl dissolved into higher pitched shouts and catcalls. The windup was on in a heartbeat, and I was glad, headache and all. Santiago came out with a series of overhand punches. One might normally call them "wild overhand bombs," but the fact was, some of them were landing, and not just on Monaco's arms. This pushed the crowd's noise level up each time, if only for a spike.

Monaco was no slouch. He seemed a little more fit than Santiago and possessed a more sophisticated repertoire. Santiago's blows, whether over the top or from some other more conventional direction, were not by any means free. Monaco made his opponent pay with a left jab or one-two combination of his own. I scored the first three rounds for Santiago. They were all very close, but Santiago dominated each one as the aggressor, dishing out just a bit more than he took.

The fourth round was so close I called it a draw. In doing so I had broken the Zach Clayton cardinal rule, but rules were made to be broken on occasion. In round four, not even one of the exchanges appeared to be dominated by either fighter, which was an extreme rarity. After fifty-five fights, I had a cardinal rule of my own—if the task of picking the winner of a round brought you all the way to the next round, it was a draw.

Round five, however, was a carryover from round four in a different way. In round four you could see the very beginnings of exhaustion from Santiago, and now in the fifth you could see it in more than just faint body language. Santiago was fighting in flurries then backing off to gather himself and catch his breath. For his part, Monaco was steady. His boxed European style, which was to stand up straight almost all the time. He gave you a duck here, a bob and weave there, but his head was usually a lollipop on a stick. This approach was either bold or foolish depending upon the results. The results in the fifth and sixth rounds were that Monaco held his own but still failed to dominate.

In the seventh, there was a palpable letdown from Santiago. For a minute or so, he let loose on Monaco, hitting him with roundhouse blows and getting away as fast as he could. Then for another minute or so, Santiago back-peddled. He was managing the clock, as they say, checking his own fuel gauge frequently and trying to make it to the next round.

In the final minute of the round, Santiago's lunge at Monaco landed the two fighters in a clinch. Perched on my pillow cushion with a clear view of Santiago's face, I saw him wipe his eyes with his right hand glove. As the glove slowly came away, you could see his eyes were closed now, maybe catching a catnap he had missed earlier in the week during the days following the birth of his child. The same way a ten-minute nap often seemed to produce an hour of true rest, Santiago seemed to be hoping to pull a few extra intervals of recuperation from the clinch. But George Coyle rudely interrupted Santiago's slumber.

Between rounds, Santiago's corner was like an OR at a busy hospital. His trainer and cut men were rubbing the fighter's arms and legs to revive his circulation. Blood and sweat were wiped. Salves and ointments were applied. Towels and palms slapped Santiago's face like a Skin Bracer commercial on speed. Over the murmur of several competing Dr. Frankensteins, Santiago's manager was edging Santiago to one more minute of glory.

"Ju got 'em. He's yours, man! This is your fight, remember that. Hit him en la cabeza. Don't let him take you to ten, ju got that?" In between the words I could understand, were Spanish words I could not. I knew a little Italian and caught the gist. It was Spanglish at its absolute best, and somehow not one iota of meaning was lost even on the not quite bilingual.

The eighth round looked to be almost a replay of the seventh, with Santiago coming out on a head of steam. Until the clinch. The clinch in this round really never happened. When the fighters pulled in close, Monaco threw a flurry of rabbit punches that ended in his grabbing Santiago around the body and throwing him to the canvass. Were this a wrestling match, it might have been worth two points. But after seeing Santiago back to his feet, referee Coyle signaled to both myself and Harold Lederman that this takedown was no knockdown. It was not my place to agree or disagree, but I happened to agree. For the books, it was as if the takedown never happened.

In reality, however, it had happened. Back on his feet, Santiago looked as if he wanted to stay down a little longer. Somehow, though, he found a way to come right back at Monaco with another flurry of overhand blows. That the crowd volume had now risen to its highest level yet was of no consequence to me. I gave Santiago credit for running as he did on fumes, and with it the round.

Santiago didn't have it in the ninth round. The minute or so of real fighting he had been getting away with in the previous rounds was now more like thirty seconds, and it wasn't very effective. Midway through the round, a determined Santiago ventured in to get Monaco for what looked to be the last time. But Monaco grabbed Santiago's arms and locked them up. Referee Coyle pried apart the two fighters, sweeping away Monaco's hold and issuing the fighter a stern warning. It was clear now that Santiago wasn't the only one out there who was exhausted.

When the round was over, I was about to score it for Monaco, but Coyle leaned through the ropes and told me to give the round to Santiago. The holding disqualified the round for Monaco. I felt as if this was somehow payback for the takedown the round before, which was not penalized. In any case, I did as I was instructed.

Santiago came out for the tenth and final round like a hungry tiger let out of a cage in a meat market. It was the first round all over again except with less precision and more desperation. It was as if Santiago derived some inspiration from his wife a few days earlier in the final pangs of her delivery. When you know you're near the end, you don't know what you're capable of. The final round was all Santiago's.

With the fight over, there wasn't much to do except write in the tenth round score, tally up the rounds, and make a few other quick notations. But I was writing in slow motion. The crowd noise was deafening, making this simple task a challenge. It was hard not to turn my head ever so slightly, and when I did, with my peripheral vision I spotted Bob now sitting behind and slightly to the left of me. He made a hand gesture telling me to finish doing what I was doing.

Before I could either consider what made my husband move in to guard my flank or finish the task at hand, two men with Felt Forum security asked me to follow them. On our way to an area behind a curtain, they explained this was a precaution. "For what?" I asked. They explained it was to make sure I finished okay. I didn't need a gun lap like Eduardo Santiago, only to stop moving for a moment. But while I was moving, I saw the crowd fully for the very first time. There were about a million Puerto Ricans living in New York, and it seemed roughly half of them were at the Felt Forum. And just about every one was shouting "San-Tee-Ah-Go!"

I stood behind the curtain surrounded by uniforms. My head came to about the top buttons. Beyond the curtain, the natives were restless. As I looked back down at my scorecard, there really wasn't much adding to do. I had it 9-0-1 for Santiago, including the ninth round which Coyle had taken from Monaco. It looked a little strange finally tallied up, because it was a close fight on a round by round basis. But the truth was, there wasn't a single thing on my card I wanted to change or would change.

After my card left my hand, it must have made it back to the ring via telegraph. No sooner did my bodyguards lead me out from the curtain than the ring announcer declared the fight a draw. As in all the previous bouts, there were no further details. Unfortunately, the Devil was in those very details.

The crowd was on its feet now and not to get a little stretching in. A few programs flew down from above. Angry fans swore and pointed. A few pointed toward me. I looked around for cops, real New York City cops, but there were only a few and they were taking in the outburst. Meanwhile, in their infinite wisdom, the Felt Forum had quickly started the four-round post-windup fight. Welterweights George Fakaras and Julio Garcia were pushed out into the middle of the ring like frightened kids tossed into the deep end of the pool by sadistic swimming instructors.

Fakaras of Long Island had exactly three pro fights under his belt, and Garcia of Newark had exactly one—a fight two weeks earlier against Fakaras that ended in a draw. Eager as they were to launch their careers, they hadn't bargained for this. The notion was to create a distraction for the wildly disgruntled masses, but the Felt Forum might as well have been the Roman Coliseum feeding prisoners to the lions.

I found my seat with the cushion, my husband still sitting in his just behind and to the left. All I could think about was how annoyed I was that I had missed a minute of the first round. How could I possibly judge a fight I hadn't seen? What kind of place was this? This would never happen in Philadelphia.

Just then a bottle whizzed right by my left ear and hit the side of the ring. It sounded like an incoming missile on the shores of Omaha Beach. And there it was on the floor, a bottle of Jim Beam smashed against the hard concrete floor of the arena instead of against my skull. It had missed by inches. I breathed maybe twice, neither one a full breath, and a second bottle came down on my right side, this one with a lower pitched whir and missing by a good two feet.

Deputy Commissioners Morris and Scicca were both climbing into the ring now. The extra bout—that dangling participle—was no more. I wondered what did it, the first bottle or the second. Whichever, the age old Fakaras-Garcia rivalry would have to be settled some other time and, hopefully, some other place. There was no reason not to take in the view now. I was certainly scared the third bottle was going to be a strike after ball one and ball two.

At the same time, I was seeing things I had never seen before and would perhaps never see again. A New York City police officer, one of the few if not the finest, was hit in the head by a paper cup filled with soda. Ceiling tiles were spinning down like amateur, un-flight worthy Frisbees, yet another advantage of having a low roof. Seat cushions followed and not because the rabid crowd wanted me to see better. Some of the cushions had been set on fire, as angry but resourceful cigar smoking lunatic fight fans were wont to do.

Then came the show stopper. A couch was hurled down from the top rows. I guessed the mob had snatched it from one of the office booths. As it arced its way down to about the fifteenth row, I noticed that like the seat cushions, the couch too had been set on fire. Yes, I had lived to see a flying flaming couch. I hadn't seen everything there was to see in the world, but I had just gotten a little closer.

I became aware that only a few seconds had passed since the last fight was called off. It wasn't my nature to gawk at grizzly or macabre sites, but I realized what I was actually doing was looking for my dad, aunt, and uncle. I couldn't spot them and hoped in the confusion they would spot us. Until at least one of those things happened, I could continue putting together the puzzle pieces.

The ring announcer had declared the windup a draw. Two years of philosophy at the University of Wisconsin and fourteen years of decoding excuses from my kids made this one a slam dunk. Neither Coyle nor Lederman had scored the fight for Santiago or it would have been Santiago's and at least some of the couches would have been saved. Coyle and Lederman did not have it for Monaco, or the Italian would have won and the Felt Forum by now would have burned to the ground. So, either the two other officials had scored the fight a 5-5 majority draw or one had scored it a draw and the other for Monaco, making it a consensus draw.

It began to dawn on me that the angry masses not only didn't know I scored the fight their way—and in sweeping fashion—but that they probably thought the novice woman judge, the misfit, was the cause of their plight in the first place. Of course, even if I had scored it a draw or for Monaco, it would have taken more than just little old me to create a stalemate. There was no great logic in whatever terrible thoughts they might have had regarding Carol Polis. It was the logic of flaming couches.

At ringside, even as I was ready to duck a flaming seat cushion, I found myself talking to staff and reporters. We were brothers and sisters in arms. Trench warfare brings people closer. Some asked me how I liked my first professional fight in New York. "Fine," I said, "right until that bottle of Jim Beam whipped by my head." Someone else asked me if I was ever coming back. "Absolutely," I said, "so long as they'll have me."

Right about then someone leaked out that Coyle and Lederman both had the fight 5-5 for a majority draw, making me the odd woman out. And at 9-0-1, I was way out. How did I feel? I measured my words carefully. The mixture of officials and reporters, trench or no trench, was a powder keg. "I'm surprised," I said. "But I respect the other officials. Almost every round was close. You lean a little the other way in a couple of rounds and suddenly you have a different fight."

With that, I leaned away from a flying cup, getting a small brown stain on my blouse but bobbing and weaving in a style that would have made Bennie Briscoe proud. My husband was holding court on his own, telling some reporter from somewhere he had the fight 6-4 for Santiago. All I needed was Bob to start doing fights here too.

I spotted Aunt Janet spotting me, and our eye contact threw us both a lifeline. I signaled to the security guards and to Bob that it was time to get out of Dodge. We had served our time and then some. I noticed Coyle and Lederman were long gone, God bless them. Even Duran and Bobick were nowhere to be found, and who could blame them?

As we made our way up, I caught one glare after another, a few slurs, and at least one middle finger. I responded with not one, but two fingers of my own, forming a peace sign and holding it aloft like a shield.

An older generation might have misinterpreted my gesture as a victory sign. As we scooped up Dad, Aunt Janet, and Uncle Bernie, it was a victory of sorts.

In the lobby, a light fixture lay shattered on the ground not far from a velvet curtain that had been torn down, dishonoring Irving Felt. When we got out to the street, it felt like a prison break. There were blue and white patrol cars with sirens flashing lined up and around 33rd Street and filled with special NYPD forces. But the cavalry had arrived a bit late.

"Oh my God," Aunt Janet said. "It was like *West Side Story* in there."

"*West Side Story* was tame by comparison," Uncle Bernie said. "I stopped a couple of bottles with my hand."

"I just want to go home!" I said.

"I don't blame you," Aunt Janet said. "What a profession you picked. You couldn't have been a lawyer like your Uncle Bernie?"

Hell had followed Bob and me downstairs to the gritty subterranean railway station. On the platform, we were surrounded by a bunch of disgruntled fight fans who had spotted public enemy number one. "Bad judge!" they shouted. "Bad judge!" We walked calmly, taking care to make no eye contact. They should have been thanking me, not looking to crucify me. But the Man Upstairs, not Irving Felt, sent an archangel in the form of a train pulling into the station with a sign that read "Phila." We quickly left the seedy, dangerous Penn Station for the Penn Station we called home—the Penn Station that was still there—and didn't look back. I had a check for thirty dollars in my pocket and would try not to spend it all on one psychotherapist.

There was plenty of looking back from the safety and comfort of home. Although I hadn't yet gotten the title fight I wanted, there was probably more press coverage for this one. People from all over the country sent me articles like my very own clipping service. Uncle Bernie led the way, mailing me a wonderful letter from a proud uncle along with the New York pieces from the *Daily News*, the *Times*, the *Post*, and *Newsday*. Like the event, the titles were a blast: "A Bottle for that Lady at Ringside,"

"Baptism for a Judge," "Lady Judge's Garden Party a Riot." Riots, of course, are a lot nicer in hindsight.

The full back page coverage of the riot in the August 6 New York *Daily News* included a photo of me in deep thought, presumably before the couches went airborne. If you looked closely, you could see that my middle finger was pensively touching my left cheek rather than my left nostril. But the important thing was that all the writers seemed to get the bigger picture. The scores were all public information now and so was the realization that the lady judge had nothing to do with the civil unrest. The sportswriters typically had the fight 6-4 or 7-3 for Santiago. Santiago had it for Santiago, too. "I think I won nine rounds," he told the *Post*'s Henry Hecht. "Women, yeah, they vote beautiful."

Domenico Monaco was less convinced. He told Hecht, "How can two judges score it even and one score it 9-1? I guess she just can't see that good." The Monaco camp was even less kind than the fighter himself.

"She goes for the underdog psychologically," one said, "'cause she's the underdog."

"She's Spanish," remarked another. "Polis, that's a Spanish name. If she's American, I'm French."

Wrong as he was, Carol Blank Sharp Rodriguez Polis was a towering media figure for a few days, with or without the seat cushion. I even had my own scrapbook to go with it. My favorite personal quote, was, "I'm a hero in Spanish Harlem but the Mafia is after me."

The central question, however—one apparently far less media worthy—was still how any two objective officials could score a fight so differently. As much as I understood the answer, the question still nagged at me. So I called the sage, my mentor Zach Clayton. I felt like Grasshopper in the TV series *Kung Fu* trying to snatch a pebble from his master's hand. Clayton agreed with my approach and acknowledged that when scored faithfully on a round-by-round basis, the final tally could look different from the fight itself. He added, however, that if you saw a wide gap opening between the two realities, you could try moving a round or two over from the winner to the loser. He called it "shading." I felt like giving him his pebble back. I was glad I hadn't shaded and had no plans to do so ever.

Clayton, who had earned my respect long ago, wasn't the only one contradicting himself. Chairman Dooley was doing it in a bigger way, and publicly. Tuesday, the day after the melee, which he read about in the papers like everyone else, Dooley criticized Teddy Brenner, president of Madison Square Garden Boxing, for not having enough security on hand and stated the lady judge had nothing to do with the circus. And in fact, by design the rioting crowd didn't know my scoring, no matter what it had been.

But by Thursday Dooley was going after me anyway. In a typewritten warning to me on official letterhead, he picked apart my performance during and after the fight. As for the scoring itself, he wrote, "From all of the reports from various sources, it appears the fight was closer than the 9-0-1 which you recorded." He also lambasted Bob for talking to the press. But the kicker was, " . . . you talked about your scoring at ringside, and this provoked a number of people into violent action." I wondered exactly how that worked. A reporter asks me a question, the answer to which he doesn't print till the next day. A crazed, drunken fan sees into the future, agrees rather than disagrees with my scoring, and throws a couch.

A week or so later, Chairman Dooley received a letter from another prominent boxing figure with an opinion. Mark Mendel was a fight manager, attorney, and a friend of ours. He also worked closely with legendary boxing manager Jim Jacobs. In the letter, Mendel expressed how grateful Philadelphia was to have the top flight services of Judge Carol Polis as well as admiration for both New York and Dooley for seeing the light of equal rights.

As far as the fight itself was concerned, Mendel pointed out that if it was a citywide majority Dooley was interested in, the other two ring officials were the ones in the minority. Moreover, just in case Dooley ever wanted to see for himself, Jim Jacobs had filmed the entire fight from the upper reaches of the Felt Forum. It was good to have friends in high places.

While my own public battle was unfolding in August, Watergate reached its climax. The "smoking gun" tape had been released, on which Richard Nixon and H.R. Haldeman were clearly and audibly heard plotting to have the CIA lie to the FBI on behalf of the White House. That was the final round for Nixon, a TKO. On August 8, he announced his resignation from the highest office in the land. The following afternoon he was giving a peace sign of his own before being whisked away from the South Lawn in a helicopter.

Somewhere, my mother was ecstatic. I was doing fine myself. They wouldn't have Richard Nixon to kick around anymore. But they would still have Carol Polis. That was okay, though. I kicked back.

My father, Solo Blank

My mother, Dorothy Blank

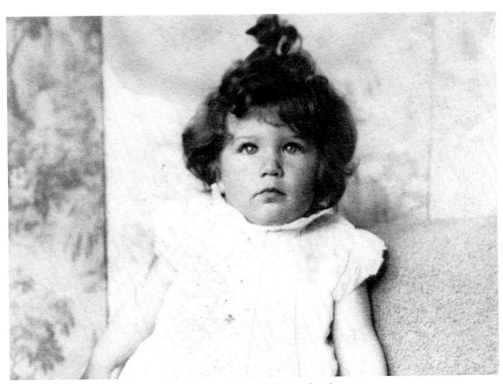

That's me, the future judge.

University of Wisconsin, Madison

Pennsylvania Governor Shapp, Bob Polis and me
being sworn in on February 1st, 1973.

With Philadelphia Mayor, Frank Rizzo.

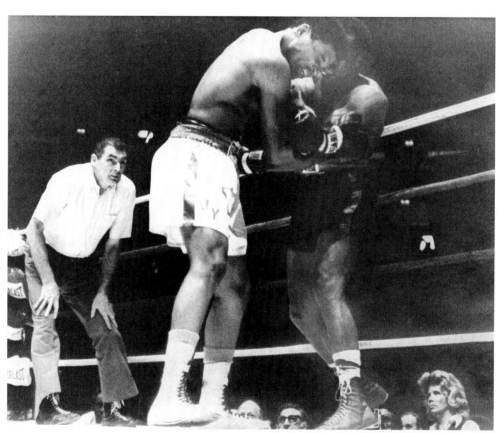

Judging my first official fight at The Spectrum in Philadelphia, Jimmy Young vs Ernie Shavers, February 19th, 1973.

With Ali at his Pennsylvania training camp.

AMERICA'S BRAVE NEW LADY OF BOXING

When America's first woman boxing judge Carol Polis made her debut at Madison Square Garden, the crowd became so violent she was lucky to leave in one piece.

With Sugar Ray Leonard in Las Vegas.

With Marvis Frazier (Joe Frazier's son) in Philadelphia.

Chuck Wepner (Bayonne Bleeder).
The *Rocky* story was
based on his life.

Eugene "Cyclone" Hart,
the best left-hander
I ever saw.

ROBERTO DURAN
Junior Middleweight Champion

Roberto Duran,
my favorite fighter.

Jimmy Young

Sugar Ray Leonard

Larry Holmes,
heavyweight champ.

Marvelous Marvin Hagler

Evander Holyfield

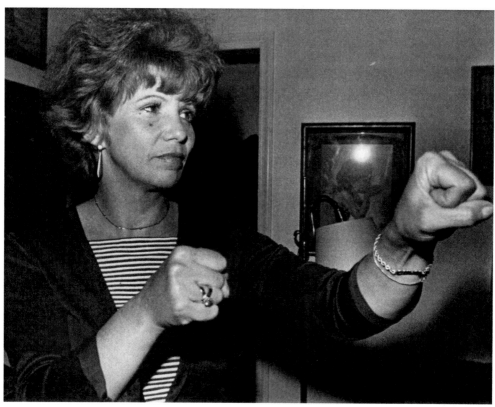

Practicing the correct stance.

Judging a fight at The Blue Horizon, Philadelphia.

Zach Clayton,
commissioner who had me
appointed on February 1st, 1973
by Governor Milton Shapp.

With Jersey Joe Wolcott,
in New Jersey.

Sitting ringside, pre-fight in New York.

Sonny Liston & Manager
Georgie Katz

Former WBA President
Rodrigo Sanchez.

Nick Keriositis, title fight supervisor from Illinois for a Las Vegas
fight, boxing historian Bert Sugar, Rita Keriositis.

Evander Holyfield and me in Atlantic City, New Jersey.

With Floyd Patterson, the youngest ever
heavyweight champ, in Philadelphia.

With Virgil Hill in Bismark,
North Dakota.

With Roberto Duran
in Panama.

With Vito Antuofermo
in New York.

Receiving "runner up"
award for official of the
year, from WBA President,
Gilberto Mendoza.

With Referee
Frank Cappucino
in Philadelphia.

With Nino Benvenuti,
in Italy.

My favorite photo taken in Rome,
sitting on Spanish steps.

RINGSIDE WITH BOXING JUDGE CAROL POLIS

Bill Kent: You are America's first female boxing judge, you're a Philadelphia native and you're still not How is this possible?

Carol Polis: I don but I'm still trying. I age to get into *Rocky*

Kent: How come see you in the movie?

Polis: I'm there for a hundredth of a fract second. There's a poin the camera pans the ri I'm in the judge's seat guess you can see *thought* I could see me.

Kent: You weren't s

Polis: After all the spent—three days, two Blue Horizon, and one Civic Center—I *know* that movie, if not in fac in spirit.

Kent: What's Don like?

Polis: I know him well—I've judged fights he's had a fighter. He's moter, and they do the ness while I do the figh we're friends. I'm fr enough with promoters s I could give them all a hug hugged all the promote least once.

Kent: How is Don Ki a hugger?

Polis: He's O.K. He's tall.

Kent: Did you wan judge the match betw Holyfield and Foreman?

Polis: I would've love have judged the Forem Holyfield fight this past Ap think both are terrific fight Seems like the Geritol ge ation wanted to see if Fore still had it, while the yup wanted Holyfield to win.

Besides title fights, I've also

judged ones you don't hear much about, at the Blue Horizon and other

surrounded—at 5 feet tall, I'm surrounded pretty easily. One

after the fight I found myself

on the back of a program. At the end of the evening, he

turned it into Zack Clayto who was then the Pennsylv State Athletic Commi r in Philadelphia, and ee. Zack said, "Keep Then, over a year and turned in scores when to the fights. Zack wou e on-the-spot questior the rules and reg l studied.

nt: You got interested?

is: I had to hang o y ex, so I figured, if yc eat him, join him. So t myself. I made an e become involved. On ack in 1973, at intermis efore a windup at th am, Zack came up to m d, "Lady, I have goc nd bad news for you d news is that you hav e to Harrisburg." An od news was that I g pointment to boxin

: Are there other fe ges now?

I guess—this is ju because I don't kno e in all the associa here are about 15 of u a great job, but it t-time. I get a phon go. Sometimes it's a Horizon, sometime d, in France, Japar outh America.

What do you do be ps?

I'm a licensed realtc ckbroker, but there' doing with thos t now. I've worke ince model at Straw Plymouth Meeting er my grandson an g my life story. Sounds like it'll be knockout.

Polis: Oh, please.

PHOTOGRAPH BY I. GEORGE BILYK

Packing a punch

Carol Polis has made a real impact in a very male sport.

By Rick O'Brien
INQUIRER SUBURBAN STAFF

She is in many ways a typical grandmother. Her hobbies include going to flea markets and garage sales, reading books, listening to music, and enjoying the company of her two dogs.

And, of course, doting on her four grandchildren whenever possible.

So where was Carol Polis headed on a Friday evening earlier this month? To a game of bingo at a local church hall? To an early-bird dinner with a few of her re...

W...
h...
N...

th...
ju...
a...
n...
1...
d...

Scoring a Match

Here are the seven considerations that boxing judge Carol Polis uses in scoring a fight.

■ Aggressiveness
■ Clean hitting
■ Cleverness of blows
■ Defensive skills
■ Effectiveness of blows
■ Fouls
■ Technical violations

— Rick O'Brien

endured plenty of criticism and taunting from spectators.

Controversy — and flying bottles — followed one fight at New York's Felt Forum in 1974. She had scored the bout (under the old 10-point system) 9-0-1; the other judge and referee both had it 5-5.

And then there was the scary night about a decade ago at Philadelphia's Blue Horizon, a legendary boxing club on North Broad Street.

"I was surrounded by about 12 men after a fight," Polis said. "They asked me why my score didn't go in the favor of their fighter. I simply said, 'Better luck ...' ... of the building as ...

Greenville, Maine

"She's the godmother of boxing," ... said. "When I assign Carol to a fight, I know I'm going to get a fair and quality score."

On this rainy night, Polis is judging fights at World Gym on Roosevelt Boulevard. It is a long way from Madison Square Garden or the First Union Spectrum, where she officiated a heavyweight bout between Mike Tyson and Buster Mathis in December 1995. But she shows the same professionalism.

"No matter who is fighting, you have to concentrate 100 percent on what you're doing," Polis said. "That's the approach I've always taken."

After judging a bunch of undercard pairings, Polis and two other officials score the main bout between Jacqui Frazier-Lyde, daughter of former heavyweight champion Joe Frazier, and Atlanta's Kendra Lenhart.

Claiming the Women's International Boxing Federation 168-pound title and the vacant Global Boxing Union super-middleweight championship, Frazier-Lyde posted a 10-round, unanimous-decision victory.

is going to appoint you as the first ... boxing judge in the country."

Polis' judging career began Feb. 18, 1973, when Jimmy Young squared off against Earnie Shavers at the Spectrum.

What advice did Clayton give Polis?

"He said, 'Be a man when you're judging fights. Look at each round as a full fight. And don't call any round a draw.'"

■

Polis — who was licensed with the World Boxing Association and International Boxing Federation/United States Boxing Association — judged nearly 30 title fights from 1979 to 1996.

She officiated all over the country, from Philadelphia to Las Vegas, and in other countries, including Denmark, France, Italy, Japan, Panama and Venezuela.

"I was the first woman to judge a title fight in Europe," said Polis, referring to a 1980 bout in Copenhagen, Denmark. "Title fights are very exciting. There's so much at stake for the fighters. It makes you feel important."

In the 1970s and '80s, when she was breaking ground as a female judge, Polis

What's My Line? and To Tell the Truth in the 1970s is just as happy scoring a fight in a dimly lit, smoke-filled neighborhood gym.

She said the Blue Horizon is her favorite place, despite what can be a tough and raucous crowd.

"It's a great atmosphere," Polis said. "But you better know your stuff when you walk in there. The people really know boxing, and they aren't afraid to speak their mind."

Polis works part time for a collections agency and lives in a townhouse — a pair of boxing gloves worn by Joe Frazier hang on a dining-room wall — with her grandson, Larry Sharp. The 17-year-old is a junior at Germantown Academy and plays guard for the basketball team.

And whenever the phone rings to judge a fight, she's quick to answer.

"In all the time I've been doing this, I don't think I've ever turned down a job," Polis said.

Contact suburban staff writer Rick O'Brien at 610-313-8019 or robrien@phillynews.com

My son Kenny Sharp
with his dog, Herman.

My daughter Margie, Tim &
Samantha Lynne Adamsky.

My son Jimmy, Sophie Devin, and Nora Sharp.

My daughter, Carol Paula and Larry, North Wales, Pennsylvania.

My grandson, Larry Sharp, in June 2004 at his
Germantown Academy High School Graduation.

CHAPTER TEN
GOING FOR BROKE

When my mother passed away she left each of us—my sister Nancy, my brother Arthur, and me—about fifty thousand dollars. I was grateful for the security it provided, but that security was more mental than financial. With the long overdue divorce from Bob finalized in 1978, I was once again a single mom with four kids, and when you did the math it was simple. If we lived off of that money it would be gone in a few short years. And if it wasn't gone by then, college tuition would eat up what was left in a hurry. So I held a lot of garage sales and was always working.

One of my longer and more eventful gigs was working at the Sherman Inn—formerly the Sheraton—in Fort Washington. Bill, the hotel manager, interviewed me in the coffee shop and asked me a few straightforward questions. The fourth question was the killer—which hotels had I worked at before. As a boxing judge I had slept and eaten in plenty of hotels, but unless you counted the bouts I had judged right on the premises, I had never actually worked in a hotel. So I went back to question three and leapt ahead to question five, something you could never do in a fifteen-round main event. I flopped around in the coffee shop booth, mumbled something about the Edgewater Beach Hotel in Madison, Wisconsin, where I went to college, and generally let the ambient noise of clanging coffee cups and saucers fill in the blanks.

I got the job, and I quickly made up for my lack of hotel experience by working several jobs at once. To the naked eye it looked like I was simply working the front desk. But in one spot I took care of the check-ins and in another spot I did the check-outs. A step to the left and I worked the cash register. Two steps to the right and I was Miss National Car Rental. A few more steps to the right and I was the switchboard operator. In the morning I did all the wake-up calls, even when I needed one myself. I was good at sounding perky in the morning when neither I nor the other party was. I picked up that skill during my job as Mom. So one month into my stint at the Sherman Inn, I felt like I had been working in hotels all my life.

I wore one more hat all my own. There was so much drama from day to day I started taking notes—mental and written—for a book or movie one day. Some people checked in for an hour. When it was two people checking in for an hour, you had an idea what they were doing. When it was one person, you didn't know and you didn't want to know. Sometimes one person checked in and another followed, stayed a few minutes, then left. That could have been a drug deal, but detective was not one of my hats. Sometimes some shady people would check in for several days and never come up for air. You hoped no one died in there. And then someone did.

The cleaning staff discovered the body in the bathtub. A woman had checked in, unpacked, set her things around the room, and placed a mirror on the sink. The mirror was pointed down at the bathtub. The woman climbed fully clothed into the bathtub, placed a pillow over her stomach, took a gun, and shot herself through the pillow. Apparently she knew what she was doing. You don't get a second shot with something like that. She must have looked at the reflection of herself and the gun in the mirror and lined it up just right before pulling the trigger. It was tragic and horrible, but she was the Annie Oakley of the Sherman Inn.

The police arrived along with two homicide detectives. The owner was hiding somewhere. Bill told me to take care of everything, so now I had a few more jobs. One of those jobs was to make sure the guests were cleared out of the lobby before the body was taken out. I was Miss Hospitality.

Toward the end of 1980 I had worn out my hats if not my welcome. Bill had been fired, though none of us knew exactly why. He had always been a decent manager as far as I could tell. One of our guests was the regional manager for Eastman-Kodak. He was a gentleman and seemed to think I had my act together, enough to offer me a job in the regional office at Eastman-Kodak. I told him it might be interesting. The Sheraton

Corporation had just taken over the hotel again, and whenever that happened the new owners liked to bring in their own people. So with the writing on the wall, I got the picture and took the offer.

Whether it was called the Sheraton, the Sherman, or the Sheraton again, the hotel in Fort Washington was the gift that kept giving. Months into my new job at Eastman-Kodak I got a knock on the door from the police. The hotel owner had given them my address, as the police were investigating a group of criminals who were using the hotel as their base of operations. I felt a chill, because I knew exactly who they were talking about. These were not the type of people who took a wake-up call. They were a black militant group that used to check in and stay in. They wore quasi-military garb. The leader was an intense looking man in his early thirties we called "The Major" because of how proudly he wore his uniform and the respect—or fear—he commanded.

The staff and I considered these people to be primarily a drug gang. Their hours, patterns, and visitors suggested just that. The detectives explained there was a whole lot more to it. Right there in room 311 at the Sheraton/Sherman/Sheraton they were planning to bomb cars and buildings in Philadelphia. This was the age of radical groups like MOVE. Drug money funded the bombs, and it was hard to know where the pushing stopped and the terror started.

I picked out The Major right away from the ID book. I picked out a few more characters, and the detectives told me I was right on every one. Not bad for a check-in-check-out-rent-a-car lady. The detectives were so impressed they asked me to testify. That was a first round TKO if I had ever heard one. I flat out refused. I had been, for all practical purposes, the face of the hotel. These people would recognize me in an instant. We could slap a red wig and big dark glasses on me when I took the stand, but it wouldn't matter. Before long detectives would be investigating the bombing of my house.

They were not happy, but they understood. Especially with a family to protect I was not too eager to appear before a judge. Of course, I still was one myself. In fact, that career had started to take off, literally.

After officiating at hundreds and hundreds of local fights, I decided it was time to see the world. So I applied to the World Boxing Association.

The World Boxing Association, or WBA, was one of the top, if not the top, professional boxing associations on the planet. They were based in Panama and governed title fights all over the world, especially in South America. The WBA's main rival was the World Boxing Council, or WBC. The WBC was closely tied to Don King and had more of a foothold in the United States. There was always controversy between these organizations and within the sport of boxing as a whole. That controversy was even greater in the late '70s and early '80s than ever. Most championship belts were split, with one fighter holding the WBA title and another holding the WBC title. Occasionally the two sides agreed to a unification bout, but that was not easy to arrange, especially if it didn't work to Don King's advantage.

Perhaps most famously, in 1978 Leon Spinx defeated Muhammad Ali to win both the WBA and WBC heavyweight crowns. But Spinx didn't hold them both for very long. When Spinx's camp signed on for a rematch against Ali, Don King objected. Ali wasn't a Don King fighter and Ken Norton was. So King's people unceremoniously stripped Leon Spinx of his WBC title and handed it to Ken Norton. Larry Holmes—another King fighter—then defeated Ken Norton for the WBC heavyweight crown. Ali defeated Spinx in the rematch to regain the WBA heavyweight crown. And suddenly there were countless millions of dollars lined up to see Muhammad Ali and Larry Holmes fight an epic unification bout.

Of the two organizations, I decided to go for the WBA. They seemed more open and transparent, and I had already had enough direct involvement with Don King for at least one lifetime. My application process was simple and informal. I wrote a letter to WBA President Mandry Galindez explaining who I was and my extensive experience. A couple of weeks later I received a letter back from Galindez stating that he had received my letter and explaining that there were no immediate openings for boxing judges. He addressed me in the letter as "Mr. Carl Polis." I was willing to accept that there were no slots for Mr. Carl Polis.

But it was Ms. Carol Polis I was concerned with.

I knew a picture was worth a thousand words, and a good picture at least two thousand. So I found a photo of me in a bathing suit taken a few summers before when my girlfriends and I were at a local swimming pool. The photo was from the waist up. We thought we were the last word, and my two-piece bathing suit was a bit provocative. So I took an address label, licked the back of it, and stuck it across my chest. This was self-censorship at its best. I put the photo into the envelope with my letter back explaining that this woman still had her heart set on the WBA.

Apparently Ms. Carol Polis scored a knockout. The following week I received a letter back from Mandry Galindez. In it Galindez explained—or confessed—that he spent a solid hour trying to peel off the address label from my photo. That was an hour he could have spent putting Ali and Holmes together in the ring, but for those sixty minutes I guess I was tops. In any case, sticker or no sticker, I was now the first woman ever appointed as a judge in the World Boxing Association.

The following week my phone rang. It was Mandry Galindez, and he wasn't calling for Carl. Galindez explained that he was going to be arriving in New York in a few days and asked if I would meet him. I told him I was sorry, I had a prior engagement. My concern was he was still looking to scratch off the rest of that label. Nonetheless, Galindez asked me where I wanted to officiate my first WBA fight. I wanted to say Italy, because that was my dream fight, my favorite spot on the globe. But there were many more fights in Las Vegas, and I was a practical woman with mouths to feed. So I said Vegas.

By 1979, my oldest son, Jimmy, had started Penn State. Kenny would be enrolling at Temple the following year. Margie and Carol Paula were in high school. Things were a little easier regarding baby sitting, because my kids were no longer babies. When I went out on a date or to judge a local fight, the oldest kid in the house could keep an eye on the others and all our pets for a few hours.

My champion in this regard was Kenny. Whatever his age, babysitter present or not, when I returned home there was always someone watching out the window for me. Kenny worried about me the way I worried about him and everyone else. And I worried about him for worrying about me. But the kids were older now. The timing of the WBA appointment was good and was no coincidence. I would still need a house sitter, but the opportunity to travel the country and the world now and again was more feasible.

While one door opened, a second one opened as well. Bill, my former manager from the hotel, called to explain he was now a stock broker working with one of the biggest investment firms in Philadelphia. I had a stock broker's license myself, so I automatically understood what he was doing. You started by calling everyone you knew to see if they would open an account. In this case, I didn't see any harm in it. I got along well with Bill at the Sherman. The money my mother had left me was practically gathering dust. So if a good broker could give me a leg up in the rough market of the late '70s, I was all for it. Maybe after I was all done paying tuition for four kids I'd still have something to retire on.

I made a small down payment on my future on April 8, 1979, the day of my first ever title fight. At Caesar's Palace in Las Vegas, WBA bantamweight Jorge Lujan of Panama was getting ready to defend his crown against the challenger, Cleo Garcia of Nicaragua. I didn't know much about these fighters except that Lujan was coming in with a much better record. But I certainly knew how to judge a fifteen round fight with a ten point must system.

What I didn't know how to do was dodge Mandry Galindez. We were now in the same city, and when I ran into him in the lobby he looked at me like he was trying to pull the address sticker off with his eyes. So I bobbed and weaved like Muhammad Ali and got out of there. Down by the Caesar's Palace pool, Larry Holmes was giving jump rope lessons. Holmes was the current WBC heavyweight champion and waiting to fight Mike Weaver at Madison Square Garden. When I saw Mandry Galindez at the other end of the pool and considered what I was wearing, I did some skipping of my own, back inside.

The Lujan-Garcia fight was a sleeper. I called most of the first seven rounds a draw, breaking the cardinal rule set forth by my mentor Zach Clayton. But this wasn't a result of my own indecisiveness. This was what happened when you had two boxers and no punches. Referee Davey Pearl stopped the fight two minutes and twenty-nine seconds into the fifteenth round, as Lujan finally had Garcia staggering. I couldn't say Pearl *mercifully* stopped the fight, because with thirty-one seconds to go he could just as easily have let the bout die a natural death. I also couldn't complain. I had always dreamed of judging a championship fight, and I now I had lived that dream—snoozing, bobbing, and weaving aside.

After the fight, I attended the Don King "Peace Celebration" at the hotel. I didn't know exactly what a "Peace Celebration" was, so I figured it was a party Don King threw anytime there wasn't a brawl after the scheduled fight. But in reality it was dinner and dancing and a lot of fun. I made friends with Rodrigo Sanchez, a WBA official who seemed like a nice guy. He was no stalker, and no one was stalking him. In fact, he seemed kind of lonely sitting in the corner, and I always made a point of getting people involved.

That was not a calculated move. That was me. But when being yourself pays off, life is beautiful. Rodrigo Sanchez was soon appointed the new WBA President, and I started getting more assignments. I was lucky, because it could have been the other way around. Usually when a new president took over an organization, as an official you had to start from scratch. It was a lot like the hotel business. But that wasn't the case here.

The first notable assignment was the junior middleweight title fight in April 1980. This one was about as far from the Nevada desert as possible. Copenhagen in April is not particularly cold but it isn't exactly spring either. Spring comes just a little late in Denmark, as the Baltic Sea keeps the air cool a few extra weeks. I would have taken this assignment in any climate, though. It made me the first woman ever to judge a professional fight in Europe. Not to mention the first to judge a title fight.

On the bus from the hotel to the arena, Rodrigo Sanchez thanked me before I could thank him. In Las Vegas, he said, everyone else hovered around President Galindez. That's the way people were. That is, except for me. And, Sanchez said, he would never forget it. There was that old saying about being nice to people on your way up, and it applied to all continents.

Brondby Hallen was a sleek, modern arena—exactly what you would expect from a country known for cleanliness and efficiency. The building featured a large but simple slanted roof with huge exposed laminated beams. Below was a polished wooden floor surrounded on four sides by about five thousand seats without a visible blemish on any of them. This was not only far from Las Vegas. It was far from the Blue Horizon.

Ayub Kalule was the reigning champion. Born in South Africa, he had relocated to Denmark quite some time ago. No one in the world wondered why a black man, especially one with means, would want to leave apartheid. I didn't know exactly how he had chosen Denmark out of all the countries in the world, but it was safe to say it was as far from Johannesburg as it was from Philadelphia or Las Vegas. Denmark, as many Jewish people knew, was a nation of independent minded, freedom loving people. During World War II, thousands of Danish families hid Jewish Danes and refugees in their homes and ultimately helped them flee across the Baltic Sea to safety in neutral Sweden.

Kalule had never lost a fight. No one had ever managed even to bring him to a draw. Of his thirty-two victories, a handful came from knockouts, but most were from technical knockouts. Emiliano Villa was from Colombia and brought in a record of thirty-eight wins, five losses, and three draws. None of those few losses had come in recent years, and Villa was clearly deserving of a title fight.

Both fighters got what they had bargained for, and so had the crowd in Copenhagen. I noticed a television camera panning in on me now and again between rounds, but the real celebrities were in the ring. The fighters combined the best of the heavier weights with the best of the lighter weights. Like the lighter weights, they were fast and agile. Like the heavier weights, they were broad shouldered and fairly massive. A punch from either one could be the first of many or the last one you would ever remember.

As the fight got underway, the strange thing was Villa carried himself in the ring more like the champ and Kalule more like the challenger. Villa anchored himself in one spot for a minute or so at a time, while Kalule came to him, threw some punches, and danced around Villa. But when the two fighters occupied the same space, there was a flurry. Villa swung more from below and Kalule more from above, so there was a real dynamic at work.

The first few rounds were like a negotiation. Each round was close. But in the middle rounds, the fight really took off. The fighters mixed it up for longer and longer periods. Plenty of punches landed. At one point the champ went down when Villa hit him hard in the midsection. Kalule fell straight backwards, more from losing his balance than from the blow itself, and got right up. Within perhaps three seconds he and Villa were going right back at it.

By the eighth round the fight had become furious. Villa remained anchored and Kalule kept circling him, but the jabs and hooks were as fast as any I had ever seen and in bunches. This squeaky clean city was getting a bloodbath reminiscent of the Vikings, and they loved it. Neither fighter showed any real sign of tiredness. These were truly the best athletes in the world.

The eleventh round was perhaps the most dramatic. At the end of the round, like any other, the fighters went to their corners. But after about twenty seconds, Villa's corner man waved his hands at the referee, and the fight was over. Villa had been hit in the face so many times his eyes were severely swollen and bloody, and he could barely see. You wouldn't have known from the round that this was coming. Villa had landed many effective blows and neither fighter seemed the least bit dazed after the bell. Villa, in fact, had walked to his corner like he was taking a seat in a restaurant. For me, it was two title fights under my belt in two hemispheres and no decisions.

That was a good thing, but not because of the weight taken off my shoulders. Those of us in the profession knew most of the serious injuries took place in the thirteenth, fourteenth, and fifteenth rounds. In fact, there was talk in boxing of limiting all title fights to twelve rounds. My personal belief was that fifteen rounds made a true champion, but no one wanted to see anyone really hurt.

There was dinner and dancing after the fight. I did the jitterbug with Joe Santarpia, my fellow judge, who hailed from New York. Then I was moved up a division or two. My next partner was the current dance champion of Denmark. I did my best box step and held my breath when we dipped. Unlike Villa, I got up again.

We had a day and a half before the flight back, so in the morning I took a walk and wound up sitting on a bench in the park across the street from the hotel. It was April 17, my mother's birthday, and I wanted to spend some time alone thinking about her. As I sat there eating a pastry so flaky it melted in my mouth, a middle aged man in tattered clothing approached me. He was carrying a satchel in his right hand and a satchel in his left. And then I realized the same long odds that had brought me halfway around the world were working overtime. Probably the only bagman in all of Copenhagen was sitting next to me. And when my thoughts shifted from my mother to what I could give him, he gave me something—a little doll.

It started to snow a little later. I had heard about black snow but didn't believe it was real. Unfortunately it was, and it was now falling all around me. In Philadelphia, black snow was white snow that lay along the curb in piles and absorbed a week's worth of city soot. In Copenhagen, apparently, it came down that way. Someone said it had to do with all the coal the Danish burned for electricity. Maybe. But between the black snow, the bagman, and being the first woman to judge a pro fight in Europe, I was feeling more special by the minute.

In the afternoon, a few of us took a bus to the water's edge. There, sitting on a rock a few hundred feet out in the water was the famous Little Mermaid statue. The statue was cast in 1913 in honor of the story by Hans Christian Andersen. For a mermaid less than five feet tall sitting on a rock in the sea, it had had a pretty controversial life. The ballet dancer who posed for it disallowed her body from being replicated once she found out it was to be a naked statue. So the sculptor used the ballet dancer's head and the body of his own wife.

But the statue was vandalized numerous times for reasons of politics and mischief. Once in 1954, citizens of Copenhagen awoke to find the Little Mermaid's head missing. They put on a new head and moved the mermaid's rock a little farther out in the water. In fact, they moved it out farther every time someone vandalized it, so that one day it might wind up in Sweden with all the other refuges. But what else could they do? What else besides put a mailing label over her bare breast?

Back at home, two days into my new job at Eastman-Kodak, I received one of those nerve-wracking, out-of-the-blue, frustrating telegrams I always welcomed with open arms. I had been selected to judge the WBA bantamweight title fight that coming weekend in Miami. The last thing in the world a newly stamped employee is supposed to do is ask for the Friday off so she can spend a three-day weekend in Florida. But ask I did. There was no way in the world I wasn't going. I was told by management I could lose my job, and I said that was their decision. They knew boxing came first when I took the job, and I wasn't pulling any punches.

I got that Friday off, which made the trip even better. Not that Miami was Copenhagen, and not that the jai alai court where the fight was being held was anything other a jai alai court. But the challenger, Joltin' Jeff Chandler, was a true Philadelphia home town fighter. Unlike so many perfectly legitimate fighters who came to train in Philadelphia, Chandler was actually born there. He trained in the same Juniper Gym where Matthew Saad Muhammad had trained and fought one memorable bout after another in venues such as the Upper Darby Forum, the Blue Horizon, and of course the Spectrum.

If he could beat Julian Solis of Puerto Rico, Chandler would become the first US fighter to hold the 118-lb. title since 1943. With a bodyweight, a hometown and an underdog status the same as mine, Jeff Chandler was for now my counterpart in the ring, and not going down to Miami to see this through would be like getting knocked out myself.

I supposed there wasn't a single quality fighter coming out of Philadelphia that wasn't in some way colorful, and Jeff Chandler was no exception. Chandler turned pro after only two amateur fights under the guidance of his manager, Arnold Giovanetti. Chandler won his first professional fight, and then his manager disappeared. Literally. In 1976, Arnold Giovanetti's car was found parked at Philadelphia International Airport. Giovanetti was never seen again.

Back at the Juniper Gym, Chandler asked Matthew Saad Muhammad's trainer, Willie O'Neill, to step in. But Willie had a criminal record and saw the hurdles for getting a manager's license as insurmountable. So Willie had his wife, Becky, step in for him. KO Becky, as she became known, was a character herself. At four-foot-seven and 82 pounds, she made me look like a heavyweight. Becky had a show business past, touring the vaudeville circuit under the name Tiny Barron. As KO Becky in her later life, she brought vaudeville to the ring. When Jeff Chandler fought, KO Becky stood ringside twirling her two impossibly long ponytails and waving an American flag so big you could have wrapped four of her in it.

Whether it was his manager's ponytails, the warm weather in Miami, the sight of a completely neutral Philadelphia judge at ringside, or the fighter's own skill, the 5,556 people jammed into the jai alai court watched Jeff Chandler pick apart Solis. At least five thousand of them were Spanish speaking, but the hometown advantage wasn't enough for Solis. Chandler was a very fast, methodical challenger. He kept his focus on a relatively small area consisting of the opponent's head and upper body and rarely strayed from trying to find an opening in that zone.

In the fourteenth round, he found the opening. Chandler was awarded a technical knockout, becoming the first American bantamweight world champ in a generation. When the fight was called, I had Chandler well ahead at 128-118. Referee Carlos Berrocal had Chandler out in front 129-122. Amazingly, judge Caesar Ramos had Chandler ahead by only a single point, 125-124. None of it mattered much, though. Three title fights and not a single one where my scoring counted.

I was relieved when I got back to Fort Washington, PA. The house was not immaculate but no worse than I had left it, and both my girls were no worse than I had left them. Even though Margie and Carol Paula were in high school, there was no chance I would ever leave them alone during one of my long trips.

It felt like I had been through more house sitters and agencies than bantamweight fights. I even had a married couple housesit at one point, but there was one big liability. When the sitters brought friends over, there was suddenly a wildcard. And when the friends brought friends it was chaos. I made a collect call here and there from whatever state or faraway country I was in, but from that distance and disposition you heard what the people on the other end wanted you to hear. So when I traveled, there was tension, and when the fight was over some of the tension was still there. This time, however, the young lady I had hired had her act together.

The relief didn't last long. Just as with a lot of my junk mail, I wasn't in the habit of opening and reading the statement from my broker. But on a day of catching up and organizing around the house, I got the shock of a lifetime. My fifty-thousand dollar investment was down to about four hundred dollars. Before full-fledged panic, I dashed around the kitchen and found a couple of the other statement envelopes and ripped them open. One had my total portfolio at around a thousand dollars. Another had it around six hundred. Then I panicked.

I was still breathless when I called Bill. I asked him if there was some kind of error, and he told me calmly—too calmly—no. I asked him what the heck he had invested my money in, and he listed a few stocks. I hadn't heard of any of them. He told me not to worry, it would all work out. So I worried. It seemed Bill and his top-three big time investment firm were indulging in the market vice du jour—penny stocks. And pennies were what I was left with.

The next person I called was a woman I had worked with at the Sherman Hotel. Normally it wasn't any of my business exactly why a fellow employee was fired, even if he was my manager. But now it was my business. She told me he was stealing from the hotel. She didn't have all the details, but Frank the night auditor did. Frank explained it was credit card fraud. Bill would alter the tape in the credit card machine somehow, which would allow him to pocket cash from the register and not be discovered. I didn't understand all of it, but I had heard enough.

I called an attorney with experience in securities fraud. He explained there were two options—go to court or go to arbitration. Court was expensive, he said. A lot of cases stopped, started, and stopped again, with the legal meter running the whole time. Even if we were awarded the whole fifty thousand dollars, there might not be much left for me. Arbitration was done through the Securities and Exchange Commission and was much quicker. In fact, it was one day and that was it. On the negative side, the panel's decision for all practical purposes was binding. As in the market—at least a fair market—you rolled the dice and lived with the results.

We opted for arbitration. We understood it wasn't a slam-dunk. I hadn't kept up with my statements. I was busy. I was a mom. I was a jet-setter. All of it sounded a lot like the dog eating your homework. But we agreed that I would be candid about that. While I was at it, we agreed I should be forward with the fact that, like my stock broker, I held a stock broker's license. I would add that, license or not, I was not an expert in investments and was relying on my broker for that. That was the truth.

Some truths, however, were best kept to yourself. The dirt I had dug up on Bill made Bill look bad but made me look even worse. Hiring as your broker your ex-manager who was an out and out criminal fell clearly into the fool-me-twice-my-fault category. The fact that I didn't know then what I knew now would be of no use. How much due diligence could a person avoid before it looked like a lifestyle?

The most important thing of all, my attorney said, was that when I testified before the arbitration panel in no way was I to shed a tear. That wouldn't be a problem, I told him. I shed all my tears when I opened the statement envelope.

The day of the hearing it was raining cats and dogs in Philadelphia.

Having been barred from shedding tears, I thought perhaps God was shedding them for me. As we shared an umbrella, my attorney shared a thought. Whatever he told the panel on my behalf, he explained, the case would depend entirely on my testimony. "Thanks," I said. "I guess I needed you like a hole in the head."

The panel consisted of three people. They were heavy hitters. One gentleman, the head of the panel, was the head of the SEC in the state of Delaware. The other two, one a man the other a woman, were attorneys and experts in the field. I felt as if I had been here before. It was a game show, and its name was *To Tell the Truth*.

Bill's testimony was what I expected. The market was struggling as of late and many investors had taken losses. He hadn't done anything unorthodox and the plaintiff, especially with her broker's license, should have understood that with the potential of profit comes risk. I glared at him, and then a thought crystallized in my mind. This was probably worse than negligence or stupidity on his part. This was probably a scam. There was, somewhere, a tale of the tape. But I didn't have the tape.

When it was my turn to testify, I understood I was in the ring now, not at ringside. I knew that feeling in my stomach. I was nervous. It had happened many times before when I spoke to an audience—or appeared in front of a national television audience. But this was worse. It wasn't a stutter or a slip I was worried about. My family's future was riding on this. So I decided to go for broke.

I explained simply who I was and how I got to this point. Yes, I had a stock broker's license, but it was something I studied for after my kids were in bed so I would have something more in common with my then husband. I had sold stock to exactly three people in my life and two of them were my parents. Yes, I should have read my statements more often, but that wouldn't have changed the outcome, perhaps merely staunched the bleeding. The most important thing was that this was all I had in the world. I had told Bill to buy a diverse mix of dependable stocks, not to spin a roulette wheel with my life. Then I turned and looked over at him.

"You are an animal. I trusted you. You were supposed to be a friend. You were supposed to be a professional. But you took it all. You destroyed my life. You destroyed my kids' future. You are an animal."

Not a tear shed. At least not on the outside.

My attorney and I waited for about an hour in an outer room, and the decision came back. I won! It was two to one in my favor. It was more than a little ironic. There was no knockout punch. No technical knockout. Here were three judges deciding my fate. And suddenly I had a little more empathy for the underdogs of this world. For the Davids taking on the Goliaths. Without that knockout blow—that lucky slingshot to the forehead—you were at the mercy of a judge. Or three. I had no other recourse. What was I going to do, toss a burning couch down from the mezzanine?

In Judaism, eighteen is a lucky number. Eighteen is represented by the Hebrew letter Chet, which is the first letter in the word "chai," or "life." A week after the hearing I learned via mail that I was awarded eighteen thousand dollars. Fifty thousand would have been a luckier number. That was thirty-two thousand dollars gone missing that could never rise, fall, and hopefully rise some more over the next twenty or thirty years and provide a cushion of sorts. Six was my attorney's lucky number. He got six thousand. That left me with just twelve thousand, and that was going straight into bonds. This fighter was disappointed with her purse. But victory was sweet. Bill was barred for life from selling stocks.

I was glad I didn't lie down in the ring. It was a matter of principle—the personal kind. My mother and father did more than leave me some assets. They left me fortitude and a sense of justice. I didn't want to be Marlon Brando lamenting to Karl Malden in *On the Waterfront*. I didn't ever want to tell myself or anyone else, "I coulda been a contender."

CHAPTER ELEVEN
DON'T CRY FOR ME, CÓRDOBA

Winter in Philadelphia is a lot like a heavyweight bout. It goes twelve weeks, maybe fifteen. The Christmas light show at Wanamaker's can help get you through the first few weeks, and the Mummer's Parade up Broad Street can take you through New Year's Day. But after the early rounds you need more than pomp and hype. By the end of the first week of January, you're staggering across mounds of snow on the sidewalk to put out the garbage and just hoping the car will start.

On January 8 of 1982, my winter bout ended in a TKO. I received a letter from the WBA that in exactly one week I would be judging the super bantamweight title fight between Sergio Victor Palma and Jorge Lujan in Córdoba, Argentina. Argentina is at the bottom of the world, and I was now on top of the world.

When my plane lifted off the runway at Philadelphia International three days later, I still had a chill in my bones, and I knew it would be a while before it wore off. It was the coldest part of the winter in the US and the warmest part of summer in Argentina, yet this was anything but a direct route between the two. My $1,472 flight, graciously prepaid by the WBA, was really five flights. We would land in Miami, then take off again for Puerto Rico. From there it was another long hop to Rio de Janeiro, Brazil, a skip to Buenos Aires, and a jump to Córdoba.

Here I was in seat 23D already tired from a sleepless night of anticipation on my Fort Washington mattress. Anyone hearing this might have told me there was no problem, as I had time to relax and catch up. But I didn't sleep on planes.

I wasn't afraid to fly. Far from it. But takeoffs were momentous occasions and small miracles. Landings were momentous occasions and larger miracles. I felt I had to pay attention. In between, we were up in the air, and that didn't seem like a place to sleep either. When my kids needed some sleep they said they had to "crash." No crashing for me.

In truth, I faded in and out, grabbing a minute nod here, five minutes there. In between I sorted out what I had just left and where I was going. Margie and Carol Paula were going to be okay. I had a reliable married couple watching the house for me. That seemed like the perfect antidote to chronic babysitter problems. With a married couple, there was no boyfriend or girlfriend to invite over. And a party, if there was one, was just a dinner party. The job at Eastman-Kodak was safe and sound as well. Warm weather notwithstanding, the potential problems were ahead of me, not behind.

You didn't have to be an expert in world politics to know Argentina was having trouble. Argentina was always having trouble. Since breaking away from Spain in the early 1800s, the country's history was fraught with power struggles and violence. Argentina was run by dictators for over a century, and if you weren't of European descent and preferably from one of the established families, your status was anywhere from second class citizen to peasant.

The legacy of this system was a constant battle between left and right extremists, who when you stepped back, looked strangely similar to each other. Every so often a revolution broke out, power changed hands, and the next coup simmered underground. There were grand experiments with in democracy, as when President Roque Saenz Peña established universal suffrage and the country's first secret ballot in 1912. But the legacy of authoritarian rule and special privilege was the gift that kept giving. Even Juan Perón and his celebrated folk heroine wife Eva—with all their socially conscious policies on behalf of laborers and the poor—came to power in 1946 through a coup and stayed in power with the help of a meddlesome military and strong censorship. The Peróns closed more newspapers than the invention of television.

The Argentina I was headed to at about 600 miles per hour was probably even worse. In 1976, Perón's third wife and widow, Isabel, was removed from the presidency by *coup d'état*, putting a military dictatorship back in charge. For the past several years Argentina was undergoing a "National Reorganization Process." Reorganization was what you did to a company with under-trained managers or to a sock drawer with too many unmatched socks. Reorganization in Argentina was the disappearance of thousands of citizens in the middle of the night. It was the imprisonment, forced labor, torture, and murder of the opposition or the perceived opposition. It was rule by fear.

Fear, of course, can't rule forever. Eventually desperation takes over. Although the word Argentina meant "silver," the peso was getting weaker by the minute and the public debt becoming greater. A few landings from now I was going to see a great fight. I just hoped it took place in the ring.

It wasn't my first trip to South America. In August I flew to Caracas, Venezuela to judge the featherweight title fight between Eusebio Pedroza and Carlos Pinango. The defending champion, Pedroza, won by a technical knockout leaving me with a record of four title fights on three continents and no decisions. The trip was somewhat uneventful other than seeing a lot of black squirrels and gas on sale for 19 cents a gallon. The biggest shock was leaving warm summery Philadelphia and landing in cold wintery Caracas. So perhaps I had nothing to fear from Argentina.

The weight of the world began to lift even before I got to the lower hemisphere. In Miami we picked up the other judge, Stuart Winston. Stuart was a character and was also the head of the umpires for the United States Tennis Association. Anyone who thought umpiring a tennis match was a breeze compared to judging a fight obviously hadn't seen some of the abuse dished out over the last few years by the likes of John McEnroe and a few of his peers. As an official, when I saw a line judge publicly humiliated over a ball maybe a hair off the line, I wanted to get out on the court and issue a right hook of my own.

In Buenos Aires we picked up Roberto Ramirez, our referee, who under WBA rules would also score the fight as a judge. Ramirez was a family man whose regular job was with the phone company. Roberto and I got along great, and we made a deal. He would be my Spanish translator in

Argentina. Not that I couldn't understand a word of Spanish. I understood most of the words. But sometimes when Spanish was spoken to me rapid-fire, I couldn't put together all the pieces. Sometimes they didn't seem like pieces but rather a long new word that needed to be dissected. Sometimes Spanish sounded to me like a tape recorder being played backwards.

I had had two years of Latin and five-and-a-half years of French. I had also studied Italian in night classes. So I had romance languages covered, kind of. I could understand Italian and for the most part speak it. But I couldn't demonstrate in Italian that I had a sense of humor. I had to leave that to the Italians. I could do better than get by in French. Basically, I had such a diverse collection of romance language nouns, verbs, and adjectives in my brain I could stumble along indefinitely. Usually by the third or fourth day in a foreign country I just about got the hang of it. And then it was time to leave.

It was not time to leave Buenos Aires yet. Roberto, Stuart and I had a few hours before our flight to Córdoba, and the powers that be had plans for us. The powers that be, in this case, were not a dark military junta. Rather, they were Juan Carlos "Tito" Lectore. Tito Lectore was Sergio DePalma's manager as well as the promoter of the fight. They did things a little differently down in Argentina, where a man in the complicated world of professional boxing could wear multiple hats. Then again, we had Don King.

Tito Lectore, though, was no Don King. His reputation was solid and he was modest. And although Don King was not unattractive if you favored static electric hair, Tito Lectore was drop dead gorgeous. Sorely lacking sleep, I felt myself drifting into a Latin American daydream, a siesta, in which Tito and I began an affair below the Equator. I had to remind myself that I was on business and snap out of it. But just as soon as I had snapped out of it, the real Tito Lectore in the real Buenos Aires presented me with a very real dozen red roses. I don't care how modern, liberated, and professional she might be—a woman who doesn't thrill at the sight of a dozen red roses handed to her by a tall, dark handsome South American is hardly a woman.

Tito had a limousine drive our entourage over to Luna Park, an elaborate 8,000 seat indoor arena in Buenos Aires. There was no problem for Tito booking Luna Park, because as it so happened he owned it. The arena wasn't packed, but the hundred or so people there generated more than enough excitement on their own. Our host had arranged a press conference. We weren't even in the city of the fight yet, and already there was hype. There were microphones and cameras and rapid fire questions sounding like a tape recorder played backwards. And there was my new translator pressed into service. Roberto Ramirez played referee between me and the press, even though the press and I got along just fine.

From these reporters via Roberto, I learned that I was the first woman ever to judge a professional fight in Argentina, let alone a title fight. They said they had been awaiting my arrival for days. It was more than a little flattering that in a city whose hometown fighter, Sergio Victor Palma, was about to defend his world title, these members of the media were interested in me. That in the very arena where Palma had successfully defended his title the last two times, I was getting the majority of questions. As a judge, I didn't expect to have fans, especially so far from home.

We had some more time after the press conference, so Tito Lectore took our entourage over to the Pink House. The formal name for the Pink House was the Casa Rosada. It was a huge, ornate, somewhat Romanesque building sitting in the middle of the vast Plaza de Mayo. The Pink House was built in 1713 by colonial Spain and to this day emanated the sense of power it was supposed to. Inside sat the executive branch of the Argentine government and the president himself.

The president at this moment was Leopoldo Galtieri. The word "moment" was not inappropriate. Galtieri had been dictator since December 22, or as we in the States liked to call it, a couple of weeks ago. His predecessor hadn't lasted more than a year or so, and when things weren't going well for the military dictatorship, they liked to play musical chairs. Some things, however, could always be counted on. The death squads in Argentina reported directly to Galtieri, as they had to his predecessor and his predecessor's predecessor. The color pink belied the plans made inside, but then again pink is the color of blood with a little bleach. No one came outside to greet us, and that was actually a relief.

Our next and final flight took us about an hour west to Córdoba, near the center of the country. Regardless of who was running Argentina I felt a lot lighter now than when I had left Philadelphia. As we picked up people along the way, we also picked up steam. We were like a caravan. A traveling circus. But then a little air came out of my balloon when I reached into my pocketbook. Most of my cash was gone. It was the first time I had checked for cash in two cities. I narrowed it down to the flight from Rio when I went to the ladies room and didn't take my bag with me. Now I was really light.

I got even lighter after landing in Córdoba. My suitcase was missing. There are few feelings in life as lonely as waiting in the baggage claim area and watching to no avail as the luggage goes round and round and everybody gets theirs except you. Roberto helped me get through to the airline officials, who told me not to panic. My suitcase might arrive the following day. The truth was I was too tired to panic.

When I got to room 319 of the Crillon Hotel in Córdoba, I wanted to lie face down on the bed in the clothes on my back—now my only clothes—and sleep. After a full day of globetrotting we were only two hours ahead of Philadelphia, and I was wiped out in any time zone. But they had plans for us. They took us to a local gym for another press conference.

And it was here, wired and beyond overtired, in a gymnasium that almost could have been on North Broad Street in Philadelphia, that I really began to understand how special this event was. This was the first ever world title fight in Córdoba, which compared to Buenos Aires was something like Chicago or Philadelphia compared to New York. There was tremendous pride involved.

It was truly international in scope. I heard other languages from across the sea of microphones, and I was thrilled to hear one of those languages was Italian. So I took the liberty of answering a question without the help of a translator. How did I feel about being the first woman to officiate in the first ever title fight held in the city of Córdoba? "*Meraviglioso. E 'un onore assoluto!*" ("Wonderful. It is an absolute honor!") More questions poured my way, in batches that were both thrilling and almost embarrassing. If Buenos Aires was a red carpet treatment, Córdoba was a coronation. I could have been Eva Perón. Who needed money and clothing?

My second wind had been nice and my third wind nicer, but back in Room 319 there was no fourth wind. As I drifted off I just hoped I wouldn't have a repeat performance of some earlier first nights in a given city. There were times I would wake up in the middle of the night and have no idea what country I was in. That feeling of amnesia might last a minute or, if I was unlucky, a lot longer. I might have to get up and look out the window before it all came back to me. But luckily, that didn't happen in Room 319. I faded in and out of sleep without ever sleeping perfectly or forgetting my whereabouts. When I woke up for good around 7 AM, I had one thought and one thought only. I needed a new dress.

The Crillon Hotel was tucked into one corner of a square. Some of the other guests at breakfast told me not to worry about venturing out myself if I felt like it, because whatever was going on inside the Pink House and inside the prison camps, Córdoba was as safe as could be. As I began my stroll down the main connecting boulevard, I knew they were right. The street was clean and the people friendly. When you see city dwellers who feel perfectly safe, it's contagious. The city was well policed, but not so well policed that there was reason to be concerned.

I walked into a clothing shop and using some of the allowance money provided by the WBA and bought myself a white cotton dress. It was sleeveless, about knee length, and best of all a lot less expensive than it should have been. The dollar-to-peso exchange rate was very favorable, so whatever was troubling the people inside the Pink House was working well for me so far.

As I strolled along the promenade, now wearing my competitively priced white dress, people looked over at me and pointed from time to time. Others stopped, smiled, and said hello. They knew who I was and what I was doing here, and they looked like they had seen a celebrity. They were outgoing and they were knowledgeable, but they weren't psychic. I invested a few pesos in a newspaper, *Matutino*, and quickly found a photo of yours truly. I had on the dress from the travel day before. Thank God I had a new outfit on today.

I stopped in to eat at a little restaurant with a bar in the front, something that reminded me of a trattoria in Italy. The waiter was a nice middle-aged gentleman named Luis who spoke to me in broken English in return for my broken Spanish. By the third course we discovered that we both knew Italian, and Luis was thrilled to discover I was the lady judge, or in Italian, "giudice." Not long after dessert I ran into Luis again on the promenade. We were like old friends by now, and when I asked him in Italian if he was on a break, he explained in the same language that he was the restaurant manager and that the break was anytime he wanted it.

We went strolling and poking our noses into this store and that. I wasn't looking for anything in particular, and Luis gave me window shopping advice. Then I received a surprise I hadn't bargained for. An attractive olive skinned woman a bit younger than Luis spotted us on the promenade. Luis gave her a big hug, and I thought I might be in trouble. What if this was his girlfriend? It wasn't. Luis introduced me in Spanish to Marita, "mi esposa," his wife. In the United States, a wife spotting her husband on the street laughing with a strange woman in a sleeveless white dress might have earned me a dirty look. In Philadelphia it might have gotten me an interrogation. On a bright summer day near the bottom of the world, it got me a hug from Marita. It was a big, friendly hug with no pretense. And then she kept going.

The ticket office for the fight was two doors down from the hotel, and from the length of the line it looked like a sellout. My pay for the event was fixed, but with each ticket purchased I felt validated. I sat on a low wall, as anonymously as possible, and tried to take it all in. But within a few minutes I was recognized. And when a crowd sees a crowd, they crowd around some more. Within a few minutes the police had to come over and disperse my impromptu fan club. I loved it. I wanted more, but the sober judge in me didn't want to milk it.

The siesta was starting soon in any case, and I figured I'd take mine in room 319. That required walking through the hotel lobby, and that act could no longer be taken for granted. There were more reporters and camera crews lying in wait there as well as countless guests wanting to shake my hand and exchange a few words in their home language. By the time I was back up in my room and collapsing onto the bed, my pretty white dress already looked like it had done some road work.

When I came to later in the afternoon, among my first thoughts was whether my suitcase had arrived at the airport. When I spotted an envelope slipped under the room door, my hopes were rising. They were still rising when I removed a note, which was handwritten on Crillon Hotel stationery. But the note seemed way too long to tell me my luggage was waiting for me at the front desk. At the top were the words "Private and Confidential." Unless it was the inventory from my suitcase, something was wrong. I felt a little queasy. But at least it was in English.

"Dear Carol,

You may remember me as the Anglo-Argentine who introduced myself to you in the hotel lobby. I was fascinated by your charming manners and other attributes. I was a tremendous boxing fan during the days of Pink Pavloller, Ike Williams, Hial Havilan and others of that vintage, being boxing champion of my high school in 1936. A long time ago because I am now 61, a revival of my interest in boxing had again been aroused by the prominence of someone like you on the boxing scene.

"You mentioned you were leaving Argentina right away, and I'm returning to the villa to join my family on Saturday morning for the last ten days of our annual vacation. I know you will be tremendously busy this evening, but I really would like to see you before we part ways. I shall be out on business until about 4 PM, most likely in my room, number 315, or downstairs.

"Please be kind enough to write me a short note to tell me if we can meet perhaps this evening sometime to enjoy a liaison between us without

your enormous entourage. Let me know if you can join the celebration for a time, and when the excitement has withered down perhaps I can kidnap you for an hour or two and hear your comments about the match over a meal or a bottle of champagne. I would be at your disposal for as long a time as you can afford to give me if this would be my good fortune.

"In short, I do anxiously hope we can get together at whatever time you can make it. We are next door neighbors at the hotel on the third floor (Room 315 and you 319) so please shove a note under my door letting me know how the cookie crumbles, but please don't disappoint me. Have a wonderful day, and may the best man win. I now look forward to your note.

Yours anxiously,
Alfredo
p.s.: Please trust this message is fully confidential, as I will yours."

My first reaction was to make sure the room door was locked. My next thought was about certain phrasings. When someone said "Please don't disappoint me," they didn't really mean the "please." This was someone used to getting his way. It had "stalker" written all over it. The worst part was that I couldn't simply tell myself out of sight out of mind. I had been within his sights in the lobby. I met so many people and shook so many hands I couldn't picture who it might be, and for the most part I didn't want to. There was no great comfort in the solitude of my room, though there was some. From memory I reviewed the sequence of rooms along the hallway: 315, 317, 319 . . . . Thank God for Room 317.

Unfortunately, there was no note waiting for me downstairs at the hotel and no luggage. Feeling as if someone was watching me, I minimized my time in the lobby on the way out to the big reception. The reception was held in a large restaurant a few blocks away and was such a grandiose affair it took the edge off my paranoia. Everyone from the WBA representatives to my fellow officials to the Governor of Córdoba was in attendance, and with tango music filling the air they sat as down at a few long tables.

Food came out on heaping Lazy Susans which the waiters placed on the table. I followed everyone else's lead, scooping sausages, goat meat, kiwi, and avocados off of the Lazy Susans as fast as they spun and putting food on the plate in front of me. After three or four minutes, the waiters would swap out our plates for clean ones. After a few more minutes, the old Lazy Susans went back and new ones came out, and we started all over again. It was a South American food orgy.

It could have been a twenty-five course meal. Somewhere around course nine or ten, I started feeling heavy and sedate. Had this been the night of the fight, I would have stopped at course three. You couldn't judge a fight effectively while bloated and woozy. Like the fighters themselves, you had to be a little hungry and edgy. But all I faced tonight was my bed, and I wanted nothing more than to sleep like a rock. So I spun and ate and spun and ate, the entire time being careful not to spray my white dress with gravy. As it was, the dress already had a large crease and a couple of small wrinkles. The last thing it needed was a blood stain.

As the wheels began to slow down, speeches were given and presentations were made. There were at least two Spanish-to-English translators with us, and one of them was helping the governor present me with a silver sculpture in the shape of a cow bone, perhaps a thigh. Someone explained that the gauchos—the indigenous cowboys—played some kind of traditional game with cow bones, so that this honor was similar to being presented in America with a silver horseshoe. I had never turned down anything silver in my life, and with a bunch of Argentine generals staring at me, I certainly wasn't going to start now.

When my turn came to talk to the generals, it felt a little like walking in front of a firing squad. They were in uniform and so austere. These were fixtures of an autocratic state, like a mob but legal. They were somber, and I imagined these were the same expressionless faces that decided between life and death for the helpless. Their stares, however, were not the somberness of a judge. A judge made rulings, and his face was full of discernment. These generals made decrees.

I had met many celebrities in my life, and it always struck me that they were entirely normal people whom many thought they knew but few really did. Yet the celebrities were, at least, entirely knowable. These generals were not knowable. And if you could know them you wouldn't want to.

The broad-shouldered mustached one in the middle wanted to know if I had children. I told my translator, yes, I had four. The general then wanted to know what their ages were. I told my translator that in the United States a woman did not state the age of her children, because that would give away her own age.

There was a delay in the conversation equal to the time it took the translator to translate. During translation, I stood and waited like a contestant on a game show, or perhaps more like a defendant at a tribunal. Then, as the final clause in my final sentence left the translator's lips, a smile swept across the general's face. It spread to the two generals flanking him, and then there was even the beginning of laughter in the brigade. Like a fighter who saw blood, I saw a reprieve, and I went in for the kill. "I apologize for my dress, which is wrinkled. But you must understand that back in the United States, wrinkled is in."

There was another delay, and this time at the end of the tunnel there were huge smiles and guffaws. I had cracked up a military dictatorship. And no matter what lay in store for Argentina, I would sleep like a baby tonight.

Estadio Córdoba was an oval shaped soccer stadium that probably seated thirty thousand. Tonight it was more like fifty thousand. The ring was set up midfield, and thousands upon thousands of bleacher seats were set up on all four surrounding sides. Literally every seat was filled, and the atmosphere was electric. The sky was black by about 9 PM, and the stars looked like tiny sparkling crystals. I felt newly alive, and the stars served as a backdrop. I was no astronomer, but I could tell right away this was a foreign sky with unfamiliar star configurations. This was something you normally took for granted. If you traveled from Philadelphia south to Florida, there were differences, but this difference was absolute. You were in another reality.

I knew the national anthems were coming. The last one played would be Argentina's. When you were a judge visiting from another country, you got the same due as a visiting fighter. So when *The Star Spangled Banner* began playing over the public address system, I was ready. But I wasn't ready for what followed. At one end of the stadium was a huge scoreboard with a video screen. The screen lit up like the marquee in front of a Broadway theater. There was a bright illuminated pattern of light bulbs encircling a name, and that name was "Carol Polis, USA." Immediately below was a video rendering of Old Glory waving in the wind.

The crowd cheered and screamed like it was the final seconds of the fifteenth round of a close fight. The real fight was between me and my tears. I was doing everything possible to hold them back, including biting my tongue. Whenever I left American soil, I always tried to carry myself with dignity, especially knowing that I represented my country. There were moments when I thought maybe I was being too cautious, but this unforgettable spectacle and the deafening welcome reminded me what it was all about.

In the US, criticizing the way things worked was our national pastime, and that was fine while standing on home soil. On foreign soil, however, no matter how cynical you were in your own backyard, you took pride in who you were and where you came from. If the people of Argentina understood it, how could I not? So I kept biting my tongue, gave the crowd the peace sign and hoped Harry Winston's name would appear on the marquee any second. I could take only so much euphoria.

I had a chance to catch my breath during the preliminary bouts. One of the many perks of officiating a title fight was being assigned to judge only the main event. So I sat on the press side, equidistant from the ring corners, a row back from the table I would shortly occupy. The judge whose seat I would take was Jorge Waldo Mandritti, and we became friends down in the trenches. And I also made quick friends with a handsome Argentine gentleman sitting next to me.

As an off-duty judge, I not only watched the action in the ring, but also the action around the other side of it. Jorge Luján's manager, Aurelio "Yeyo" Cortés, had been animated and quirky my entire time in Córdoba, and now just prior to his fighter's grand entrance was no exception. Cortés made an appearance or two ringside, milled about, admonished a few people, and exited back down the aisle. I couldn't tell what his purpose was except perhaps burning off some nervous energy.

If he was nervous, I understood why. When I had judged Jorge Luján in Las Vegas back in '79, Luján was so patient it made me sleepier than a twenty-five course meal. I didn't know much about the Argentine world champion Sergio Victor Palma, but if he was an aggressive fighter he had a great chance to defend his title against Luján. Luján had lost three straight fights coming in. He had lost his bantamweight title to Julian Solis, then lost his challenge to Philadelphia hometown favorite Jeff Chandler, who had beaten Solis. That was the fight I skipped out of work for to judge in Miami. It was a small world, and I was quickly becoming a player in the worldwide bantamweight soap opera. Luján then lost a non-title fight to Roberto Rubaldino. The fight at hand, between Palma and Luján, was for the world super bantamweight title.

People asked me from time to time what the difference was between a title fight and a "super" title fight. Did it mean one fighter flew around the ring in a cape and the other threw kryptonite at him? Not exactly. The "super" designation was meant to unify the title among the various boxing organizations—the WBA, WBC, WBO, and the IBF. How they decided who could contend for the super title was often somewhat of a mystery, and this fight was no exception. By any measure, it should have been Jeff Chandler in the ring tonight against Palma. But I could only judge what was in front of me.

When Sergio Victor Palma was led into the ring, there were not only deafening roars from the fifty thousand in attendance. There was a massive fireworks display. By its timing it wasn't so much a celebration of the event as of the national bantamweight hero. Meanwhile, Luján's manager, Cortés, was ranting and making fireworks of his own.

As the fight got through the early rounds, Luján was more

aggressive than he had been in Las Vegas. The truth was he had to be. Palma was a dangerous fighter. He swung almost equally with the left and right. His punches were thrown from either side and from various angles. This was very disconcerting to Lujan, as it would be to any 119-pound fighter. He had a hard time getting settled around Palma, who pushed forward constantly, a bit like a barroom brawler. It couldn't have helped Lujan or his manager that the entire crowd kept chanting "Argentina! Argentina!"

In the middle rounds, Lujan measured up. His answer to Palma's ambidextrousness was to duck, crouch, and pop up again almost as quickly as Palma could throw a flurry of punches. Lujan's hands moved even more than Palma's but not always in the form of effective punches. By my count, Palma was the ring captain in the majority of rounds.

Lujan's mental count was probably similar. In the eleventh round he needed to make something happen to take control of the fight, but the only thing that happened was a clinch between the two fighters. As the seconds ticked off, Lujan became as frustrated as his manager and bit Palma on the shoulder. In a land known for beef, the challenger had gotten a mouthful of Grade A, and Roberto Ramirez called it out before Lujan could swallow.

Our referee pulled the fighters apart, issued a warning to Lujan, and then a message to the judges. He held up a finger to me then swung around to show the same finger to Harry Winston. That meant we both had to deduct a point from Lujan in the round. The sign language was necessary, because now the faithful Argentines were even louder than the fireworks they had set off earlier. It was also fortunate that my suitcase had finally arrived at the hotel earlier in the day. I swapped out my white dress for a red one, which aside from not looking lived in would not show all the blood spots.

When the bell rang ending the fifteenth and final round, I could feel the beginning of chaos in the stadium. The elements were there. The hometown crowd wanted vindication but wasn't sure it was coming. There was a low grumble that hearkened back to the Felt Forum and Annapolis and anywhere in history the masses wanted to finish a fight themselves. And there was the nut job manager in the ring trying to finish his own fight. Between the noise and the language barrier I couldn't make out a thing Cortés was saying, yet I understood every word of it.

I had a duty to remain at my seat until the scores were read, and I did, just barely. All three of us had Palma as the winner by four points—a unanimous decision. The roar of the crowd reached a crescendo without getting much less menacing. Maybe they were reacting to Cortés's childish antics in the ring. I didn't want to wait around for the post-fight psychoanalysis. My tall handsome friend said "Vamos!" and we went.

There was a reception back at the hotel. Receptions were always better after the hometown fighter won, so we were treated to more tango and twenty-five more courses. A couple of handsome young professional soccer players practically asked to come back to America with me but I explained there was no room in my suitcase. Somewhere between courses eight and nine, Sergio Victor Palma walked in and the attendees erupted in applause. Palma was a poet of sorts and read one of his works before presenting me with a miniature red and white leather boxing glove with his name embroidered on it. I thanked him and said I could have used it on my way out of the stadium.

A couple of courses later, Jorge Lujan and his manager walked in, and the room became subdued. Lujan was quiet and polite. He appeared banged up, which made me feel bad for Lujan but even more certain in my decision. And then the dreaded moment— Manager Cortés walked up to me and started in. He stared at me as a defendant might stare at a criminal court judge who had just wrongly sentenced him to life in prison. There was no translator handy, but I made out the gist of it: "Why didn't you go for my fighter? Why?" He kept calling me "Polly." As if I wanted a cracker. All I really wanted was to hide somewhere.

I explained to him in simple English: "I am sorry your fighter didn't win. Better luck next time." For good measure I threw in a *"Buena suerte!"* in Spanish and a *"Bona fortuna!"* in Italian. In any language I wanted out.

I managed to leave Argentina in one piece and without being gobbled up by my secret admirer. But I did not manage to leave with my reputation intact. Five title fights and finally a decision. And, as I had suspected, not without a price. In my wake, Cortés the Killer had accused all three officials of having been bought. My source of information was WBA Officials Chairman Alberto Aleman, who sent me packets of newspaper clippings. So chivalrous was Aleman that he sent English translations of these articles along with personal notes underscoring his confidence in me and in all the WBA officials.

Cortés was crazier than I had given him credit for. He accused the referee of "blocking up" his fighter's style, as if Roberto Ramirez was holding Lujan's arms when Palma was pounding him. Cortés called Stuart Winston a "cartoon character" and claimed he made loud predictions that Palma would win. Cortés even accused Palma of biting Lujan, rather than the other way around. That was hard to digest.

As for Carol Polis, at least Cortés was consistent. He called me "Polly" even in the press. Whereas everyone's language skills at some point fell short on one front or another, Cortés made his deficiencies work to his advantage. He claimed that during our brief, unpleasant interaction at the post-fight reception I told him I thought Lujan had won. If you put this guy in the UN, he would have started World War III inside of a week.

I wrote letters back to Aleman, and slowly but surely via Air Mail I was vindicated along with my peers. In March of 1982 the WBA banned Cortés from the sport of boxing to the extent they could.

I could have gloated that Cortés the Killer went the way of Bill the Stock broker. But something much more important was going on. In April, Galtieri had Argentine forces invade the British held Falkland Islands. For a few weeks the world watched closely to see if the invasion would hold up against Margaret Thatcher's forces and if Galitieri's ploy would successfully distract Argentina from its sorry political state.

By June the British retook the Falklands, and days later the military dictator and mass murderer Galitieri was removed from office. In the following months, elections were held and democracy was restored to Argentina. If I had learned anything in my life it was that justice was usually far too late, but it was still justice. Aleman wrote me a heartfelt letter of apology, and I wrote back the truth—that no one needed to cry for me.

CHAPTER TWELVE
WHAT HAPPENS IN VEGAS

From time to time, people would ask me if I ever thought about the possibility of a fighter dying in the ring when I judged a fight. My answer was yes, I thought about it, but as little as possible. I prayed it would never happen and then pushed it out of my mind. At least until the next person asked the question.

But toward the end of 1982 the question was getting harder to avoid. On November 13, at Caesars Palace in Las Vegas, WBA lightweight champion Ray "Boom Boom" Mancini was fighting South Korean challenger Duk Koo Kim in a fifteen round title fight. Like many quality lightweight fights, it was fast, furious, and evenly matched. In the thirteenth round, Mancini started getting the best of Kim, who looked tired but kept bouncing back for more exchanges.

In the fourteenth round, Mancini, whose own face was cut up, smelled blood, and it wasn't his own. For better or for worse, this was the mark of a champion. With the bell, Mancini came out more like a bull than a lightweight. He charged Kim, caught him with a left and a right, and then less than a second later another right, this one so powerful and direct to Kim's face that the South Korean fell straight back. It's never good when anyone falls straight back, and that includes professional fighters. The back of Kim's head hit the canvas hard. Unbelievably, Kim got up after only a few seconds and staggered with the intention of throwing a few more punches. But referee Richard Greene called a TKO, letting Mancini keep his WBA lightweight belt at least till another fight.

The crowd at Caesars Palace went wild, not only for the display of ring skills but because Mancini was an American from Ohio and the closest thing they had to a modern Raging Bull. Mancini's father was a couple of rows away starting a celebration of his own. But all jubilation ended a few moments later when Kim collapsed and went into a coma. Four days later, with Kim's mother at his side having flown halfway around the world, doctors removed the patient's life support system.

Overnight, the possibility of death in the ring had become less abstract for the sport of boxing and even less abstract for me. Then, on December 6, I received a telegram informing me that I had two days to get to Las Vegas to judge the December 10 heavyweight title fight between WBA champion Mike Weaver and challenger Michael Dokes. The bout was to be held in the very same Caesars Palace where only four weeks earlier Duk Koo Kim had sustained life ending injuries.

On December 8 my morning flight took off for Denver, where I would pick up a flight to Las Vegas. I should have been ecstatic to have gotten one of my original wishes upon being appointed a judge. I was finally going to officiate at a world heavyweight title fight. Not that I was a heavyweight elitist. Just the opposite. The middleweights on down were generally faster and more skillful, not to mention that their fights usually went longer. Whenever I spoke to someone who called himself a boxing fan and it turned out that all he really knew were the heavyweights, I stopped the conversation a bit early, like a heavyweight fight. That wasn't really a fan. That was a spectator. I didn't want a sluggish fifteen-round conversation.

But still, there were great heavyweights and, therefore, great heavyweight fights. The aura about a heavyweight title fight was undeniable. The heavyweights' size and strength made them the most dangerous men in the world. The anticipation leading up to the fight always had something extra, making that ring the center of the universe at least for a night. And with the heavyweights, everyone was conscious of the same thing—the fight could end at any moment with one punch.

But the questions on my mind weighed even heavier. I always told my kids to reason things out but not to rationalize. In the face of numerous cries to ban the sport of boxing altogether, I wondered if *I* was rationalizing. *No*, I thought. *I'm not*. Boxing, I reminded myself, was safer than football, and just about no one wanted to ban that. In boxing, the punches were above the belt and cushioned by regulation gloves. Fighters took a physical before the bout, and a licensed physician—the ring doctor—was by law ringside the entire fight.

Yet there was now a firestorm surrounding the sport as it took a good look at itself. In response to the death of Kim, the WBC held a series of meetings. The result was a series of rule changes intended to make boxing safer. Fifteen round fights were abolished, with twelve rounds becoming the maximum. The time between rounds was lengthened from 60 seconds to 90. When a fighter was severely shaken up, the referee could issue a standing eight count. And when a fighter was knocked out, there would be a mandatory minimum 45-day layoff before his next fight. Prior to returning to the ring, the fighter would have to present the results of a CAT scan to the state athletic commission.

The irony with the rule changes was that the death of Duk Koo Kim occurred in a WBA event. The WBC reacted as it should have, even though there was an element of closing the barn door after the horse got away. But what about the WBA itself? It still hadn't held its conclave, and here I was 20,000 feet above the Earth soaring to the next WBA title fight.

I was certainly glad I wasn't Richard Greene, the referee at the Mancini-Kim fight. I knew if the rest of us had heavy hearts, Greene had to be changed forever. The death of a loved one or anyone for that matter in your presence was horrible, but the pain eventually faded when you knew there was nothing you could have done. If, however, you knew there was something you could have done, there was no fading. The memory of exactly where you could have intervened played on an endless loop in your mind. Unlike a referee or a ring doctor, as a judge you never had the ability to stop the fight. But God forbid something like that ever happened on my watch, there would be little consolation. I would always know I was part of it.

After a short layover in Denver, I boarded the plane to Las Vegas, which was going to be a one-hour hop. On line near me was Larry Holmes, the current heavyweight champ of the WBC. He was headed to Caesars Palace, too, but not to fight. Holmes was doing the commentary for HBO, which had paid two million dollars for the Weaver-Dokes broadcast rights. Holmes would have a unique perspective. The winner of the fight would, as WBA champion, be next in line to fight him in a heavyweight unification bout. Holmes had beaten Mike Weaver in a brawl of a fight in 1979, but Weaver was now a more skilled and experienced fighter. Dokes had, to date, won twenty-five fights, lost none, and fought to a draw once. Either way, the unification fight would be a good one and Holmes—the Easton Assassin—was ready to go. But in boxing, especially these days, the logical course was often the last one followed, especially where Don King was involved.

Holmes mumbled a lot. I wrote it off to my trouble hearing a man over a foot taller than I was in a crowded airport. Still, I hoped he had it a little more together by the bell for round one. Millions around the world would be listening. I was listening with one ear. The other was still listening to my own thoughts regarding the cloud over the Dokes-Weaver fight. And then a stewardess in her thirties with shoulder length brunette hair approached me. I thought maybe I was bumped from the flight. It was nothing like that. I hadn't even gotten to Vegas and I was already being pressed into service.

The crew was two stewardesses short for the flight, and the one who made it wanted to know if I would fill in. I looked at it from her perspective. I was wearing a blue velvet blazer and a nice pair of jeans. I had been thirty-nine and holding for several years and was getting pretty good at it. Perky was no problem for me. I supposed I gave off the right kind of vibe. In any case, I would make at least as good a stewardess as Larry Holmes would make a color commentator.

"Would I?" I said. "I'd love it!"

The stewardess popped an apron on me and explained that they wouldn't be able to pay me. She asked if there was something they could give me in lieu of cash. "Yes," I said, eyeballing a crate stocked with little bottles of Seagram's 7 and Cutty Sark. "I have a lot of friends who drink and a lot of Christmas presents to give out." We had a deal.

I fit right in. No one noticed a thing, with the possible exception of

Larry Holmes, who must have thought the WBA didn't pay their officials nearly enough. I walked up and down the aisle, gave out a lifetime's worth of pretzel bags, poured gallons of cranberry juice eight ounces at a time, and chatted up a storm. When a passenger asked me for the weather in Las Vegas, I said, "Sunny, dry, and about eighty." How far off could I have been?

Not far off at all, it turned out. Vegas felt like Vegas. The lobby of Caesars Palace was packed in anticipation of the fight, and celebrities were everywhere. Robert Vaughn, star of the 1960s TV series *The Man from U.N.C.L.E.*, was checking in. But before I could check in behind him, I saw Nick Nolte standing off to the side and I dropped everything. He was with a gorgeous blonde woman almost as tall as he was, and I figured a short gorgeous blonde would balance it out. Nolte's new movie, *48 Hrs.*, with co-star Eddie Murphy, was debuting that very weekend.

"Mr. Nolte," I said, "I loved you in *North Dallas Forty*." I hadn't seen it but if it was about football players and starred Nick Nolte, I was sure I would have loved it.

"Oh, thank you very much," he said with a smile. "I'd like you to meet my new wife."

"Congratulations to both of you!" I said. "What takes you away from your big box-office weekend debut?"

"We're here to see the fight," Nolte said.

"Me, too. Believe it or not, I'm going to be judging it."

"Really?" Nolte's bride said. "That's fabulous."

"Any tips for an amateur bettor?" Nolte asked.

"I'll let you know right after the fight," I said. "In the meantime, could I trouble you for an autograph?"

"Of course," Nolte said. "What would you like me to write?"

"Oh," I said, "just write: 'In memory of our most wonderful night together.'"

He wrote it out exactly that way, and with a smile.

"Good luck with the fight!" he said.

"Good luck with opening weekend!"

Caesars gave me the honeymoon suite. There were pink velvet walls, a ceiling mirror over the bed, and an enormous sunken hot tub in the bathroom. On the dresser were two tickets to the Wayne Newton concert. These sort of perks underscored the fact that I was flying solo. They should have saved them for Nick Nolte and his bride. But that wasn't going to stop me from enjoying everything. I had at least forty-eight hours to do so.

In the evening I visited the Dokes and Weaver camps, both of which were located within Caesars. I ran into the other judges, Mike Glenna and Jerry Roth, as well as the referee, Joey Curtis. Curtis was in his mid-fifties, with silvery grey hair. He owned a construction business in Las Vegas and had a good reputation. Refereeing was not something he even needed to do. He simply loved boxing.

As before any title fight, everyone was up and at their best. But here in the hotel there was an asterisk. Just a few feet from Joey Curtis, reporters and insiders were talking about how he might handle the recent tragedy in the very same ring only weeks before. The next time in the water, even if it wasn't you who drowned, was always a big question mark. When fear crept in, you either got right out of the water or you went in way over your head just to make a point.

In the sport of pugilism, however, especially when it involved Don King, there were always multiple asterisks and many layers of doubt. Superimposed over the specter of Duk Koo Kim's death was the cloud of King's influence. Don King was the promoter of the event and his son, Carl, was Dokes' manager. Mike Weaver was managed by a different Don, Don Manuel. Don Manuel's goal in life was to make as much money as possible for his fighter without the help of Don King. But that was like trying to sell olive oil behind the back of Don Corleone.

Don King had filed a suit against Don Manuel claiming the two had a prior agreement to match Dokes and Weaver which prevented Manuel from putting Weaver in the ring with anyone else. Manuel filed a countersuit preventing King from promoting any Weaver fight in the state of California. The legal nuances were harder to follow than a right hook from Roberto Duran.

Meanwhile, not much actual fighting was getting done, at least not with fists. Weaver's scheduled fight with Randall "Tex" Cobb was postponed three times due to training injuries. Then, in June, Michael Dokes was injured in a fight he wasn't even part of. After the title fight between Larry Holmes and contender Gerry Cooney, Dokes got into a scuffle with the Las Vegas police and injured his knee. Though still undefeated in the ring, Dokes now had a blemish outside of it. The blemishes for boxing, meanwhile, piled up.

Ironically, by not fighting, the fighters achieved or at least equalled a record of sorts. Due to his long layoff—even longer than Dokes'—Weaver was now the underdog. Las Vegas oddsmakers had the challenger as the 11-4 favorite. Only three other heavyweights had ever defended their titles as underdogs: Jersey Joe Wolcott in 1952 against Rocky Marciano, Muhammad Ali in 1965 against Sonny Liston, and Leon Spinks against Ali in 1978. And the only reason this fight was going forward was that a court had ordered it.

No matter who won the fight, Weaver or Dokes, boxing stood to lose. No one who thought it through could expect a unification bout. If Mike Weaver won the fight, Don King wouldn't let him fight his champion, Larry Holmes. Instead, King would make sure—through contracts, cash, courts, smoke and mirrors—that his son Carl's fighter, Dokes, got another shot at the WBA title. If Dokes beat Weaver, King would effectively control both the WBA and WBC heavyweight belts. If the two fighters then squared off for the unification, unless there was a draw King would lose one of his belts. If you were King, why dethrone yourself?

The next morning I ran into Don King in the hotel lobby. I was as tired of hearing the rumors of a fix as I was thinking about the possibility of another fatality in the ring. I just wanted to enjoy myself until it was time for the opening bell. So in a moment of bizarre clarity, I walked up to King and asked him flat out, "Who's going to win the fight?" As if the end of my sentence was the beginning of his, he replied, "Dokes."

It didn't mean all that much. It didn't mean there was a fix and it didn't mean Don King knew the winner for sure. And it didn't exempt me from calling every moment of the fight as I saw it. Nothing would ever do that. It simply let me move on. I thanked Don King and walked toward the dining room.

The fact of the matter was Don King was not to blame for the sorry state of boxing's heavyweight division. The Nevada Athletic Commission, the New York State Athletic Commission, and just about every other regulating authority in between were to blame. Until they made it illegal for a promoter to also be a manager, nothing much would change. Don King was a man who should have walked around with an attorney sewn onto his arm. He was a shark. He would be the first to tell you that. But the regulating bodies gave this shark and others a warm body of water filled with tuna to swim in.

I had a lovely day planned. When I was in Vegas, I liked to go swimming in the morning and spend the afternoon playing the slots. I was not what you'd call a big time gambler. I usually played with nickels and I liked to partner with someone sitting next to me, not because it cut my stake down to two-and-a-half cents, but for the camaraderie. My peak performance was a couple of years earlier when I started with five nickels and wound up with about a hundred dollars. Makes you wish you started with five whole dollars.

On this day I let it all hang out and played with quarters. The elderly gentleman to my right and I wound up splitting twelve dollars in winnings. The cigarette smoke didn't get to me, nor did the constant sound of bells and coins. What did distract me, however, was the announcement about every fifteen minutes over the hotel public address system: "Princess Fatima. Princess Fatima, please come to the front desk." I had heard it all morning when I was swimming, and here it was again. Each time I stopped my crawl, my sidestroke, or my one-armed bandit pull and looked around. I expected to see a beautiful young lady in a white gown floating by. But there was no Princess Fatima.

On the day of the fight we had a buffet lunch at the hotel. Across the room with his entourage sat Sugar Ray Leonard. Sugar Ray, named Ray Charles Leonard by birth for his mother's favorite singer, was at twenty-six already considered one of the greatest fighters of his generation. As a welterweight, he had beaten my favorite fighter, Roberto Duran, in the Louisiana Superdome, with Duran famously telling the referee in the eighth round, "No mas!"

Only a year and three months ago, right here in this very hotel, Leonard defeated Thomas Hearns in fourteen grueling rounds to unify the WBA and WBC welterweight titles. *Ring* Magazine called it the fight of the year for 1981, but it came at a price, leaving Leonard's left eye severely battered. Leonard successfully defended his title the following February but found out shortly afterwards he had a detached retina. He withdrew for a few months, declining to schedule any more fights.

And then on November 9, 1982, Leonard announced that he was retiring. He told Howard Cosell and some friends it wasn't a question of his retina, which had healed, or of trying to avoid a middleweight bout with Marvelous Marvin Haggler. Leonard said what few twenty-six-year-old prodigies of any vocation had the courage to say—that he just didn't feel the drive anymore.

So here he was at world famous Caesars as purely a spectator. Leonard had been retired for all of a month and seemed to be at peace with it, though one had to wonder why he returned so quickly to the scene of the crime. I walked over and introduced myself as one of the judges for tonight's title fight, and Leonard immediately asked me to sit down. He was very articulate and still, obviously, in excellent condition. He was not inclined to blow up forty pounds after a fight, like Duran was prone to do. You got the impression Leonard would never blow up.

While telling Sugar Ray about my amazing trip to Argentina the previous winter, one of his people took our picture, which I would absolutely have to get a copy of for my scrapbook. As I smiled for the camera, I heard it again: "Princess Fatima. Princess Fatima, please come to the front desk." At this point I had to know who in the heck was Princess Fatima. But if I didn't ask the kindly gentleman who had shared my slot machine the day before, I wasn't going to ask the great Sugar Ray Leonard. Especially at the same time I was asking him for his autograph.

As he signed and I looked closely at his hand, it struck me that Sugar Ray Leonard didn't exactly look like a fighter. His hand had an elegant shape. His body was not bulky but more like that of a ballet dancer. Knowing that he could take apart another man in the ring, I couldn't quite say he was dainty, but for the moment that was my working adjective.

The strange thing was many of the fighters had a dainty side, even if it wasn't at all physical. The two heavyweights who would attempt to demolish each other in a few hours were no exception. Mike Weaver was an aspiring minister who relaxed by playing a baby grand piano. Michael Dokes was a gourmet cook who designed his own clothes. Both of them, like so many fighters, hoped to invest their money wisely and get out of the ring while they still had their youth, looks, and mental acuteness. Few of them did. There was almost always the bad investment advice, the lust for one more mega-purse, and ego to believe they could still take on anyone.

When I sat back down with Mike Glenna, Jerry Roth, and some of the WBA officials, I just couldn't stand it anymore. I had to ask.

"Who is Princess Fatima? I mean, where is she, where is she from, and how come they keep paging her?"

The guys looked at each other and looked back at me like I was a kid at camp who didn't know how to tie a sailor's knot.

"Carol," Mike Glenna said. "Princess Fatima is no princess."

"She's not?"

"'Princess Fatima' means 'Would any available hooker please come to the front desk.'"

As evening fell, the indoor arena at Caesars was packed with 4,400 spectators. The last preliminary bout was nearly over. I was getting ready to take my seat, which was on the opposite side of the ring from the WBA commissioner, with the other judges taking positions along the remaining two sides of the ring. Dokes was making his way into the arena with pomp, circumstance, and a fur coat down to his feet. Not to be outdone, his manager's father, Don King, strutted in with frosted hair to the rafters, the ever-present bow tie, and a multimillion dollar smile. Right behind him was his secretary, Connie. They walked right towards me and never veered off, finally stopping right in front of me.

"Hey, lady judge," King said. "How about you take a picture of me and Connie over here?"

He had to be referring to the cheap disposable camera I had in my hand.

"Of course," I said. "I'd be happy to."

They posed and I snapped. Then I took down Don King's address for when the film came back from the developer. I recognized the address. It was his office, the office of the King, precisely where I started a run of high profile, sometimes highly controversial fights leading me all the way to Caesars Palace. If I had any complaints about the fight, I would know where not to send them. Strangely, Muhammad Ali's personal photographer was within earshot of us. Either King was still on the outs with Ali's crew or he had tremendous faith in my $6.95 Kodak.

With moments to go before the opening bell, I made sure of the fighters' trunks—Dokes in white, Weaver in red. They were both black fighters with similar builds, but this was a practical, not a racial matter. In moments of entanglement and confusion, knowing the trunks, the socks and the shoes, was always a good idea. Now Dokes walked around the ring and tossed several long-stem red roses down to various women at ringside. One of the recipients was his mother, whom he credited with everything he had. I wasn't so sure who the others were and wasn't so sure I wanted to know. None of the roses landed in my lap, and given the paranoia surrounding the fight it was just as well.

At the bell, the two fighters came out swinging. This was rare for a heavyweight fight and even rarer for a heavyweight title fight. They stood face to face opposite of my side of the ring and just delivered, almost flat-footed. Weaver punched more from the sides, Dokes more from the inside. There was some body contact. When Weaver missed completely with a left hook, the momentum pulled his whole body rightward. As he recovered to face his opponent, Dokes hit Weaver with a fast right-left combination. The left hook of the pair hit Weaver's jaw about as hard as one human being could hit another and Weaver went down immediately. Only forty-six seconds had elapsed.

Weaver bounced right back up, and referee Joey Curtis paced over to give the dazed fighter a few moments to get his wits together. Weaver seemed to indicate with a nod of his head that he was ready to spar again, and Curtis retreated. But as Dokes backed Weaver into the corner, all the champion could do was put his hands up to his face. Dokes rained blows on him, hitting Weaver's hands, forearms, and elbows.

Then some punches made it to Weaver's body, and Joey Curtis moved in to separate the fighters. This looked like the ten thousand referees before him separating two fighters in a clinch. The difference was in this fight, a moment later, Joey Curtis lifted Dokes' hands in the air ending the fight one minute and fifty-six seconds into the first round, making him the new WBA world heavyweight champion.

I was confused, because Weaver seemed sluggish but not incoherent. Curtis never asked for the ring doctor's opinion. And then I got even more confused, because a few seconds later Dokes leaped in the air and then crumpled to the canvas. People from all sides rushed into the ring, some to check Dokes' condition, others to check Weaver's, and still others for no apparent reason at all. The crowd grew loud and menacing. I knew the chorus all too well, as if I had been baptized to the soundtrack. "Bullshit, Bullshit, Bullshit . . . ." And the low, ominous, sickening hum.

More people rushed toward the ring and into it. I no longer had a clear view into the ring as all sorts of self-appointed gangsters got in the way. There seemed to be a massive tug-of-war surrounding the championship belt, as if Weaver's camp holding onto it a minute or two longer would look better in the record books. And I wondered why I was still standing by my seat and not running for cover. There was a reason. The ring announcer had never announced the official outcome of the fight. I supposed he didn't want to fan the flames any further, and once I realized he had no intention of ever making the announcement, I was out of there.

The plane ride home was calm. There were no shoving matches in the aisle, and people were handing me pretzels and cranberry juice instead of the other way around. The irony of pandemonium was sometimes you learned a lot more after the fight by watching the TV recaps than you did ringside as a paid official. Dokes had jumped in celebration and injured his leg in the process. It was the first time I had seen the loser standing and the winner on the canvas, but lately everything had been upside down. When interviewed, Joey Curtis said the ghosts of the Mancini-Kim fight had nothing to do with his decision to end the fight so abruptly. And the Pope was Jewish. Death made people gun-shy. That was called being human. You had to worry about the ones who never flinched.

Back in Philadelphia my friends consoled me. I explained there was nothing to be consoled about. Naturally I brought my 'A" game to any fight, especially a heavyweight title fight. And naturally I wanted a chance to perform just like any heavyweight. But no one needed to feel sorry for me and the $1,500 I had just put in the bank any more than they needed to feel sorry for Mike Weaver after making $1.2 million for 116 seconds of questionable work. We were both richer, and more importantly we were both alive.

Weaver-Dokes was given a second shot by the WBA. In May 1983 at the Dunes Hotel in Las Vegas, Mike Weaver, Michael Dokes, and the WBA itself restored some of their collective luster. The second fight turned out to be the diametric opposite of the first one, this one going the full fifteen rounds and ending in a draw. A different referee was used as well as a new group of judges except for Jerry Roth. That was more than okay with me. I had left my troubles in the desert and wanted them to stay there for a while.

Not everyone was so fortunate. Three months after watching her son fade away in a Las Vegas hospital, Duk Koo Kim's mother took her own life by drinking a bottle of pesticide. A few months later, on July 1, 1983, referee Richard Greene committed suicide. As a mother, I felt it. As an official, I felt it. There were so many levels to these fights and so many levels in life. On at least one of those levels I questioned myself. What would I be if I didn't?

CHAPTER THIRTEEN
HAGGLING

When the green light went on it was like the opening bell of a round. I came out of my corner, not so much swinging as listening. Eastman-Kodak was a top company, and district support representative was a decent paying job. But you took your lumps and bruises. You sat among a half-dozen reps in a small room and took calls all morning and afternoon. You wore a headset, stared into a computer terminal, and typed in problems—a broken copier, a malfunctioning microfiche system, a printer on the fritz.

It was 911 for the photographic world. You bobbed and weaved around customers jabs, ducked the right hooks, and asked the right questions so you could dispatch a service man and send the customer back to his corner.

Like a boxer, a district support representative required training. For our training we went north to Rochester, New York. We called it "Rotten-chester." Every building looked the same, like an industrial version of *The Stepford Wives*. You walked in to the designated building beneath the neon letter "E" and spent the day learning the protocols of the System 34 mainframe computer. This went on for a week, which felt like a month.

Back in Philadelphia, you were in the ring all day, but it felt more like a fishbowl. Supervisors looked at you, looked at the green light, and looked back at you to see how long before you answered the bell. The pressure was tremendous. The other reps and I used to joke that any day now they were going to surround us with Plexiglass and throw in raw meat at lunchtime. That would give us an extra hour of productivity. Then I suggested that first thing in the morning they hook us up to a catheter and eliminate breaks altogether.

So when on Tuesday October 16, 1984 I received a telegram

informing me that I had been selected to judge the Hagler-Hamsho world middleweight title fight in New York, it was like a fairytale, and I was Cinderella. This would be my ninth title fight, but strange as it sounds, it wasn't just another title fight. The build-up to the fight was tremendous. It wasn't something you needed to be a fight fan to hear about. It was everywhere—the fight of the year.

I loved traveling to faraway places and having a pugilistic adventure few people back home were aware of. But this was the tops—a heavily covered title fight in Madison Square Garden. I thought the celebrated middleweights of the time—Hagler, Duran, Hearns, Leonard—were well matched with the middleweights of any era or, for that matter, the best fighters of any division *and* any era. Out of the chaos of a half-dozen rival boxing organizations with ugly fight fixing rumors and heavyweight mismatches ending in the first round came what was shaping up to be a new golden era of middleweights. And I was going to be front, center, and without a headset.

All of that wasn't even the highlight. The WBA supervisor, Alberto Aleman, informed me by phone that I was going to be part of history. There were three women judges picked to officiate the various fights on the card at the Garden that Friday night, and it was Aleman's opinion that the time had come to assign them all to the same fight—the main event. The added publicity couldn't hurt the door or the HBO viewership, and the three women in question were veterans. He was right on both counts.

When you think of a protégé, you usually don't think of someone eighteen years your senior. But Eva Shain followed me into the ranks of professional boxing judge by about a year. And she had done well. The fight between the defending champion Marvelous Marvin Hagler and top ranked contender Mustafa Hamsho would be Eva's fifteenth title fight, compared to my ninth. I didn't begrudge her anything. She was a lovely woman married to a great guy. Eva's husband, Frank Shain, was a longtime ring announcer. Frank was what you would call a raconteur, full of funny stories he made even funnier. We all knew at least half of this business was about making friends and lobbying, and Eva was fortunate to have her husband Frank lobbying for her.

The other judge in our triumvirate was Carol Castellano, who followed me and Eva into the world's roughest profession. In spite of the lovely first name, I didn't know Carol personally and only knew a little about her. She was from New York and had judged eighteen title fights in her career to date. Her husband, Tony, was also a boxing judge. Husbands had brought all three of us into the ring, and theirs were still around. I was happy for them and glad they had judged so many title fights.

Like a broken clock that was right twice a day, women sometimes fit the stereotype. But there was no jealousy here. As the chance to make history yet again sunk in, all I could feel was excitement and pride for all of us. I had in my own way opened a door, and other capable women had walked through it. Now we would all walk together through another door. It wasn't about who had more title fights under their belt. It was about how, collectively, we had forty under our tent.

I left the house Thursday morning at seven and drove out to New Jersey to pick up my brother, Arthur, who worked in New York. Arthur wasn't looking to shadow me on my triumphant return after ten years. We just both liked the idea of having some company on the way in. The train from Trenton into Penn Station was about an hour and a half and a chance to catch up and settle in before a frenzied two days.

Marvin Hagler and I shared the same birthday—May 23. We weren't born in the same year. Hagler was thirty and I was still holding on to thirty-nine for dear life. But if you've ever met someone born on the same day of the year as yourself, even if you dismissed astrology out of hand, you knew they shared some important traits with you. Hagler was strong, steady, and consistently tough. He was goal-oriented. How else could you compile a record of fifty-nine wins against only two defeats and two draws? Forty-nine of those victories came by knockouts.

Hagler grew up in Newark, New Jersey, a particularly tough town on an East Coast full of tough towns. In 1967 during the Newark riots, the tenement in which the Haglers lived was so badly vandalized, Marvin's mother moved the family not only out of the building but out of Newark.

They resettled in Brockton, Massachusetts, which was a fortuitous choice for a teenager interested in boxing. Brockton, was the home of Rocky Marciano, possibly the greatest heavyweight fighter who ever lived. Marvin Hagler started training at the well known gym owned by the Petronelli brothers, Pat and Goody. It was 1969, the same year Rocky Marciano died tragically in a plane crash. It was as if one fighter for the ages left the planet and another one took his place.

Marvin Hagler fought his way up the ladder. In the 1970s, the ladder for an ambitious, talented middleweight led straight through Philadelphia. Hagler fought Bobby Boogaloo Watts, Willie the Worm Monroe, Eugene Cyclone Hart, and Bennie Briscoe, paying dues through the nose and in the process picking up the only two losses of his career, against Watts and Monroe. It took Hagler till 1980 to take the middleweight belt, in Wembley Arena, London. There, he stopped hometown favorite Alan Minter in the third round by a technical knockout.

The fight to that point was as close as could be, and the only reason it was stopped was a cut over Minter's eye. A riot broke out at Wembley, and like me, Marvin Hagler was no stranger to a riot. Still, Hagler took both the WBC and WBA belts that night, which for a disputed fight was as close as you could come to an undisputed title.

Since then, Hagler had defended his title often without ever relinquishing it. One of those defenses came in 1981 in an eleven-round TKO over the Syrian born Mustafa Hamsho, who was now coming back for another taste and a bigger payday. Hagler was hard to figure out in the ring. His stance was listed as "ambidextrous," which meant he might face you leaning left or leaning right depending upon his strategy, and deliver punches from anywhere. Not many experts or casual observers thought Hamsho would do any better this time, but they were all willing to pay to see him try. For Hagler it was really about the opponents who lay in his future, with names equally gargantuan to his, like Thomas Hearns and perhaps Sugar Ray Leonard.

Hagler's own name was a point of contention. After he took the middleweight title, he was roused to anger because fans and sportswriters declined to place his self-appropriated nickname, "Marvelous," in front of "Marvin" when referring to the fighter. So he took this particular fight to the courts, officially changing his full name to Marvelous Marvin Hagler. It wasn't religious or moral or political as it was many years earlier with Muhammad Ali. It was just a great fighter trying to call still more attention to himself and establish order in a world too full of riots. It was personal and arrogant and maybe even a little understandable. But it wasn't marvelous.

Especially when I did a title fight in the United States, showing up was a lot like a homecoming. One after the other, or sometimes even in bunches, I ran into old friends and associates. As I made my way up the escalator above Penn Station and across Seventh Avenue to the Penta Hotel, the class reunion was in full swing. I spoke to Harold Lederman, the part time judge and full time pharmacist; Arthur Mercante Sr., the legendary referee of the first Ali-Frazier fight and many other bouts for the ages; Bert Sugar, the Damon Runyanesque editor of *The Ring* magazine; and Irv Rudd, the public relations head for Bob Arum's Top Rank, the organizer of the event. I thought that since this wasn't a Don King event, there wouldn't be much controversy. Not only was I wrong, but I was at the center of the controversy.

It was on everybody's lips. They assumed I had read a newspaper, but I hadn't. The Petronelli brothers had thrown down the gauntlet. Marvin Hagler would not accept three women judges. The word was delivered through the twin mouthpieces of Pat and Goody, a couple of real old school Italian-American trainers who no doubt amplified the message. Their reasoning, if it could be called that, was that boxing was a man's game and that three women judging together would somehow lead to an inaccurate result. So what the Hagler camp wanted from the New York State Athletic Commission was to use only one of the three of us for the Hagler-Hamsho fight.

In speaking to my friends—Arthur, Harold, Bert, Irv, and anyone else who would listen—I pulled no punches. First of all, the three of us—Eva, Carol, and Carol—did not judge this fight or any other fight "together." We weren't a committee or a knitting club or a temperance league or any other type of group for that matter. We were three individual judges, each with more title fights under our belt individually than both fighters had together. We had our eyes on the fight—often to the point of a raging headache—and didn't give a damn what the other two judges were thinking or what over-the-counter pain medication they might take after the fight.

While we were at it, I had to ask why it was that if three women were bound to call the fight wrong, one woman had a chance of calling it right? It seemed to me each of us was either competent or incompetent. My compadres all heartily agreed with me, even the grizzled veteran writer, Bert Sugar. But they knew what I knew—that this was all politics. The managers for some four-round, lightweight undercard fight had exactly zero chance of demanding something like this and getting it. They knew enough not to even try. But the Hagler camp had bargaining power by virtue of the gate and television money they were bringing in.

Technically speaking, legally speaking, if John Branca, Chairman of the New York State Athletic Commission, and Gilberto Mendoza, President of the WBA, got together and drew a line in the sand, the Hagler camp would have to stand down. Their only other option would be to walk away, breaking their contract. But these lofty agencies knew where the money was and were afraid to call a bluff. As far as they were concerned, Hagler was the hand that fed them, even though it was the same hand that slapped me and my sister officials.

The press conference was scheduled for 11 AM upstairs at Madison Square Garden. That gave me a little time to walk around outdoors on a warm fall morning. As I glanced over at the Felt Forum from across Seventh Avenue, I experienced a small flashback and then it passed. I didn't see any flaming, flying couches in my immediate future. Ten years had gone by as quickly as one or two might, but I had to be fair to time as it had been to me. A lot had happened. I had survived on my own and then some. I had been around the world doing what I loved and got paid for it. My youngest was almost ready to fly the coop. I had returned to the scene of the crime not without a few butterflies but with a lot more confidence. I could honestly say I was better off.

The streets of New York were better off too. Not that anyone could ever expect the area surrounding Penn Station, with tens of thousands of people coming and going every day, to be anything like orderly, but things were less chaotic and cleaner now. Between Mayor Koch, a conservative Democrat, and President Reagan, a conservative Republican, the pendulum had swung back towards order because as a matter of survival, it simply had to.

There were more cops on the streets. Far more. There were street vendors, but most of them seemed to have a license. There was even a grand plan to tear down and reinvent 42nd Street, the smut capital of the galaxy, and make it into some sort of family-friendly place. I would probably have to live a long time to see that, but even the reality of the plan itself said something about the direction of this mesmerizing city.

I had to enjoy the remnants of the old city while they still clung to dear life. So I bought a three-dollar pair of earrings from a street hustler about two blocks from the Garden. They probably had fallen off the back of a truck, but I was going to do them justice in front of millions of fight fans worldwide, even if I was relegated to judging an undercard bout. And no trip to New York was complete without walking up to a green metal newsstand and plucking down some spare change for a tabloid, especially if you might be in it. And I was.

The Associated Press story in the *Daily News* caught my eye first. The headline read: "For Men Only? Hagler says he won't fight Hamsho if women judge." Pat Petronelli wasn't shy about his misogyny. His quote leapt off the page: "This is a man's sport. The top bouts should be judged by men." Yes, even incompetent men, if need be. My own name jumped off the page next, and I learned that I could be reassigned to the WBA light middleweight title fight between Mike McCallum and Sean Mannion, about an hour and twenty minutes before the main event. As consolation prizes went, this wasn't the worst one imaginable. But it wasn't justice. Alberto Aleman had hired me to do the big fight. Where was he in all this? The best part of the article was Mustafa Hamsho's take on the controversy.

The world was not accustomed to an Arab man in the role of women's rights advocate, but absurd situations called for unusual gestures. "I think Hagler is plain worried," the challenger said. "And sex should have no place in the appointment of judges." Hooray! Three cheers for progress in the Middle East.

The press conference in the East Ballroom of Madison Square Garden was as anyone would expect it to be—a big deal. Between network and local cameras and microphones, plus international press, the podium was a cluster of objects waved in the faces of Hagler, Hamsho, and Bob Arum. Bob Arum was definitely not a Damon Runyanesque character. Quite the opposite. He was a Harvard Law product and for a time a higher up in the US Department of Justice until realizing at some point in the 1960s there was a whole lot more money to be made in the fight game if you knew how to bring together the biggest names in the sport and hype the event.

Arum spoke about how they expected nearly a full house Friday night but that there would be no local television blackout whatever the turnout. He addressed the "other" controversy, which was over the scheduled length of the fight. Since this was a scheduled fifteen-round fight and the WBC sanctioned only twelve-round fights, that esteemed body was threatening to strip Hagler of the WBC half of his belt. Regardless of how long the fight actually went, all Marvelous Marvin had to do was step into the ring and he was a loser. That's how crazy this business had become.

Still no mention of the female controversy. Then Bob Arum paused and said, "At this time, before we continue, I'm going to have to ask the ladies, respectfully, to leave the room." So I got up and started to leave. What else could I do? He asked politely. It was an odd request, but I wasn't about to hold a sit-in. It was a short walk up the aisle and out a side door. I looked straight ahead, trying not to be too obvious and choosing not to see if Eva Shain or Carol Castellano were somewhere behind me. I would know soon enough anyway.

They were not. Two other women joined me in the hallway. They were both a lot older than I was. Before we had the chance to discuss how uncalled for the exclusion was, a middle aged man apparently from Top Rank popped his head into the hallway. He looked amused.

"You can come back in now. Bob was just kidding. I think you took him a little too seriously. Or maybe the joke's on us."

Oh my God. There was such a thing as generous to a fault. And now there was polite to a fault. Or naïve. My father had raised me to leave the room when asked. But my father didn't run one of the two largest boxing promotion companies in the world. We walked back through the door. I was first out, so I figured it was only fair that I be first in. It was like reentering a second grade classroom after being removed for wetting yourself. The people were laughing. I would have laughed, too. Half the world was watching. I hoped they didn't talk to the other half.

Outside the East Ballroom I ran into Alberto Aleman of the WBA. Hunted him down was more like it. He confirmed what I had learned formally during the press conference—that the final decision was in the hands of Commissioner Branca. Aleman fleshed it out for me. He could force the issue but didn't feel he would accomplish anything more than antagonize the Athletic Commission. It was going to be just one of us doing the main event, and I shouldn't get my hopes up. The way things worked in the state was that the one woman picked would likely be a New Yorker or at least identified as such.

For all practical purposes, that meant either Carol Castellano or Eva Shain. Carol and her husband were from New York, and Frank and Eva were from Fort Lee, New Jersey, just over the George Washington Bridge. Like the football New York Giants, who actually played in the New Jersey Meadowlands, that was so close to New York it was the Big Apple for all practical purposes. A lot more so than Fort Washington, Pennsylvania, anyway. Besides, wherever he happened to get up and brush his teeth in the morning, Frank Shain was a man about town.

I thanked Aleman for his honesty and told him unlike the Hagler camp I would accept whatever the Commission decided. Aleman and I were like old friends. He had gone to bat for me when it counted, in

Córdoba, Argentina when my license and reputation were on the line. All that was on the line here was the biggest title fight of my life and a big feather in my cap.

I took another walk around the Garden area in the afternoon. For the first time a singular feeling, replacing the uncertainty, was sinking in—that of being ripped off. I didn't know if controversy followed me around, I followed it around, or we both somehow always wound up in the same place. But like my three-dollar earrings I felt like I had fallen off the back of a truck, only I didn't know where I was going to land.

Over at Macy's, I walked up to the perfume counter and took a spritz of something on my left wrist. It was nice, like linen hung out to dry in the sun, but I knew I could do better. The next smelled like white lilies, and the next like fresh daisies. I just kept going until I must have sampled fifty perfumes. Each scent masked the one before it, but none of them covered up the stench of the politics I was in the middle of. None of them made my disappointment smell like roses.

It wasn't often you were cheated out of a gig by someone who shared your birthday. But right there at the perfume counter at Macy's I decided I not only still had my birthday but also the qualities that went with it. Goal-oriented and free-thinking, I was ambidextrous, at least emotionally. It was clear I wasn't going to sit in the judge's chair for Hagler-Hamsho no matter how vociferously I objected. But there were a lot of other ways to win this fight. These few blocks were teeming with opportunities, and I was going to go out and get them.

The following day, Friday, the day of the fight, I came out swinging. I spoke to Bobby Lee, who ran the IBF/USBA. Bobby suggested I come to one of his meetings in the near future and join his organization. That would mean doing more high-profile fights in the US and Europe and more paydays. I schmoozed with several officials from Top Rank, and none of them brought up the laughing stock incident from the press conference. Maybe they were just being polite. Maybe they found it endearing. Hopefully they had just forgotten about it, forever.

The jackpot came in the form of Roberto Sabatini, who was a top boxing promoter in Italy. I was always lobbying the WBA to give me an assignment in Italy. Of course I had been there before at my own expense, but being paid to enjoy the most beautiful country on Earth would be the pinnacle for me. I loved the people, the architecture, and the entire way of life. Everything in Italy looked as if it was bathed in golden sunshine. I must have lived there in a past life. But it was my future in this life I was concerned about, and the way I hit it off with Roberto Sabatini, I was sure I was now one step closer to returning.

At the same time, I wasn't done fighting the main event. What I really needed was an advocate who, unlike Aleman, wasn't serving two masters. Someone who was himself an unabashed fighter. That person was Jimmy Binns, Pennsylvania State Athletic Commissioner. Binns was a tough, well dressed, unabashed lawyer who had made a fortune in litigation prior to putting on Commissioner's gloves. Jimmy was my advocate. But Jimmy was not here, at least not yet. I wasn't able to reach him on the phone. The one-man flotilla from the Commonwealth hadn't sailed in yet. And I was still just a free-floating out-of-state judge, like a fish out of water.

Later in the morning I became a refugee of still another sort. Word on the grapevine was Mustafa Hamsho had let the New York State Athletic Commission know he did not want a Jewish judge officiating his fight. Three steps back for progress in the Middle East to go with the three steps forward. Syria, under various names and oppressive regimes, had been hostile to Israel, in its many incarnations, for thousands of years. I could understand the misplaced national pride, if not outright forgive it. But the fact of the matter was Mustafa Hamsho had been living in Brooklyn for the last three years.

Suddenly I had three things going against me—I was a woman, an out-of-towner, and Jewish. I wondered what the fourth strike would be—a new height requirement? So when I walked into the weigh-in at 11 AM and was told I was off the Hagler-Hamsho fight, it wasn't exactly a surprise right hook. It was a glancing blow at best. The strange thing was the selection of judges—Eva Shain, Harold Lederman, and Vincent

Rainone. Of the three, only Rainone wasn't Jewish. I supposed once you put a large enough variety of prejudices in play, they started to cancel each other out.

Hamsho weighed in a half pound over. If anti-Semitism had mass, that might have explained it. He had a few hours to work it off. Most of us knew it wouldn't matter. He was going to get beaten in the ring, and badly.

My assignment was, actually, better than a consolation prize. The WBA Light Middleweight title, currently vacant, was nothing to shake a stick at. Mike McCallum was undefeated at 21-0 and considered so capable a fighter that his name was bandied about as a possible opponent for the heavier middleweight kings, like Duran and Hearns. A victory for McCallum would bring home a world title for the small country of Jamaica.

Meanwhile, at twenty-nine wins, five losses, and one draw, Sean Mannion was a strong underdog. He had beaten a string of top contenders and veterans on his way up and was a hero to legions of Irish Catholic fight fans in Boston. In fact, rumor had it that so many of them were coming down for the fight, Amtrak had to add five trains to the Boston-New York route.

Aside from facing a crowd of proud Irishmen, McCallum—Irish surname and all—had another opponent, grief. Few people seemed to know it, but only three months earlier his fianceé, the mother of his young child, had died. Under those circumstances, just getting into the ring was an accomplishment.

Right outside the weigh-in, I ran into Jimmy Binns. I asked him where he had been in my hour of need, and the answer was with a client. Too little, too late, but still wearing a two thousand dollar suit. At least in this case he was apologizing to me. Once, a couple of years earlier, Jimmy asked me out of the blue if I had ever been "approached." No one in the history of mankind thought faster on his feet than Groucho Marx, so when my eyebrows went up like Captain Spaulding's, playing up the suggestiveness of the question, I had bought myself a few seconds to think a little more, vaudeville style. No, Jimmy insisted, with the air of a man used to having lunch with federal and state judges, this was a serious question.

"Yes," I said. "Once that I can remember. The night before a North American title fight, I got a call from the manager of one of the fighters, who let me know he had requested me for the fight. I told him, wonderful. Then, the other fighter's manager called to tell me the same thing. I told them they should talk to each other and start a Carol Polis fan club."

"Any other time you can remember?"

"Not really," I said. "They don't need me. Why go to one of the three judges when you can go directly to the other fighter?"

"Well," he said, "maybe as an insurance policy . . . ."

"Mr. Binns," I said, "I'll be very honest with you. If somebody came to me and said 'I will give you one million dollars to make sure that you judge the fight for fighter A,' I'd be a liar if I said I wouldn't think about it. Actually, Mr. Binns, my price has gone down to $500,000."

Jimmy rolled his eyes and walked away. This wasn't a courtroom, and I wasn't going to be interrogated. Especially over something hypothetical.

But here, following the weigh-in, the atmosphere and feeling were very different. I didn't have any explaining to do. The rest of the boxing world did. So we joked that with all my extracurricular activities, we would one day honeymoon in Italy right after a title fight, courtesy of the WBA.

My extracurricular activities continued throughout the afternoon. I met the head of a sporting goods company who thought it would be great if, as boxing's first woman judge, I represented a line of clothing and wore it ringside. He was not kidding. He had a list of manufacturers for me to contact. So long as I didn't have to wear a billboard I was game.

An hour later, a woman named Pam Burke arranged to meet me in my hotel room and ask me a few questions. This, fortunately, wasn't another interrogation. Instead, there were cameras and a crew. Pam was a producer for an HBO series called "Bread and Butter," which explored the lifestyles of women who worked in a variety of fields. They were more interested in what I made for breakfast than the kind of turmoil I went through leading up to a fight. So I gave them what they wanted, over easy, and they ate it up.

In the Penta lobby, somewhere between endorsements and interviews, I ran across Marvelous Marvin Hagler and his wife, Bertha, the mother of their five children. She was reasonably attractive but had prominent buck teeth. It was beyond me why a man earning multiple seven-figure paydays wouldn't set aside five figures to have his wife's teeth fixed. But I didn't have much time to chew on it.

Not far behind their champion fighter and his over-biting wife were his overbearing co-managers. I met Pat and Goody Petronelli. They knew who I was, were somehow glad to see me, and even gave me a couple of Hagler publicity shots. I smiled and took them. I wasn't about to lecture these guys. They were men around sixty whose views were set in granite. A woman was a two-hundred-and-fifty-pound kitchen slave who stirred the sauce while the men stepped out in pointed black shoes with their compadres. I wished them luck, but in this case they wouldn't need it.

On my way down to ringside, I saw Carol Castellano run, not walk, contradicting that famous song by the Ventures. I knew what she was doing. We all knew. She was securing the camera seat. Beyond being veterans of dozens of bloody title and non-title fights spanning the four corners of the globe, we all knew the four corners of the ring, and we all wanted the judge's seat the television camera would be on most of the time. We all wanted to be seen by our friends, family, Francis Ford Copolla and whoever else might be watching at home. But *this* Carol didn't run for that seat. *This* Carol was a lady.

Mannion, the Irish-American, was in the green trunks, but I didn't need to memorize trunk colors, sock colors or anything else to distinguish these two fighters. McCallum, the fierce Jamaican, established himself early. He punched straight on and from the sides, as well as from the lower regions with uppercuts. Mannion stayed with straight ahead punches for the most part. McCallum figured out fast that by taking his time and landing more blows than his opponent, he was going to win round after round. I could attest that he would.

Mannion was as tough and heroic as the legends he represented and never backed down. He bounced on his feet, became the aggressor whenever he could, and took a lot of blows to the head. At one point, in round nine, he cut McCallum off in a corner and hit him with a flurry of rights and lefts that had the Jamaican dazed and staggering. At least the Irish portion of the crowd rose to its feet, maybe more, and it got loud in the Garden. But they might have known what I knew. Unless Mannion somehow finished the job in the next minute, McCallum would regain his bearings and go back to Plan A for the final rounds.

That's what he did. By the final round, number 15, Mannion had a bloody nose that was already a few rounds old. There was mutual admiration, as neither fighter had ever before had to go beyond ten rounds in the entirety of his career. There would be no WBC title tonight for this marathon, but the WBA light middleweight title was definitely McCallum's, and his opponent had nothing to apologize for.

Neither did I. By going fifteen rounds, I has proved my worth to this near capacity crowd as had referee Tony Perez, judge Johnny LoBianco, and even the camera-hogging Carol Castellano. We had gone the distance. I was tired and felt each mile in my own way. And that was that. Unlike in the Commonwealth of Pennsylvnia, Jimmy Binns country, there was no designated seat in the first row for an off-duty judge. I found a seat a few rows back and got ready to enjoy the world middleweight title fight.

Both Hagler and Hamsho came out punching, even brawling. They swung hard and missed a lot. Hamsho ducked as well as any middleweight I had ever seen, leaning his whole upper body forward quickly and at exactly the right time as Hagler's right and left hooks shot over him like missiles. The presence of Arthur Mercante in the ring was unmistakable. He was like a third fighter, strutting like a confident pro and ready to take the bull by the horns if he saw something he didn't like.

In the second round the furious brawl-and-duck pace continued.

Hagler landed one solid right punch to the side of Hamsho's face that opened up a cut and had the crowd on their feet. There was a lot of fast work on Hamsho's mug between rounds, and in the third round the Syrian was ducking a lot less. The question was if that was a good idea, and the answer was no. Hagler started landing blows, and Hamsho, now trying to stand straight, was grabbing onto the champion at times.

Mercante was more involved now, like the crowd, who smelled blood. The referee could be heard shouting, "Don't hold and punch," a reference to Hamsho's desperation. When a fighter clutched like that, it was a sure sign he was overwhelmed. With the referee not tolerating the holds, Hamsho tried to mix it straight up with Hagler, and a furious exchange had Hamsho on the canvas a minute and a half into the round. After an eight count, Hamsho stood and reentered the slaughter house. Hagler saw his next opportunity, swung like greased subway turnstiles at rush hour, and put Hamsho right back down. The Syrian's manger, Al Certo, jumped into the ring and hovered over his fighter almost before he hit the canvass. Mercante appeared a bit surprised, but the manager knew when to say "No mas!" in Arabic.

There was almost no regret for me. Had I been in Eva Shain's seat or either of the others, I would have had something new and interesting on my resume but no new judging under my belt. Anyone can judge a romp.

Sometimes you see another human being, across a train seat but at the same time across decades of life and pain, and you know you're going to make a connection. The first words could be anything, but the tracks are already laid. That was the case with the young Spanish woman sitting next to me on the train back to Trenton. She couldn't have been more than nineteen. She was pretty, but half her beauty lay somewhere spilled out on an apartment floor. I was no Jimmy Binns, but I was a district support representative, and the right questions usually rolled off my tongue, along with answers I sometimes couldn't stand to hear.

Her grandfather had sexually abused her for years. Her parents blamed her, and she turned to heavy drugs. She was on a weekend leave from a rehabilitation clinic and wrestling with the same question she had long wrestled with—why go on living. But really, she wanted to live. She wanted to live more than anything in the world, and her deep brown eyes were just looking into mine to give her a reason.

I told her that her grandfather was an animal and her parents were dead flat wrong. I told her to stop protecting all of them in her mind. It was time to recognize the truth and protect herself. Once she could do that, there would be no need for drugs. I told her I had never gone through anything like that but I had been through a lot, and it was definitely, absolutely possible to get high on life. It was a high that reemerged and persisted no matter what happened, and the power became stronger each time you got back on your feet. But she had to remember, she couldn't do it all herself. She had to open her heart and accept help.

As we pulled into Trenton, she thanked me. And I thanked her. I could see from her expression she had no idea why I would do that. But I had to. Amidst all my clever moves, all my jockeying for position, and all my ducking, I needed to remember what it really was like to be up against the ropes.

CHAPTER FOURTEEN
SOMEONE IN MY CORNER

I'm sitting with my ten-day-old granddaughter in Terminal D of Philadelphia International Airport. She is looking up at me in her one-piece baby blue pajamas, swaddled in the blanket they gave us just today at Sacred Heart Hospital. As long as I am holding her time is frozen. I hear arrivals and departures being announced every minute but they are not for us.

We could stay here forever. She came into the world under horrible circumstances, but in our ten days together she has become the light of my life. In her tiny blue eyes I see heaven. I see generations of my family—strong, timeless, pure. I can only hope she sees the same as she looks up at me. I can only hope she trusts me. That she understands this is the hardest possible thing in the world for me to do but that I have to do it for her. She stops crying and looks, and for that moment I am sure she understands. She knows how much I love her.

I hear an arriving flight from Chicago announced and I am bargaining in my head for another fifteen minutes. Another ten minutes. Maybe, just maybe it's a different flight. Chicago is a big city. But I look down the long corridor of carpet and steel with a hundred deplaning passengers and I know my time is up. I see a lady in her early thirties walking toward me, and from the photo she sent I know it's her. For some reason she's dragging behind her a huge black plastic garbage bag that must be too heavy to lift. I have no idea what is in the bag and I don't want to know.

The bag is getting closer. The lady is taking step after step but I am the one walking the plank. An invisible hand is gripping my heart and crushing it. I can't breathe and I can't imagine ever breathing again. I want to know what it is I'm experiencing. And then I know. I'm *dying*. *I'm dying*.

* * *

You can feel like you're dying and live to tell about it. I knew that for a fact. One afternoon in December 1984, I was cleaning my younger daughter's room and I found a piece of paper with a doctor's letterhead. I read it and it said her "due date" was in April. My heart was suddenly in a vise clamp. I didn't know where to put myself. So I forced a breath or two and continued cleaning my daughter's room.

I knew it was true the instant my crushed heart told me it was. I got on the phone and called the doctor listed at the top of the paper I had found. I wanted to know how far along my daughter was. He told me it looked a little past four months, and that's how he came up with the due date. Simple math on one hand, but not for me. I was busy refiguring everything. I never had a clue. She wore layered clothing. Who would be looking for signs? She was only seventeen.

She was my youngest of four. She was a great kid. She was good natured and a competent student. But at fourteen or fifteen she started running with a rough crowd. My oldest son was always surrounded by wonderful kids. My next son a little less so, and my older daughter even less. By the early '80s something seemed to be lost. The good kids were still there, but they were thinning out, and my youngest fell prey.

A couple of weeks later I spoke to the doctor again and asked him about the possibility of an abortion. He told me he was Catholic. I told him I wasn't asking about his religion just about the viability of the procedure and about my daughter's future. He told me it was a moot point because of the stage of the pregnancy.

I made some calls and tracked down my daughter one day at her boyfriend's mother's house. The mother didn't seem up in arms over the situation. I told her to put my daughter on the phone, and I told her I expected her, the father of the baby, and his mother in my kitchen tonight so we could discuss the options. That night we went through the entire range of possibilities. The boyfriend's mother was unwilling to step away from her job. The boyfriend had asked my daughter to marry him, and she said no. The guy was not husband material, and I was glad she was smart enough to know, however late in the game. I had already made a few calls regarding adoption, but she refused to give up the child. To her credit, she wanted the baby.

I was experienced enough to know what was coming next. I was forty-eight and had raised four children, largely by myself. I had an education, but my 'life' education came from my father, who always said there was no such word in the English language as can't. "Can't," he said, "really means *won't*." So I could and I would. I reminded myself that I had seen and done just about everything and lived to tell about it. I had a stock broker's license. I sold industrial real estate. I managed a hotel where a woman checked in, put a pillow over her stomach, and shot herself to death. And, of course, I was the first woman on the entire planet ever to judge a professional fight.

Raising four kids mostly on my own was a juggling act more demanding than judging a fight and perhaps even harder than being in the ring. I was pulling money out of my official's fee to pay the babysitter, getting up at the crack of dawn to send four kids off to school, then running off to my bread and butter job. Over the years the toll of all this was something I didn't think about too much, but it was there.

In my mid-forties I saw light at the end of the tunnel. I was proud of my kids, and one by one they were going off to college. At the same time, I loved getting assignments for title fights around the world—Argentina, Venezuela, Denmark, Japan. I was now on the cusp of having something I hadn't had in a very long time—a life of my own. And I earned it.

Yes, I knew what was coming next. My daughter was keeping the baby. But I was the one who would be taking care of it. At forty-eight, near the bell for round fifteen of a fight that had taken my entire adult life, I was going right back in the ring for round one.

My daughter's due date was April 21, 1985. It came and went. Two days later I had a fight to officiate at the Blue Horizon in Philadelphia, about forty-five minutes from our house in Fort Washington, Pennsylvania. Around six o'clock in the evening as I was getting ready to leave, my daughter told me she thought she was getting labor pains. I handed her a piece of paper and told her if the contractions continued to write down the times.

I officiated four of the six fights that night. It was a bloodbath, but that was nothing unusual. They were mostly local boxers battling not just the other fighter but fighting for a sliver of attention in the most demanding, competitive sport in the world. The catcalls from the old timers sitting up in the cramped mezzanine of the building fell to the canvas like little bombs. There was a brutal technical knockout in the second round of an eight-rounder and a knockout in the third round of a four-rounder.

These bouts were hard on the loser but not as hard on me. For me, any fight that didn't go the distance was a reprieve. The ones requiring a decision were tests of a judge's ability to concentrate without missing a beat and somehow come out with a final score beyond reproach. For the fighter, the blows came from outside. For the judge, they came from inside. By the end of the night, I usually had my reward for a job well done—a raging headache.

This night was no exception. But it was worse than usual. The pounding in my skull was coming in closer and closer intervals. That meant one thing for a fighter and another for a judge. For the mother of a seventeen year old girl going into labor, it meant something entirely different.

My daughter's water broke. When I got home I walked in the back door alone and walked out the front with my daughter in tow never even putting down my purse. We got to Sacred Heart Hospital around 11:30 at night. I had never met the obstetrician before, but he acted as if he knew me and wanted to know if I was going into the delivery room to watch. "Well," I said, "I've given birth four times, but I have no idea what it looks like." The doctor handed me a cap and gown, and we were off to graduation.

My normally unshakable daughter was screaming. They weren't the intermittent yelps you heard at the dentist's office before the Novocain set in. There was no anesthesia because there was no time. The screams were long and loud and connected and there was nothing I could do for my daughter except hold her hand. I looked down and felt right at home.

Unbelievable, I thought. *From one bloody arena to another.*

The baby's head pushed out. The lady who thought she had seen it all—and that was me—realized that until now, she hadn't. There were more screams, and they weren't all from the new mother. I heard my daughter yelling, "I will never do this again as long as I live!" At the exact same time I heard myself shouting, "This is the most beautiful thing I have ever seen in my life." Hopefully we both meant it.

We weren't out of the woods yet. The doctor announced the umbilical cord was wrapped around the baby's head twice. I thought, Why is he telling me that? This is his arena, not mine. So I said, "You're the doctor. I'm sure you'll be able to take care of it." He did. And because of the cords I couldn't tell whether it was a boy or a girl. That was the doctor's arena, too. It was a boy!

The nurses cleaned the baby and wrapped him in a blanket. I was euphoric and told them to give my daughter something for the pain. One of the nurses gave me something instead. Then Grandma got to hold the baby. I took him in my arms, all six pounds ten ounces, and stood there breathless. He had my heart instantly. It was amazing. The most beautiful thing I had ever seen in my life had just gotten more beautiful.

She named him Lawrence Christopher Sharp. A few weeks into the baby's life, my daughter's pediatrician called me back. The idea of adoption hadn't been ruled out entirely. The doctor told me he had been walking in his backyard doing a lot of thinking and had come up with two Catholic couples who were willing to adopt. I thanked him but explained we were not going to go that route. When I got off the phone I thanked him again in my mind, because our brief conversation crystallized everything for me. Larry was ours. I made a promise to myself right then that I would do everything in my power to give him as normal a life as possible.

There was nothing normal about it. At least not for a while. In the morning when I drove off to work I kept thinking something might happen to the baby while I was gone. In my mind I would see my daughter running out of the house without the baby. I drove distraught through the streets of Fort Washington praying to God nothing would happen. I sat on the train to downtown Philadelphia like a zombie. At work I was haunted.

Until one day I stopped the car. I pulled a U-turn and drove back up the block. I picked up the baby, put on his little coat, grabbed his bag, and put him in his car seat. We drove to the station together. I took him on the train. Where other commuters were flipping through box scores and stock prices, I was cradling my grandson and feeding him his bottle. At work I was given some slack because my brother ran the office. I held the phone with one hand, the baby with the other, and Larry learned more about selling industrial real estate than any two-month-old on the planet.

And I learned more about what was sustainable and what was not. I had to quit working for a while to get things under control. Over the next few years I surfed one wave after another, smoothing the waters for my three-and-a-half year old grandson and turning an exhausted fifty years old in the process. As a reward I saw Larry turn into a wonderful little boy. I had custody and some calm. At this age I took what little relief I could get, and it turned out to be very little. On a cold night in late February of 1989, my daughter told me she was in trouble again. I was in trouble, too.

I remained wired and wide awake for two days and two nights. I wrapped my mind around every possibility. Once Larry was in school full time, I could drop him off and leave the new baby with a sitter I would find. I didn't know who the father of the new baby was, but I suspected it was the same as the first. Now that the other grandmother helped out once in a while, maybe she would help a little more, and perhaps I could bring the new baby to work on the other days. I knew how to carry a baby on a train. I knew how to get things done at the office. I was a veteran of the impossible.

I had to fight off the tears in synagogue. I spotted the rabbi walking out of his study and felt a little awkward asking him for a minute of his time as I was not a member of the congregation. But he invited me to step back inside and have a seat. My tears flowed. "I'm fifty-two years old. I can't raise another child. I just can't. It wouldn't be fair to the child. I'd have to go on welfare. I already have a small grandson at home that I'm raising."

I decided on adoption. There was no other way. I asked the rabbi if he knew of a Jewish couple that wanted to adopt. They just had to be good people, really, and if they were Jewish that was ideal. The rabbi told me he needed to think about it and he would call me at seven that same night.

He called at seven on the dot. That was a trait I appreciated. The rabbi told me I was not going to believe this, but a couple who were members had been trying unsuccessfully for years to have a baby. They had given up hope and were looking into adoption. But just today the woman had gone to the doctor and found out she was pregnant. Her best friend, however, lived in Chicago with her husband and had also been trying for many years. She was still looking for her miracle.

I gave the rabbi my name and address and asked him to have the woman in Chicago write me a letter explaining why they wanted to adopt. I also requested a photo of the couple. The rabbi said he would oblige and in the meantime all I had to do was wait.

I was never very good at waiting, and now was certainly no exception. I noticed an issue of *Time* magazine with a feature article on the complexities of adoption. Laws varied from state to state, and arrangements could fall through at the last minute. I couldn't have that happen. The article mentioned Lawrence Raphael, an attorney with a toll free number who specialized in adoptions. I had once gotten assigned to a major fight by walking into legendary promoter Don King's office and introducing myself. There was no point in being shy. I called Lawrence Raphael to discuss my case and told him we were expecting in July. He told me he would gladly get involved.

The letter I got from Sandra, the prospective adoptive mother, had everything in it I could have hoped for. Her husband, Stephen, sounded like he would make an ideal father. From the photo I could see they were a kind-hearted couple. I wrote a frank letter back expressing my gratitude. Maybe, just maybe we were all out of the woods.

As the due date neared, so did the woods once more. My daughter's OB/GYN stepped out into the waiting area and asked me to come back into the examination room. They had just performed an ultrasound and discovered the baby was getting smaller. We had eight weeks to go, with grandchild and grandma both hanging on by a thread.

With three weeks to go the thread got thinner. My attorney called to say the adoptive parents wanted to speak to me and would I accept a call at five o'clock the following day. "Of course," I said. When the phone rang the next day, right on time, it was Sandra. I figured it would be a good idea to talk before we eventually met. But now, she explained, I couldn't count on it. She and Stephen had spent the past weekend reconsidering the adoption given the difficulty of the pregnancy and the fertility drugs that were becoming available.

I told Sandra the baby was gaining weight and that she had my assurance the baby would be healthy. Sandra said it was only fair of her to let me know what they were thinking. I begged her to hang in there. When I got off the phone I wanted to scream and cry, and I did both.

Like hundreds of fighters I had watched over the years from ringside, I got up quickly and dusted myself off. The next morning I started making phone calls. I needed a back-up in case Sandra and her husband lost their nerve entirely. I did get one bite. The office at nearby Gwynedd-Mercy College knew of a couple that was looking to adopt. I asked that they call my attorney as soon as possible. I called my attorney as well and had him scour the country. When I wasn't making phone calls, I prayed to God.

God answered my prayers in the back of an '83 Buick LeSabre. My daughter Carol Paula gave birth in her girlfriend's car in the driveway of Sacred Heart Hospital. The doctors and nurses took the baby inside and cleaned her up. *Her.* I learned it was a girl born in that car when I got the phone call at four in the afternoon.

The nuns at Sacred Heart Hospital were dressed in white and floating around the maternity ward. Angelic though they were, I asked them to fly away for a while and leave me with the baby. There I sat with her in a rocking chair explaining everything—how she got here, what I had done to protect her, and how no harm would ever come to her again.

How sorry I was to have to give her up but what a wonderful life she was going to have. I believed she understood every word. I had to believe. It was the only thing that kept me sane. I didn't know who was going to take her. The one person who really wanted her was right here in the rocking chair. I would be back every day.

God was working overtime. Sandra called a couple days later to say she and Stephen had a change of heart. They would be the ones. *That was wonderful*, I thought. *But they had put me through hell and I was not quite back*. I spoke with the sincerity and directness of someone who had just escaped from a burning building. I let them know I was giving them the greatest gift any human being could give to another. All I was asking in return was once a year to receive a letter telling me how my granddaughter was doing. With the letter would be two current photos of the child, one for me and one for the biological mother. I would send back a small gift. Sandra agreed to it. It would all be done through the attorney.

This fateful day was arranged by the attorney, too. The rendezvous at Philadelphia International. The arrival of the adoptive mother with her paralegal. Their impending flight right back to Chicago. My daughter's accompanying them on the flight back so that the adoption could be completed legally in the state of Illinois. Even the scheduled visit to a pediatrician in Chicago. Everything but the huge black plastic garbage bag.

I shake Sandra's hand and then the young lady paralegal's but there is no hug from me. I am not ready to hand over the baby. I fumble for the papers from Sacred Heart Hospital for hand delivery to the pediatrician in Chicago. We talk about what a great attorney Larry Raphael is and how hot it is this July beyond the tall windows, out on the runway. Sandra snaps one photo after another of the baby, my daughter, and me. I am not feeling photogenic and am just barely together enough to spread a blanket on the floor of the terminal and give diaper changing lessons.

My diapering lesson is complete, but my feeding lesson is interrupted. They are announcing a departing flight to Chicago on the public address system. There must be a mistake. The flight in was not more than forty-five minutes ago and it seems more like five. My reprieve is over. I feel like a prisoner on death row bargaining for an extra course with my last meal.

I hand over the baby and say, "Take good care of her." What else is there to say? The words do nothing for me. Absolutely nothing. The terrible sensation of breath escaping me is back with a vengeance, and this time it's for keeps. Inexplicably, the words of Muhammad Ali fill my head—his admission moments after fighting fourteen exhausting rounds against an indomitable Joe Frazier in the Philippines. "This is the closest to death I've ever been."

Me too. The big black garbage bag is moving away, down the corridor, getting smaller and smaller. And so is my sweet little girl. My thoughts are now wrapped around something Ali said to me when we met years ago. It wasn't something anyone would ever expect him to say. He said anyone can fight, but it takes a real man to walk away. *But how on Earth am I ever going to walk away from this?*

I can't. I sit down right there in the airport and sob uncontrollably. I realize how many tears I had held back for weeks, for months, and I flood the airport with a dam that has burst. It doesn't matter. Death by drowning. Death by broken heart. Take your pick.

Someone taps me on the shoulder. I look up and catch my breath for an instant. It's a nicely dressed man around thirty.

"Is there anything I can do for you?" he asks.

"Yes," I say. "Can you give me a hug?"

I stand and he opens his arm. I grip tight and he grips just as tight. We keep hugging and I cry some more. Somehow a piece of me returns. Then another piece. After five minutes we let go and he has something to tell me.

"I want you to know," he says. "I was sitting behind you the whole time. Right over there. And I could tell what was going on."

"You could?" I say.

"Yes," he says. "And I just want to tell you I think you're one hell of a woman."

I sob again. I am still sad beyond description, but I am no longer empty. I am whole. And suddenly I understand Ali. I understand what every strong person had that kept them going one more round or allowed them to walk away. I had someone in my corner.

CHAPTER FIFTEEN
ODD WOMAN OUT

I didn't own an answering machine. In 1989, that put me in the minority. But as far as I was concerned I *was* an answering machine. I had to answer to my real estate clients and to my brother, who ran the company. I had to answer to the Pennsylvania State Athletic Commission and the World Boxing Association. And I had to answer to my grandson, Larry. So answering the phone at home didn't seem like any great feat. But when I picked up the phone around dinnertime one Monday, I wished I had the real machine.

It was a man's voice on the other end, perhaps in his thirties, fairly articulate. He wanted to speak to Carol Polis. This was my last chance to play answering machine. It didn't sound good, like he wanted something from me. He didn't ask for Carol Sharp, the name most people in my life knew me by. Carol Polis was my boxing name. But like a tape set to "play," I answered. "Speaking!"

The caller was from the EEOC, which he explained was the United States Equal Employment Opportunity Commission. I had heard of it, but just in case, he elaborated. The EEOC was created to enforce Title VII of the Civil Rights Act of 1964. This act, most closely associated with the civil rights struggles of African-Americans, legally protected numerous minorities, and Title VII prohibited employment discrimination based on race, color, national origin, and sex. That was great. I certainly didn't have a problem with that. But I did have one problem, I didn't have any such complaint, and I told him so.

Eva Shain, however, did. The gentleman explained that the woman who had followed my footsteps into the world of professional boxing was seventy and believed she was being pushed by the World Boxing Association into retirement based on her age. As a result, she had filed a complaint of age discrimination with the EEOC. The agency was currently doing an investigation into the matter and would likely be filing a suit against the WBA. The gentleman said that Ms. Shain had given them my name as someone who might be interested in joining the suit.

"Absolutely not."

"I think you might be interested in hearing the merits of the case before making up your mind."

"I'll listen," I said. "But I don't want to waste any of your time. I don't have a gripe with the WBA."

"But you might someday."

"If I have to retire at some point, I'll retire."

That point was a long way off. I'd be Eva Shain's age in eighteen years. But the man from the EEOC gave me the hard sell. He played the civic duty card for a while, then the female solidarity card. Then it was back to the self-interest card. I told him I had too many dishes to clean to sort it all out at the moment but that I would really have to think about it. That wasn't a lie. I would have to think about it. As for a decision, that was already made.

I wasn't the type of person to bite the hand that feeds me. The battle against age discrimination was a legitimate one. But it wasn't mine, especially not in this case. The WBA, like Commissioner Zach Clayton before it, had shown a lot of faith and guts just by appointing me. Maybe one day the organization would erase some of that good will by letting me go, but they could never change the fact that they stuck their neck out for me or strike from my memory all the wonderful places I had traveled as a result.

I liked Eva Shain, and I saw her point. I hadn't heard a thing about a rule or even the consideration of such a rule. But if it was true, there was no logical reason for a mandatory retirement age in our profession. You weren't exchanging blows in the ring. And you weren't the referee, who chased and corralled the fighters in the ring. You were just sitting there, ringside, in a chair or a high stool. Of course you had to be quick, but unless you developed some sort of mental impairment or Alzheimer's disease, I really didn't know why you couldn't judge into your nineties. So if I was Eva Shain I might do the same thing. But I was Carol Polis with a four-year-old grandson to raise. Eva Shain would have to get into the ring without me on this one. I already had too many bells to answer.

Larry was developing into a wonderful kid. He was smart, already athletic, and the type of young man who really listened and tried to do his best. I never regretted for a moment effectively taking over as parent. But that didn't mean I liked everything that went with the territory. When I raised my four children, I saw clearly that as I approached my fifties new opportunities would open up. One by one the kids left the house and the vision became clearer. Then Larry came along and the vision got cloudy. In terms of the rest of my life, it was a little like being sent back to "Go" without collecting two hundred dollars. I had a little boy in the house who depended on me for everything. I couldn't go gallivanting around the world. But I still made one or two trips per year to somewhere exotic to judge a title fight and make some money. I looked forward to those rare occasions, and I wasn't going to give them up for Uncle Sam, Eva Shain, or even my own family.

I was doing more for my family than ever. When I left the Plexiglass fishbowl at Eastman-Kodak and went to work selling industrial real estate, I was doing at least as much for my brother, Arthur, as he was doing for me. The industrial real estate game wasn't like the residential and commercial real estate business. Instead of houses and small office buildings in your area you dealt in huge manufacturing facilities, warehouses, and distribution centers throughout the country. The industrial real estate game was like an all or nothing proposition involving multimillion-dollar facilities. The stakes were higher and the deals fewer and farther between. If you expected a steady stream of small to medium commissions, industrial real estate wasn't for you.

In the office we had books listing available properties along with their SIC code. But if you were relying on these listings for your leads you were going to be beaten to the punch. You had to know what was going on in the world. And what was going on was American garment facilities were emptying out as jobs went overseas because of cheap labor. Most important of all, you had to know people in industry.

Arthur, for instance, knew a big shot at Levi-Strauss, a great example of a legendary American company becoming less American every day. Levi had dozens of factories and warehouses being dumped faster than you could take off a pair of straight-leg jeans. Arthur's friend would let him know the next property to go on the auction block. We would then find a co-broker in that part of the country. Without a co-broker, the traveling could become overwhelming.

I knew people, too. I made it my business to know them. I made a lot of cold calls, and I came to understand a fundamental truth, one I already knew from the world of sports. The world was often upside down for a woman. If one aspect of the game was harder, there was every reason to hang in there, because odds were another aspect would be easier. So it was with cold calls.

The typical corporate office was stacked at the front with women receptionists and executive secretaries. This was who you got when you made a cold call. I called them the guard dogs. A man, especially one with a sonorous voice, could get through the guard dogs and to the executives fairly easily. When a woman called, the guard dogs got rabid. They growled and barked and kicked up a little dust. That was okay. I threw them a bone. I calmed them down. Whether that meant scratching behind their ears or convincing them I already knew their master, I did it, and more often than not it worked.

Once a man got through to the department head, director of real estate, whoever, he had a false sense of security. The top guns at these Fortune 500 companies breathed different air than the rest of us. Everyone wanted something from them, and the next man in line was no one special. But an amiable woman who knew of a great warehouse in their area and could fly in to meet with them was like a ray of sunshine. I got even luckier when I spoke to the top man at Boeing in Seattle, Washington. His secretary was out sick, so he picked up the phone like an intern and we became good buddies—the part-time boxing judge from Philadelphia and the head of one of the largest aerospace companies in the free world.

No matter who you were schmoozing with and hopefully, eventually, closing a deal with, you needed a big cushion to lean on. I didn't have a cushion. All I had was a slow, steady draw against future commission provided by my brother. That was what I lived on and what put most of the food on the table for Larry and for my grown kids, to the degree that I still could help them. The draw wasn't always what it should be. That was the way the world worked. That was the way America worked. And now that was the way my family worked.

The way the EEOC worked was like a good middleweight fighter. They were relentless. They hit hard, and they hit often. They called the house about once a week to get me against the ropes and work me over. The lefts and rights and jabs were always pretty much the same. They told me this was my duty. This was my responsibility. This was in my own best interest. Lurking in the background, unspoken, was the notion that cooperating was my actual legal responsibility. I figured if they could truly compel me to testify they would have already done so. But I thought maybe they were waiting for the right opening to land that big right hook It got to the point where I was afraid to answer the phone. I needed guard dogs of my own.

I let the World Boxing Association know what was going on. That wasn't like walking next door and telling your neighbor that the postman dropped something in your box by accident. The WBA home office was in Panama. When you called it was expensive, and it was hard to get someone on the phone who spoke English. Whenever I received a telegram from the WBA that wasn't clear, I tried the phone, and it was hard enough clarifying a relatively straightforward matter regarding an upcoming assignment. The matter with the EEOC was more abstract, and I wasn't even sure *I* understood it correctly.

So I wrote a couple of letters to El Presidente, Gilberto Mendoza. I wanted to be on record as having been approached and, more importantly, as having refused. While sitting down at the kitchen table I could easily have written another letter, to Eva Shain, letting her know I didn't appreciate her giving the EEOC my name and number, but I thought better of it.

Months into the harassment, I hadn't heard back from the WBA by phone, telegram, or mail. What I really needed was some counsel. But between rounds I had a big job, a little kid, and local fights to judge. I did some research, though. The head of the EEOC at the time, Clarence Thomas, was appointed by President Reagan. Thomas was a black man who didn't fit the stereotypical mold of a black politician or lawmaker. Although he was the product of a broken home and grew up fairly poor, his grandfather instilled in him a tremendous sense of self-reliance.

Politically, that translated into abhorrence for affirmative action or any policy for that matter that gave special treatment to black citizens in the white world. Instead, Clarence Thomas' desire for black Americans was that they work fervently to thrive in their own businesses and build an insulated black community from within. Exactly what that meant for the EEOC was not clear. The agency's mission seemed somewhat at odds with its director's personal values. That was not an accident on Ronald Reagan's part.

Yet the agency continued to exist and function. Perhaps this particular suit, against the WBA, in being a fight against age discrimination, was more in line with the sort of goals Clarence Thomas wanted to pursue. Whatever the case, only a handful of people worked for the WBA, and a smaller handful were U.S. citizens.

More likely, the action was seen by the agency as a big potential feather in its cap. That was how agencies in the public eye functioned— much like people, always looking to justify their existence. Regardless, this particular agency with its pesky, harassing phone calls, could never measure up to the FBI. When the FBI agents came to my door in 1977 following the Don King fiasco in Annapolis, I was filled with awe and fear. Hearing from the EEOC was like trying to get a salesman off the phone.

In mid-November of 1989 I finally heard from the WBA via

telegram, but it had nothing to do with the EEOC. I had two weeks to get my VISA ready to go to Paris, where I would judge the light heavyweight title fight between Dwight Muhammad Qawi and Robert Daniels. I loved Paris, and that was already enough of a thrill. But in a follow-up letter I learned that the fight would be judged by three women—myself, Patricia Morse Jarman of Las Vegas, and Rosemary Grable of Detroit. Five years ago the same thing had been attempted and it fell apart before everyone's eyes. This time I had the feeling it would stick.

Maybe I felt that way because France was a laissez-faire nation culturally, where something like that didn't rise to the level of anything more than a curiosity. Or maybe I felt enough years had passed that the time for this particular watershed had arrived, quietly. Either way, maybe I was feeling more like Clarence Thomas and less like the agency he ran. Sometimes progress didn't require a lawsuit. Sometimes it didn't even require a fight, except for the one in the ring.

Attending WBA conventions seemed to become more and more critical for landing assignments. Some of the women who followed in my footsteps, including the two others picked for the upcoming fight in Paris, had attended more conventions than I had, as well as being assigned more title fights over the past few years. That didn't seem to be a coincidence. Flying to Tokyo on my budget and with my responsibilities simply to attend a convention in order to perhaps land assignments at some time in the future, was nearly out of the question. Even if I were assigned additional title fights as a result, it was questionable whether I would be able to accept.

But I did fly to Costa Rica to attend one convention and drive down to Atlantic City for another. By coincidence, the next one was in Philadelphia and only days before my departure for France. No matter what the demands of the rest of my life or my upcoming travel date, being a no-show in my home town was a no-no.

When I saw Antonio Brandino at the convention I was all smiles. Antonio was from Florence, Italy and one of several vice presidents of the WBA. We became good friends at the two title fights I had done in Italy.

Like the Italian people, he had every faith in my ability as a judge. But here in my backyard he hadn't brought exactly a vote of confidence. Antonio wasn't thrilled with three women on the upcoming card. He made it clear that two was enough. He said the promoter, the Acaries brothers of Paris, had probably pushed it solely for publicity. On that score, I didn't doubt Antonio was wrong for a minute and I told him so. And I told him I didn't blame him for saying two women was enough. For most Americans, one was enough.

On the flight over to Paris I had time to think about how lucky I had really been during the past few years. My title fight assignments ranged from the mundane to the sublime, and I was grateful for all of them. On the mundane side, in June 1986 I did the junior middleweight title fight between Buster Drayton and Carlos Santos. The location—far off, exotic Brendan Byre Arena is the New Jersey Meadowlands.

It was a work day and a work night. The main event didn't begin until 11 PM, following which I took a long drive south on the New Jersey Turnpike, an incredibly straight highway on which I did everything I could to avoid swerving. I arrived back home in Fort Washington around 5 AM with enough time left over to shower, put on fresh clothes, leave the house for work at 5:40 and sell more industrial real estate.

The year before, I had a middleweight title fight in Scranton, Pennsylvania. This was a gig through my other organization, the IBF/USBA. The contestants were John Collins and Mark Holmes, cousin of heavyweight champion Larry Holmes. Holmes, as a matter of fact, had a lot of brothers and cousins. This one was a contender in the ring, at least until the second round. In that round, Collins knocked him down three times, and referee Frank Cappuccino stopped the fight. That was a merciful act on many levels. Aside from perhaps saving Holmes' life, it spared me from Chuck Bednarik.

Bednarik was a member of the Pennsylvania State Athletic Commission and an NFL legend. Aside from his rock solid physique he had a strong jaw line and rugged good looks. I had a crush on him when he played for the Philadelphia Eagles in the 1950s and early '60s. And he literally crushed just about every opposing player who either tried to get away or got in his way. When he retired following the 1962 season, having finally won a championship with the 1960 Eagles, he was one of the last players to go both ways—offense and defense, that is. Bednarik was older than old school. In his mind there was no reason in the world to ever sit on the sidelines when there were still more butts to kick out on the field.

In one famous game against the New York Giants, Chuck Bednarik stopped star running back Frank Gifford cold, like a three-foot thick cinderblock wall stopping a Volkswagen Beetle. But that wasn't enough for Chuck. He literally picked up the stunningly handsome Gifford and threw him to the ground like a sack of potatoes. In football as in boxing, there were graceful ways to fall backwards and there were nearly lethal ways. This was nearly lethal. When Gifford hit the turf you could virtually hear the dull thud, even on a soundless highlight reel. The Giant running back seemed tiny in Bednarik's hands and was out cold for a long while.

If Bednarik was a lot nicer off the field than on it, it wasn't obvious in Scranton or in Allentown, where I had done a bunch of fights under his watch. He would bark and growl when a judge's scoring wasn't to his liking. This was really out of bounds for a commissioner, and class acts like Zach Clayton and Jimmy Binns would never second-guess a judge, especially not in public. And if for some reason they ever had to, they would do it in private and without foaming at the mouth. So in Scranton, with the benefit of a KO, it was Mark Holmes on the canvas instead of Carol Polis.

Then there was the sublime, at least in relative terms. In November of 1985 I traveled to Rimini, Italy, on the WBA's dime, to judge the junior featherweight title fight. The seat-of-the-pants lobbying I did under duress in New York during the Hagler fight had paid off in spades. Rimini sat on the Adriatic coast and with sights like the Arch of Augustus and the Tiberius Bridge was almost as full of history as Rome. Rimini was the home of the great director Fellini and inspiring of things both breathtaking and erotic. My own breathing got just a bit deeper when I saw my hotel room. It had a view of the Adriatic Sea so close and spectacular, if you didn't look down, you thought you were out there transporting silk and jewels for Caesar.

The contest between hometown fighter Loris Stecca and the champ from Puerto Rico, Victor Callejas, was almost a dead heat going into the sixth round. In that round, Callejas pummeled the Italian contender like the Huns pounding the Romans. The ring doctor wouldn't allow Stecca to answer the bell for the seventh round, and word got out fast that Callejas had broken Stecca's jaw. Then, with her son nursing his wounds in the corner, Stecca's mother jumped into the ring and went after Callejas. The champ didn't have much time to celebrate because no sooner did he put up his hands in triumph than he saw a sixty-ish irate lady coming at him with a shoe.

She chased him around the ring for a half a minute or so, waving one Prada pump in her right hand and wearing the other on her left foot, providing some of the most exciting action of the evening. Mommy actually got in one good hit on the side of the champ's head, faring slightly better than her son, before the referee stopped yet another fight involving a Stecca. I wanted to go up there myself and tell Senora Stecca that as a mother I knew all too well at some point you had to let your sons go and fight their own battles. But this was Italy.

The after-fight dinner was almost as spectacular and almost as Italian. This was another historic spot on the Adriatic Sea, but the "dons" of the community—the promoters, government officials, and local celebrities—were conspicuously absent. In America we called this being a bad sport. The Italian word was *vendetta*. But I kept both my shoes on and enjoyed every bite. I even got to be interviewed on Italian TV, so that now I was not only dwelling in my favorite land, I was a bit famous in it. During the interview I learned that I was the first ever professional woman boxing judge in Italy.

Sometimes the fight itself was a no-show. In October 1985 I traveled all the way down to Curacao for the WBA bantamweight title fight between Khaosai Galaxy and Israel Contreras. With the fight, Galaxy was honoring the king of his homeland, Thailand, as the ruler turned sixty the following year.

Curacao was one of three historically important islands in the Dutch West Indies, just north of Venezuela. It was known for trading—both the trade winds and the trading of all things valuable, including rum, spices, and of course slaves. The origin of the name "Curacao" was disputed, some saying it meant "cure" for all the sailors who successfully treated their scurvy with island grown citrus fruits, and others saying it meant "heart," as the island was somewhat heart-shaped. While there, I needed both—a cure and a heart. My dad's health wasn't good, and I took the initial flight down to neighboring Aruba only after learning that he was doing better.

When I landed in Curacao, by way of Miami and then the short hop over from Aruba, I learned the fight was postponed until November. Galaxy had gotten there a little late and, more importantly, Venezuelan TV had done the same and didn't have sufficient time to set up. Fortunately, the King of Thailand could wait a little longer to turn sixty.

As for me, I was feeling my age all dressed up and no place to go. But when I called home and found that Dad was still doing okay I had effectively positioned myself for a vacation. The rest of the positioning was with the promoters, who in light of the circumstances and my disappointment at missing the World Series or whatever was going on back home agreed to pay the full roundtrip ticket, my hotel, and half my expenses. Without ever having to judge a fight I had a lovely few days. And it's a good thing, because I never received the money for the plane fare home.

I got back to Italy in January 1987 to judge the junior welterweight title fight between Patrizio Oliva and Rodolfo Gonzalez. The site was Sicily, in the city of Agrigento on the southern coast. Agrigento was founded in the sixth century BCE by the Greeks, and there were still remnants. Everywhere there were lush green hills, grape arbors, and Greek temples. But when we were taken on a tour of the land, I saw something so historically real I had to tell the driver in Italian to stop immediately so I could get out and take a few pictures.

It was an elderly shepherd walking down a dirt road cutting across a field with a large flock of sheep. The shepherd was perhaps eighty going on a hundred and crippled, so that his walking stick seemed less a prop and more a necessity. His faithful black shaggy shepherd dog, true to his name, actually kept the sheep together, darting out to the edges of the flock to nudge the lost sheep inward. The words of the 23rd Psalm kept running through my head. Aside from the click, click, click of my Cannon F-1, the scene was truly biblical.

The fight in Agrigento was held in a circus tent with 11,500 of us packed in like sardines, appropriate enough with the island of Sardinia nearby. The fight went the distance, and all three judges called it for Oliva. There were no moms and no killer shoes, just an unusually good fight with the winner hailing from Naples. But the highlight for me came in Rome. After the fight we went over to tour and do a TV interview. During the ride back from the station, the limousine driver recognized me and told me I was known all over Italy for being fair and honest. It was probably the proudest moment in my professional life, right up there with the National Anthem being played in Córdoba, Argentina. The thrill in Rome was profound and internal. No tourist's camera could possibly capture it. Here I was in my favorite country in the world, *and I was their favorite, too.*

There was virtually no fanfare when we landed in Paris on this chilly day in late November 1989. For me that was notable and welcome. Even though we were in one of a handful of the most famous cities in the world, my reference point, ironically, was not the other exotic places I had been to. It was the Hagler-Hamsho fight in Madison Square Garden five years earlier. I still remembered the sinking feeling of exiting the train in New York and being told, over and over again, that there wouldn't be three women judges. Here in the City of Lights there was no sign of darkness. If anything, they were blasé.

That business-as-usual etiquette was welcome for more than just professional reasons. I had only three or four days in Paris, and I wanted as little of that time as possible stolen by controversy. What you really needed in Paris was a few weeks, at bare minimum. Fortunately, I had been here before, once as a boxing judge and earlier as an eighteen-year-old on a student trip, I had a diary from that trip almost long enough to make a book. So instead of lamenting the brevity of this visit or any other, I had the luxury of calling it just another chapter.

The Eiffel Tower, the Louvre, the Assemblée Nationale, and Pont Neuf, along with a couple dozen other famous attractions, were all safely painted in my diary and in my mind and didn't need a fresh coat. With limited time, I chose to spend it first at Montmarte, a hill sitting at the north end of Paris on the right bank. Tourists know this hill first and foremost by the white domed basilica that sits atop, known as Sacré Cœur.

What goes on beneath the church is certainly spiritual if not exactly religious. Montmarte is full of nightclubs and is known as an artist's community. Their alumni include Picasso, Van Gogh, Monet, and Dali, all of whom at one time had studios along these same streets. When you walked around, you could still feel the creative vibrations from a century or more ago mixed like oil paint with the artist residents of the day. On my previous trip I had lost track of time on these very streets and almost turned up late for the fight. So this time I made a conscious effort to leave by subway at a given hour.

The subway took me from the spirit to the wallet. Champs-Élysées was close to if not the most famous avenue in the world, connecting the Arc de Triumph to the Place de la Concorde. The avenue was jam packed with cafés, restaurants, theaters, and gift shops and represented about two kilometers of the highest rents to be found on the planet. Still, I thought I could get my favorite perfume in all the world here for less, because it was "local." No such luck. Shalimar perfume was even more expensive along the Champs-Élysées than it was at Wanamaker's. That didn't matter, though. Paris was and always would be a woman's city.

It was also a dog's city. Dogs were allowed in hotels and restaurants. At a restaurant a few blocks from our hotel, where I ate with the other two judges scheduled to make history, my chair was back to back with a chair in which sat a cute white poodle, French by definition. I couldn't see if he was eating crepes or escargot, but no one seemed to mind, least of all me.

I loved dogs, and I just hoped this one was a good tipper.

The restaurant had only one bathroom with no sign. It was coed by default. No sign for men or women. You just walked in and locked the door. When I did that, I wanted to unlock it fast. There was no toilet. No bidet. Just a hole in the ground. Literally. There was no toilet paper, either. I didn't think they were out of it, because there was no dispenser.

I tried to console myself. The French were liberated from passé prejudices but not always from grime. They were known to bathe in the sink on occasion. Paris was, after all, an ancient city. Then again, the Roman conquerors had running water and water closets back in the day. I was a bit fazed. Maybe this was the poodle's bathroom. If it was, I felt sorry for the poodle. I felt sorry for myself as well. But if it was good enough for de Gaulle it was good enough for me, so I squatted. This, I told myself, was a small price to pay for a progressive culture that didn't bat an eyelash at three women boxing judges. Vive la France!

At times, the entire operation—in fact, the entire milieu—seemed as cavalier as that bathroom. The promoter never set up any sort of tour for me and my "fellow" officials. There was no rules and regulations meeting. We were told what we needed to know on the fly. There was no standing eight count. There was no saved-by-the-bell provision. There was no limit to the number of knockdowns in a round. The fight would be allowed to continue as many times as the fighter could get back on his feet before a count of ten or before the referee called a technical knockout. The fight, however, was a twelve-rounder. The WBA had finally, a few years earlier, fallen in line with the WBC and eliminated those epic fifteen-rounders.

The Pavilion Baltard was a relatively small arena, seating a little over 2,000. From a distance it looked a little like a carousel building, albeit larger and rectangular. The atmosphere inside was appropriately festive, but down at ringside it was low key. Pat, Rosemary, and I were in position, and there was no turning back. I hoped the fight would go the distance, but I expected Dwight Muhammad Qawi to take Robert Daniels.

Daniels, from Miami, was only 21. Qawi was almost 37. Some people saw a large age difference as an advantage for the younger fighter, but not me. At 37 if you worked hard at keeping in shape you were still physically about 98 percent. Qawi was definitely in shape. Like other top fighters reaching his golden years, in exchange for the two percent he acquired many years of valuable experience finding his opponents' weaknesses, pacing himself, grasping the psychology of the fight, and a hundred other subtle but vital skills. Daniels had 17 wins against a single loss, compared to Qawi's 32 wins against 6 losses. But the real difference in experience wasn't fully expounded by the numbers.

Qawi had lost five years of his life to prison. He wasn't the first young man from Camden, New Jersey sent away for armed robbery, but he was probably the most successful. He learned to box in jail and emerged relatively polished in his mid-twenties. At that time, Qawi was known by his birth name, Dwight Braxton. After prison he converted to Islam. But his nickname as a boxer didn't belong to any particular religion. The Camden Buzzsaw came right at his opponents with a flurry of punches that at times appeared as a blur. I had my own nickname for Qawi—the Cement Slab, Jr., like Joe Frazier. Every fighter in the light heavyweight—or cruiserweight—division was physically solid, but the Cement Slab was in his own league. Qawi was like a freshly cut granite statue painted rich glossy brown.

He needed every intimidating quality his multiple nicknames implied. That was because Dwight Muhammad Qawi was only five-foot-five-and-a-half. It was a miracle at that height for anyone to be fighting professionally as a light heavyweight, let alone contending for a world title. Really it was a testament to Qawi's abilities as a fighter combined with his sheer will.

As the fight started, the difference in height came into play almost immediately. At 5' 11", Daniels did his best to punch from a distance. With that strategy—the same one applied by almost every professional fighter Qawi had ever faced—Daniels landed a few effective blows. But Qawi was his usual relentless self. He continually rolled forward like a tank approaching the front line. Once in a while a shell hit him, redirecting him for an instant, but he kept rolling. The Camden Buzzsaw knew that once he got inside to the other fighter, the two were fighting in the Qawi zone. Daniels knew it, too. But knowing and executing were two different things. No contender for the title wanted to be seen as perpetually backing off. So Daniels and Qawi mixed it up for short spurts, and Qawi won those brawls, landing numerous effective jabs in rapid succession along with the occasional dynamite right hook.

I had Qawi ahead four rounds to two after the first six, and so it seemed did the Parisian crowd. The second half of the fight was a little more even. Daniels stuck more to his long distance bombs. When they did get into the Qawi zone, the Slab was still the Slab, but he was less of a buzzsaw than he had been. His lefts were good, but his rights were practically non-existent.

The fight went the distance, which was a huge plus for both the WBA and the three women judges. I had it 116-113 in favor of Qawi and felt sure Pat and Rosemary would turn in similar scores. But I was wrong. Rosemary Grable scored it for Daniels by only two points. Patricia Morse Jarman had Daniels winning by a single point. It was a split decision, and I was the odd woman out. Robert Daniels was the new light heavyweight champion, and the French were not happy.

There was booing and hissing but no chance of a riot. There were too many truffles to eat and too much strolling to do along the Seine, but I was a little disappointed. Yes, it was fortunate the fight went the distance so that none of us pioneers were saddled with a free ride on our way to making history. But it would have been a lot neater and cleaner if the three who made this revolution all leaned the same way. In my mind at least, I had the right score. Rosemary and Pat had been doing this for only a few years, and I knew the pitfalls of those close rounds where a taller, perhaps more graceful fighter picked up points that weren't always deserved.

But on further reflection, the split decision was a thing of beauty. Rosemary, Pat, and Carol were not a team or a unified front. We were individuals, and individuals often disagreed. Any successful revolution in the end required each person to return to being no more than a single freethinker. We had just gotten there sooner than expected.

The next morning at breakfast I finally met Muhammad Qawi. He was not your stereotypical Black Muslim, and nothing like the militants who checked into the Sherman Inn years ago in Fort Washington. He was genial and became even more so once I told him I was from Philadelphia. The City of Brotherly Love, after all this time, was still Mecca to fighters the world over, especially Camden. I noticed Qawi's right hand was wrapped. He explained that he had injured it mid-fight and that from about the seventh round on he could no longer punch with it.

That explained a lot. He was a courageous fighter to have soldiered on like that. This was a five-and-a-half foot tall warrior who had once lost a split decision to the towering Evander Holyfield and put away the rangy Leon Spinks on a TKO in the sixth round. The night before, the injury to Qawi's hand had probably made the difference in the fight. In fact, I learned that through the first six rounds, all three judges had the exact same score.

When I arrived back home in Fort Washington, I knew there would be no messages waiting for me. Rather than with a sitter, Larry had been staying with his father's parents for a few days while I was away. I still had no answering machine, and I was as glad as ever about that. I didn't want to come home to a phone message from my friendly neighborhood EEOC caseworker.

But there was no stopping the U.S. Mail. In the pile just inside of the slot at my front door, sandwiched between a phone bill, a water bill, supermarket circulars, and a couple of clothing catalogues, was an official looking letter. I saw the logo subliminally even before I made out the individual letters: EEOC. It was with this stubborn federal agency as it was with parking tickets, moving violations and the IRS. You could run but you couldn't hide. I had a hundred other things to catch up on, but I put my bags down right there in the foyer and opened the envelope like ripping a Band-Aid off an old wound. It was a subpoena to testify in two weeks.

One good Band-Aid rip deserved another. The next morning I drove to nearby Blue Bell. With the December wind blowing against me,

I walked across the parking lot to Jimmy Binns's law office. I wasn't there as a client. That would have cost me a hundred dollars just to take off my coat. I was there as one of his officials. I sank down low in the leather chair opposite his mahogany desk. So low that Dwight Muhammad Qawi could have swung and missed. But within a minute I knew when I managed to get up again I'd be standing tall. Binns, in his usual red tie and classic pinstriped suit, told me he had also gotten a subpoena from the EEOC. The upshot was he wasn't going.

Just like that the pressure lifted. He didn't explain why he wasn't going, and he didn't tell me not to appear. It was like a hand signal from a referee. If you had been around, you knew, and if there had been a compelling reason for me to appear, there was no way he would have let me walk out of that office in the dark. And that was it. There was no formal counsel. If the great Commissioner Binns wasn't showing up, why on Earth should I?

I had the wind at my back walking back to my car. I doubted I would ever hear from the EEOC again. I was sure they had done good things for good people and would continue to do so, just as I was sure they would, along the way, continue to disrupt unwilling lives. In boxing and in life you didn't accept every fight and you took time between fights. Without selectivity and some sort of plan you wound up talking to the canvas a lot. If you were smart, determined, resourceful, and most of all patient, you might even make history. Now this was history too.

CHAPTER SIXTEEN
YOU DON'T LOOK LIKE A JUDGE

When the first *Rocky* movie came out in late 1976, my friends were astonished I wasn't running down to the local theater to see it with them. Some of them had already seen it twice. From their perspective, *Rocky* was the ultimate boxing story, the ultimate Philadelphia story, and therefore the ultimate Carol Polis story. My perspective was a little different. I had been to so many fights, including so many in Philadelphia, I didn't need to pay to see another one, real or staged. I had been to enough sweaty gyms, weigh-ins, and press conferences to last several lifetimes.

When I finally gave in, it took about ten minutes to be seduced. Stallone and the director, John G. Alvidsen, got it right at every level. The brutal intensity and day-to-day thanklessness of training was captured perfectly. The working class monotony outside the gym was right on target. The whole seedy yet glorious nature of the sport that existed beneath the radar was drawn to a tee. There were also more than a few thrills of recognition, from Stallone pounding a side of beef like Joe Frazier, to his running up the steps of the Philadelphia Museum of Art at dawn in a scene that, itself, belonged inside the museum.

And yet all the wonderful production details paled in comparison to the real attraction of *Rocky*. This was the archetypal underdog story made modern. Sylvester Stallone's Rocky Balboa was the ultimate nobody, to the point that when he is offered a shot at the heavyweight title out of the blue, he sits there oblivious mumbling about how, sure, he would appreciate the opportunity to be a sparring partner for the champion. Rocky's was a world of twenty dollars here, thirty dollars there for mixing it up in a bloodstained ring while a few dozen bloodthirsty locals placed bets.

In the space of about two hours, we get to watch a nobody come of age. Best of all, he doesn't discover his self-confidence alone. Rocky and

Adrian, his perfect mousy counterpart of a girlfriend, find their confidence and dignity together. By the final scene, with Rocky Balboa fighting Apollo Creed in what seemed to be a death match, I was up on my feet screaming with everybody else in the theater, "Kill 'em, Rocky! Kill 'em!" So much for having seen it all.

I was hooked. *Rocky* hit close to home not so much because it was filmed near my home or because it was about boxing but because it was, somehow, about me. I was Rocky with a purse.

The *Rocky* pictures continued and so did my life. Though the thrill of watching someone rise from life's rubble the first time couldn't be duplicated, *Rocky II* and *III* were decent sequels with familiar characters and fairly plausible plots. By *Rocky IV*, the magic was gone. Watching our hometown hero fight Dolph Lundgren's machine of a Soviet fighter while the fate of the free world supposedly hung in the balance was not only preposterous, it was a cliché. But by the mid-1980s, *Rocky* was not simply a series. It was a franchise, and a franchise had to produce revenue.

In April 1989, however, while I was out in Los Angeles judging a junior featherweight title fight, I met an actor by the name of John Iberia. My first glance was a foreshadowing of the conversation we were about to have, because from the side John looked a lot like Sylvester Stallone. It turned out he was Stallone's stand-in in a couple of the *Rocky* movies. A stand-in is a body-double for the star, who gets to hang out and have a drink in the trailer while the stand-in and the crew spend grueling hours setting up the lighting, camera angles, and movement of a scene.

John told me *Rocky V* would start production in January 1990 in the City of Brotherly Love. When I heard that, I was ready to run up the steps of the Art Museum.

From the time I could walk or maybe a little earlier, I wanted to be a star of the stage, the screen, or both. My parents had to endure hearing me sing every word of every song on "Your Hit Parade," sometimes on key, sometimes not. Behind my bedroom door it was more than just a sing-along with a popular radio show. It was a full musical production. When I sang "Dance Ballerina Dance," I did, holding a hairbrush like a microphone and gazing in the mirror, twirling in my pink ballerina shoes, trying somehow to stay on my toes, and at least once falling so hard I wound up with a scar on my cheekbone.

That behavior wasn't entirely abnormal for an eleven year old girl in 1947 or any other year for that matter. But for me, the dream never really ended. In 1962, for instance, as a young mom, I was doing the hairbrush thing with Frankie Valli and the Four Seasons, minus the ballerina moves. My "tour" continued right on through the '60s and '70s with the Supremes, Neil Diamond, Lionel Richie, Billy Joel, and any number of other great acts. I even took a singing class that put me up on stage in front of about two dozen slightly drunk spectators at a local night club.

On a more adult and professional basis, judging professional boxing matches—especially title fights—brought a measure of recognition, a touch of the limelight. I was there to judge, of course, and not to be seen. But the fact was I was seen. I was a small part of something much greater, but an important part. I never hid that from myself and gave interviews wherever and whenever appropriate. I had unplanned, unexpected moments—like the one in Córdoba, with my name in lights and a stadium full of people cheering—etched permanently in my memory. Being the center of attention wasn't the point of what I did, but the dream never died.

And now it took on a new life. *Rocky*—whether the first or the fifth—was boxing, underdogs, and Philadelphia. I now thought about being in *Rocky* the way my friends thought about simply seeing it. This was a must. Given who I was, what I did, and where I was in life, this was my first chance and possibly my last. I absolutely had to be in this movie.

So I took step one, which was to give John my press kit. The kit contained a resume of the fights I had done—highlighting the title fights—as well as my contact information, newspaper clippings, and some publicity shots. Aside from the one of me with Ali, maybe my favorite one was with Marvis Frazier, Joe's son. Marvis let me stage a shot of Carol the featherweight knocking him silly in the ring with a deadly left. Not only was John Iberia willing to pass along my press kit to the director, he promised to report back to me when he had any news. Suddenly I not only had an agent of sorts, but one who looked like Rocky.

Perhaps the most unusual thing about my interaction with John was that I actually had a press kit ready to go. That was not something judges usually carried around—whether judges on the bench or at ringside. But I never kidded myself about wanting to open up other doors in life and walk through. I came prepared, and not just to score a fight.

Amazingly, John called me back in October for another press kit. Not long after that he called again to say that he had gotten a part as one of the other fighters and that the director liked my press kit. "Great!" I said. "What do I do now?"

"Nothing." He said. "They should be calling you in a month or so when they set up in Philadelphia. I'll see you there."

This was some of the best news I had ever gotten. Or was it? I had days and then weeks to think about it, and I decided I wasn't that sure what the news meant. It wasn't like applying for a job and getting that job. This was merely the expectation of an audition, and the truth was I didn't even know what part I was auditioning for. Clutching an imaginary hairbrush while driving to work one morning, I considered the part of Rocky's new love interest. I was no home wrecker, but a flirtation might be just the thing to inject some life back into the series, especially if the flirtation ended with a torrid love scene. At least the champ would still be with, loosely speaking, a Philly girl.

But when I got my head out of the clouds and let the imaginary hairbrush dissolve, I set my sights on something a lot more realistic. I decided I wanted to play a boxing judge. It wasn't exactly a reach. I had been playing one in real life for almost twenty years. I hadn't seen a script, of course, but if this was a boxing movie there had to be judges, even if they didn't say a word. What better way to achieve immortality than to play myself in a movie my grandchildren could watch? I practically congratulated myself for the maturity I displayed right there on the Turnpike in rush hour traffic.

Still, there was a problem. Now that I had settled on a role, how was I going to tell the casting director? I didn't know who he was or where he was. John Iberia, meanwhile, had told me to do nothing. And there was nothing I hated doing more than nothing. So I looked up the names of a bunch of theatrical agents in the area and sent them more press kits. They all told me pretty much the same thing—that they would forward it to the casting agency hired for the movie.

I finally got a call from the casting agency just after the New Year telling me to report to their offices on the morning of January 8th. When I showed up in the Hunting Park area of Philadelphia to what was basically a makeshift office for a capacity crowd of wannabes, I was underwhelmed.

You might expect to walk in to a casting office and hear booming operatic voices singing "The Barber of Seville" and self-styled thespians rehearsing Shakespeare. But it was a cattle call and strictly banal. I found out quickly it was an audition for extras, most of whom were hoping to fill up a small square of backdrop during the Italian market scene. A big concern amongst the hopefuls in the room was the pay scale. If you were non-union, like I was, compensation for a day's work was forty dollars. If you were in SAG or AFTRA, you were looking at a cool hundred. In a room of nobodies I was less than nobody.

Then, just like on the first day at a new school or sleepaway camp, you see someone you know and the chemistry of the day changes. My first sighting, near a table where coffee and Danish were being served, was Frank Cappuccino, the legendary referee. Frank was just as glad to see me, and he wanted to play, of all things, a referee. We then ran into Ed Derien, the fight announcer, yet another local notable hoping to play himself. There was hope after all.

I was given a number, twenty-five. Having to wait for twenty-four people to screen test first wasn't ideal, but it was better than number fifty-five or ninety-five. I might have been cattle, but I was somewhere near the front of the herd. I had some time to graze and struck up a conversation with a sixty-five year old lady from New Jersey who had acted since the age of five and done countless TV commercials. She did seem familiar from this car lot or that furniture showroom. She was limber as someone half her age and did a backbend for us right there and then to prove it. Her beau was even less than half her age at twenty-one, and he was on hand just in case we needed proof of that as well. The two of them went dancing regularly. There really *was* hope.

I grazed right into another lady, this one a little closer to my age and with exactly my first name. Carol announced to me very early in our conversation that she was the Carol from the Neil Sedaka song, "Oh, Carol." I told her I thought I was. Carol looked crestfallen, as if she had to refigure the one story she had probably told to everyone she met for the last twenty-five years. I was sorry she didn't get the joke. "Sedaka" in Hebrew meant "charity." I supposed I could have been more charitable, but in a way I was. "Oh, Carol" was a really dopey song.

It was time for Carol number twenty-five to do her screen test. Mike Lemon, the casting director, introduced himself to me along with his assistant director, Meredith. Mike told me he was a big boxing fan, knew who I was, and saw me on TV all the time. When I heard that, it was "goodbye forty-dollar-a-day extra" in my mind. "Carol" was going to the top of the charts.

"Thank you," I said. "That's great. I'm looking to get the part of a judge."

"Well," Mike said. "How about being an extra in one of the crowd scenes? We need a lot of extras for those fight scenes."

"Why not a judge?" I asked

"You may *be* a judge," he said. "But you don't *look* like a judge."

With that, "Carol" dropped off the charts completely. I took a few steps over to my screen test spot and tried to shake off the hard right hook. There was this popular television commercial for Vicks Formula 44 Cough Syrup with an actor who introduced himself by saying, "I'm not a doctor, but I play one on TV." It was the reference for jokes everywhere for years, especially when someone casually asked you for medical advice. But getting passed over for a judge was no joke, and there was no Marcus Welby on the set to take care of my upset stomach. This was simply not fair. *I was a judge, and I played one on TV, too.* Why couldn't I play one in the movies?

I had a pleasant bedside manner, though, better than the casting director's. Meredith told me to hold up the paper with the number twenty-five on it and look at the camera. I was to state my name, height, and weight. I did, removing a few pounds for all the Danish I had eaten that morning. Mike told me to drop the paper and "emote." I wasn't sure what he meant. Maybe they were looking for a few bars of "Figaro." So I dropped the paper, at least getting that right.

"I'm a boxing judge," I said. "Boxing judges don't speak."

"I just need you to emote," Mike repeated. I must have looked flustered, because I was, so Meredith stepped in.

"Just tell us a little about why you want to be in the movies." That was all I needed to hear. It wasn't as if I had nothing prepared. I had been preparing my whole life.

"It all started when I was a little girl holding a hairbrush like a microphone in front of a mirror while listening to 'Your Hit Parade' on the radio. I've always loved performing. I never dreamed it would happen, but in 1973 I became the world's first woman professional boxing judge and my star has been rising ever since. I've traveled all over the world and done twenty title fights. I've met Muhammad Ali, Joe Frazier, Roberto Duran, Sugar Ray Leonard, and practically anyone you can name.

"I'd like to think I've opened the door for other women, not just in this sport but in other areas thought of as a man's world. That's a reward in itself. But one feather in my cap I've always wanted to have is a role in a big movie. Something that would top off my career and maybe get me a little tiny piece of immortality. Doing this movie—not just a movie, but a *Rocky* movie, maybe the last one—is exactly the missing puzzle piece. Now, I understand the role of love interest is apparently already taken. If something does open up, I would expect to be called. But if that doesn't happen, I would be perfectly thrilled just to be myself . . . and play, what else, a boxing judge."

Mike and Meredith smiled, and the test was over. They told me the director, Academy Award winner John G. Avildsen, would be personally reviewing the screen tests and I should expect a phone call. It was strictly

"Don't call us, we'll call you." But at least I had done my job. I had emoted and then some. "Carol" was back in the top forty.

Over the next few days when I thought about what might be going on behind closed doors in the casting office, I pictured Avildsen, Mike Lemon, Meredith, and Sylvester Stallone himself having already settled on Carol Polis to play herself and simply debating whether it should be a speaking role. And if so, what sort of part could they develop? Maybe they would show the rules meeting before the fight. Maybe the fight would be a really close decision going the wrong way so the media would surround me and ask me how I scored the fourth round, when Rocky got knocked out of the ring. Or maybe they'd show Rocky landing on me. It would be the first time I didn't crawl under the official's table for cover. Anything for fame.

When the call finally came a few days later, Meredith told me I got the part of a forty-dollar-a-day extra in the crowd scene at the Blue Horizon. I was to show up the morning of January 18 bright and early. It was a long time to wait for a decision like that one, and it felt more like a knockout.

But I wasn't down for the count. When I got to the Blue Horizon, with its ornate nineteenth century appeal, I felt like I was home. No matter how many camera and Klieg lights were set up, and no matter how many best boys, grips, and gaffers were milling about the ring, this was my venue. I had judged literally hundreds of fights here over the years. If I was going to shatter the glass ceiling for women boxing officials looking to break into the movies, there was no better place to do it than the Blue Horizon.

There were about a thousand extras milling around, and I couldn't have been the only one looking to break rank. Before I could, the crew grabbed a couple of megaphones and began to corral us. In a matter of minutes, we were all funneled down to the basement, which was strange because after moonlighting at the Blue Horizon most of my adult life, I had never been to the basement before. I didn't even know there was a basement.

It was a large, plain room with columns here and there to hold up the ring and seating area directly above us. There were chairs and tables with an impressive buffet for a thousand hungry extras. Apparently this was where the Blue Horizon did their staging for large catered events. Still, it felt more like the holding cells beneath the Roman Coliseum. The difference was I couldn't wait to go upstairs and fight the lions. Or maybe judge a couple of lions fighting each other.

In any case, Rocky Balboa wouldn't be fighting anyone. It wasn't as if the director made sure each extra had a script to review. But elements of the story for *Rocky V* had leaked out in the media and continued to leak in dribs and drabs here in the basement of the Blue Horizon. Rocky was now retired and struggling, and not just over what to do with the rest of his life. His accountant had fled the country after squandering all his money, forcing him, his wife Adrian, and their son to move out of their mansion and into a modest attached home back in their old neighborhood of Kensington. I knew what it was like to be ripped off by a financial "expert" and start over, so that was one more thing I had in common with Rocky.

As the story develops, Rocky takes a young, misguided fighter named Tommy Gunn under his wing. The ex-champ finds new meaning in life as a trainer, but it comes at a price. Rocky Jr., played by Stallone's son in real life, Sage, becomes very jealous. Then Tommy gets pulled away by a shady promoter based on Don King, leaving Rocky in the lurch with neither a protégé nor a son. The part of Tommy Gunn was being played by the real life professional fighter Tommy Morrison, who claimed to be the grandnephew of Marion Morrison, a.k.a. the great John Wayne.

Numerous aspects of the script were apparently still being worked out, including the fate of Rocky himself. There was a rumor that Rocky was going to be killed off at the end of the movie, making this the absolute last in the series. If that was the case, I didn't have much time to make my mark.

I ran into my compadres, Frank Cappuccino and Ed Derien in the basement and found out we were all in the same boat, selected as non-union extras. The big deal, apparently, was to be a union extra, not so much because of the money but because you were likely to be seated in the first five or six rows. Frank Cappuccino was still in the running to be a referee. But as far as I was concerned, it was time to strike a blow for the hometown crew. It was time to make a move.

So I wandered upstairs and outside. I had been told Sly Stallone's dressing room was in a bus in the parking lot. As usual I had to fight my way out of a corner and was willing to go straight to the top. But there were probably twenty busses in the lot, and going door to door looking for Rocky Balboa was even out of my league.

I wandered back inside from the cold to the main level, hot from Klieg lights, where the crew was staging a scene. No sign of John Iberia. I milled around and asked who was in charge, and I was pointed to Cliff Coleman, the first assistant director. Cliff was in his late forties and easily six-foot-five. I walked right up to him and started talking directly to his belly button before backing off a bit and straining my neck. I wanted to make eye contact, even if it was long-distance and painful.

"Here's my card. I want you to have that and think about something."

Cliff looked at my business card, looked at me, and looked back at the card.

"I'm going to ask you for one simple thing," I said. "You know, I'm a boxing judge in real life. I was the first woman ever to do it, and I'm still doing it. And I'm just asking for the one thing."

"And what is that?" he asked.

"I would like to sit in *my* seat."

And just like that he started to laugh. It started as a smile and a chuckle and ended up as a guffaw. He couldn't control himself. But I had to, because I certainly didn't want to cry. I stood there and wondered whether I had just finished the worst audition in the history of American cinema. What did he find so hysterical—my size, my chutzpah, or the combination of both? I might never find out, because Cliff was called back to the scene, and I decided it was time to slink back down to the basement.

Then, while starting to slink, I was stopped cold by the Italian Stallion. I literally almost knocked into him, which startled him but made me feel better about not scouring the parking lot. Sylvester Stallone was no disappointment. He was even better looking in person than in the movies. I always made a note of what boxers wore in the ring. This one, outside the ring, wore a black shirt, black pants, black socks, and black shoes. The only thing on his body not black was a gold chain hanging from his neck with a little pair of boxing gloves. He could have fit right in with a gangsta rapper's entourage.

But Sylvester Stallone, in his mid-forties, was buff. He could probably have gone one or two rounds with a real fighter, but not much more. And perhaps the most pleasing thing about Stallone, at least for me, was his height. He was five-seven, maybe five-eight, and after having just spent a few minutes damaging my neck muscles for life, it was a relief to speak at only a small angle.

"Mr. Stallone," I said. "I'm a big fan."

"Thank you," he said with no affect. It wasn't "Ay, thank you, know what I mean" like Rocky Balboa drooling words onto the pavement. It was succinct—two precise words from a professional actor.

"My name is Carol Polis, and I happen to be the very first woman ever to be a professional boxing judge. In the world. I'm from Philadelphia, and I'm thrilled to be working with you on this movie." With that I handed him my card.

"That's actually very interesting," he said.

"And of course, I'm hoping to play a judge."

"I'm sure you'd make a good one." He looked at my card a second time and put it in his pants pocket. And that was that. My ride with the Italian Stallion. He excused himself and continued walking to the ring. It wasn't the worst of all interactions. At least he didn't laugh at me.

Right behind the Stallion was actor Burt Young, Rocky's brother-in-law, Paulie. In all the *Rocky* movies, if you couldn't get to Rocky directly, you tried Paulie, and so did I. I gave away another card and another song and dance, and Paulie seemed just a little less thrilled than

"Rock." From his appearance, Burt Young could have been a truck driver or factory worker, and no doubt typecasting was part of how he landed the most lucrative movie role of his life, if not all of his roles. The most striking aspect of our brief meeting was how much skinnier Young appeared in person than on screen. They said the camera added five or ten pounds, and apparently they were right. Unfortunately what Burt Young shed off camera I would have to gain on camera. But that's show business.

I eventually returned to the holding cell downstairs to find Cliff busy dividing the masses into union and non-union. The Red Sea parted, and I was on the wrong side. Over on the other side, Cliff was selecting three judges from a group of middle-aged men. My hand went up, though it's tough to see a hand from across the sea. But I could make out the three lucky guys and knew for sure the only fight judging they had ever done was from the living room couch. My dreams sank and my heart with it. Yet almost in the same instant, they were buoyed.

Cliff walked across the room, looked down at the top of my head, and asked me to stay behind with the union people while the non-union people were led upstairs to their seats. I had been raised to believe that the good Lord had some sort of plan for me, and now evidently Cliff did, too. When he returned to the holding cell to lead the union flock upstairs to the promised land, I tried to keep my hopes in check. That became nearly impossible when Cliff pointed to the front row and told me to take a seat up there.

Upon further explanation and more precise pointing, it wasn't exactly the promised land, but it was a little closer. The seat was the last one behind the far end of a wooden table at ringside. Cliff asked me if I wanted to play a photographer. I certainly did. The role of photographer was an esteemed one in American history, from Matthew Brady during the Civil War to Weegee shooting crime scenes before the crime, to Frank Sinatra being selected by *Life* magazine to be their official shutterbug at the first Ali-Frazier fight. Besides, I had brought my own camera to take shots for my next year's Christmas card.

My camera, however, wasn't offered a part. Instead, the crew gave me a very large, heavy prop camera. There was no film in it, but it could do one thing—make a huge flash. My marching orders were to take a "picture" whenever there was a knockdown or a solid blow. The remainder of the time I was supposed to concentrate on the action. But there wasn't much action, and there were no solid blows.

Over the next several hours with one much needed break for lunch, I learned more about filmmaking than I had by watching countless films over the past half century. The "fight" was really a series of ten and twenty second exchanges completely choreographed. The choreographer was the third man in the ring, or if you counted the fake referee, the fourth man. If you counted all the cameramen, prop people, makeup artists, and crew, more like the thirty-third man. There were more people in the ring than during a Don King post-fight brawl, except these people all had jobs to do.

One makeup lady's job was to take a thick magic marker and paint bruises on the fighters. Another makeup guy's job was to do the same with cuts. When the action stopped, which was every few moments, these magicians would move their hands in a cloud and a bruised, cut, bloodied and battered fighter would miraculously emerge. They did a better job of it than real opponents. Another technician's job was to spray oil and water on the fighters every minute or so to make them look sweaty, glistening, and exhausted.

The choreographer's job was to divide the action into tiny segments, each one to be performed over and over again. Nary a blow landed, and nary one was supposed to. The actors and crew were all experts in near misses that would eventually look like landed punches, I supposed, once edited together tightly and layered with sound effects. As a photographer I made a great judge, and one thing I knew for sure—every round was a draw.

It was all fascinating, boring, and sad. Creating the illusion of a fight from dozens of sprayed and painted ballet moves was fascinating. There were scattered bricks, but these artists made you think there was a wall. It was boring, because most of what we extras did—whether as fake judges, fake photographers, or fake audience members—was wait around for the director to announce we were doing another take. The movie business was like the universe—mostly empty space punctuated by tiny bits of matter. Finally, it was sad. Part of me was still holding a hairbrush and gazing in the mirror. I still wanted to believe it was all real.

I had made it to celluloid, I thought. But I hadn't gotten my Christmas card shot with Sylvester Stallone. So a few days after the shoot I tried calling a phone number someone gave me. It was for Tony Filiti, Sylvester Stallone's step-father. I explained who I was and that all I really wanted was something for my scrapbook—a shot of me and Sly while he was still in town. Like step-father, like step-son. He was brief and polite. He didn't laugh but told me he tried not to get too involved in Sylvester's affairs. Affairs—I wished.

Just when I thought the final bell had rung on my movie career, I got a call from Meredith, who asked if I would be interested in being an extra at the big finale fight scene at the Civic Center, near Franklin Field. I was there in a flash.

On January 18, I filed in the back door of the sterile Civic Center along with ten thousand other extras who would be compensated with a free lunch and a long day of choreography. Just as I was about to take my special seat in the fifty-eighth row, I heard a scratchy sound from the PA system that was like the voice of God. It was. It was Cliff. "Will the lady boxing judge please come to the front?" Champions walked to the ring, or sauntered, or swaggered. I ran. The last person I had seen run to ringside like that was Carol Castellano before the Hagler fight. She stole my seat on that occasion, but no one was stealing it now.

It was true. I was a judge for a day and for the ages. Shooting began, and I concentrated on pretending to concentrate and managed not to get a headache. What I did get was a bladder ache. I was, plain and simple, afraid to leave my seat to go to the bathroom for fear of all the Carol Castellanos in the world. There were ten thousand of them right here under one roof. Fortunately there were enough distractions to keep mind and body together. Sage Stallone was strutting around the ring like he was the next champ. I had a nice conversation with Pat Rooney, who had been one of Mike Tyson's trainers.

I also had the thrill of a lifetime for an art aficionado, meeting LeRoy Neiman. He was playing the ring announcer, but his real talent was capturing the beauty of sports on canvas with strong, beautiful blotches of paint. All I wanted to do was talk about his artwork, and all he wanted to do was talk about my life in boxing. In a world where everyone tries to steer the conversation back to himself, it was a wonder of nature.

But the most notable distractions were the wannabe starlets who petitioned me every few minutes. In the crowd of ten thousand there must have been hundreds, and they each had the same story. They were twenty-something, reasonably attractive, wearing too much makeup, an aspiring actress, and looking to meet Sylvester Stallone. They saw me at ringside and probably figured I was part of the entourage. So they asked me questions about Sly, like where he was staying, and pushed folded handwritten notes into my hand. They were typically vapid with the personality of a ring towel.

It wasn't my style to look down on them or anyone else for that matter. I didn't want to be a judgmental judge. I just took a lot of mental notes. They were determined and I was determined. They wanted to be part of something big and so did I. The difference, I thought, was that I was persistent while they were desperate. Like the entire experience, it was fascinating, boring, and sad. And I loved every minute of it.

Someone very kind sent me a wonderful color photo a few weeks later. It was a wide angle shot on the set at the Civic Center. In the background were Sylvester Stallone and Tommy Morrison with the crew in the ring. In the foreground was an aspiring actress in a red and black dress playing a judge and star for a day, minus the hairbrush. And behind it all was a huge American flag hanging from the rafters. I had my next Christmas card.

Not long before that next Christmas I went to see *Rocky V* during opening weekend at a local theater. I thought I spotted the back of my head for a hundredth of a second at the Blue Horizon. I was almost sure I spotted a side shot of my head at the Civic Center for two hundredths of a second. It was a subliminal zip and a subliminal blur. As I closed my eyes, I recalled seeing the whoosh of a lady ringside holding a camera. The more I thought about it the more clearly I saw it and the less I believed it.

That same weekend, Kenny, who was now a professional writer for a local radio station, also went to see *Rocky V* and swore he saw me distinctly five separate times. But what are sons for?

I couldn't possibly be upset. As hard as it was to become a boxing judge in real life, it was just as hard in the movies. In that strange way, art had indeed imitated life. As for achieving immortality, however, I couldn't say *Rocky V* did the trick. For that I would have to write a book.

On set in *Rocky V* movie.

The Rocky statue in Philadelphia.

CHAPTER SEVENTEEN
REQUIEM FOR A BANTAMWEIGHT

You can always hear the clicking and the clacking in the radiation chamber. It's only a few minutes, but other than being held under water or trapped in a nightmare, it's the longest few minutes of your life. The clicks and the clacks from the machinery are harsh but controlled. They are scary and cold and have you thinking that you are the subject of some sort of experiment.

But you must get through, so you do what you have to do. After a week or two of radiation every day, you begin to realize—first unconsciously, then consciously—that there is a pattern to the clicks and clacks, a beginning, a middle, and an end. Eventually you can tell where you are in the session and when it's coming to a close. The clicks and clacks become your friends.

You are alone in the radiation chamber. Very alone. There is a technician beyond the steel and glass door to the room. He strapped you in, and he'll be back. But for now you are isolated, at the bottom of the ocean with someone watching.

You are propped up on your back, on a table and wearing a hard molded clamp on your arm and chest. But the clamp cannot do the work for you, some of the hardest work in the world—the work of being perfectly still. If you are not perfectly still, the radiation finely tuned to the depth of the tumor will begin to sear other parts of your body.

After a lifetime of being proactive, you finally get good at being still. You learn to meditate on events. There can be no giddiness or slipping away into a pleasant dream, as that would defeat the whole purpose. What you can do is soberly review details, whether they are new to you or repetitive. You can create your own clicks and clacks.

For years I would go to Abington Memorial Hospital every

November for my annual mammography. This day in mid-November 2007 was warmer than most, more like a seasonable day in early October. The only thing that made it less than leisurely was the cyst on my left breast. But I wasn't particularly concerned. My mother had been very cystic, and now that I was seventy-one years old, a cyst or two could be expected.

When the Russian diagnostic technician walked into the room to discuss my mammography, I still wasn't particularly concerned until I caught the way she sat down extra carefully next to me. I'll give her credit. She didn't waste any time. It was cancer. I said it couldn't be. She showed me the lump on the screen. It was dark and hard with a half-dozen other telltale characteristics. There was no question in her mind.

When I came home that afternoon, I climbed right upstairs, walked into the closet in my bedroom, closed the door, curled up into a ball on the floor and just sobbed. *This can't be happening*, I thought. Why me? Why now? I've worked so hard raising four children and then on the cusp of starting a new life, a fifth, a grandchild. I juggled and did things on enough shoestrings to open a footwear store and reinvented myself every month, day, hour I had to for one goal—to keep it together for their sake. To do the right thing for them, with the underlying belief that maybe, just maybe, things would eventually work out for me, too.

I thought maybe I did something wrong. Maybe the lump is the badness coming out. But God, what exactly did I do that was so wrong? How many millions of things did I do every day that were unpleasant and difficult and trying but right?

In the closet my face was pushed up against the hem of a dress. Behind it was another dress and another and another. Together they made a soft pillow for my head, and the pillow smelled like good days from the past. Days of sunshine and piles of leaves on the sidewalk and laughing with a close friend in the kitchen while the kids ran around the house and did things I didn't necessarily want to know about. It was safe in the closet. I could cry as long as I needed to. The fabric dried my tears and the ones that followed. There was no shame. I felt pain, but here my pain had distinct boundaries and no more could get in.

What if I never got up and got out of the closet? I thought. But why should I? Because I had to. Because I still had my two dogs who needed to go for a walk and depended on me. Because Larry expected to hear from me at college. Because sitting sobbing curled up in a ball on the floor of a closet was no sort of example to set. But there was one problem. I didn't think I could do it.

I tried to will myself to get up. I couldn't do it all at once. This was too terrible a Band-Aid to rip off. Worse even than a Band-Aid, it would sting for much longer, as the road stretched out before a cancer patient is long and trying. I tried to do it piecemeal. Just to pull my ahead away from the dresses. Just to sit upright. Just to tuck my hands under my thighs and push. But it wasn't happening. Each task that made up the whole became as difficult as the whole.

Then I borrowed something from my past, an image lodged firmly inside my psyche. It could have been from anyone's psyche, but I had a special claim to this one image. It was that of a boxer knocked down trying to get off the canvas. He is dazed, hurting, jarred, unfocused. But the count of ten is running. There is still a fight left. I still had things I wanted to do. I still had things I *had* to do.

No one cheered when I opened the closet door and walked out into the bedroom. But I had the beginnings of a strategy for the rest of this round and perhaps the next one. It was cancer, but we had discovered it early. It was stage one. The prognosis was good. The oncologist explained to me there would be two operations. The first one would remove the tumor. The second one, a month later, would remove two nearby lymph nodes to make sure it hadn't spread.

Even if it hadn't spread, there would be six weeks of radiation treatment following the second surgery. Even after the radiation, I would have to take a pill every day to reduce the chance of a relapse. Every day for five years, complete with side effects. I took a look at the interior of the closet and noticed the shape of my body still vaguely pressed into a pile of clothing. It would be so easy to go back in.

Things were somewhat better on a hot summer day, July 20, 2008, precisely the twenty-first day of radiation with exactly twenty-one more to go. Halfway through. Finally I heard the closing clicks and clacks and saw the technician through the glass getting ready to shut it down for the day. A few more moments and I would be able to wriggle around once more, scratch the mild itch on the right side of my nose and be myself again. I wanted to go home, but there were no more closet scenes now. I had turned the corner and had more than just a few baby steps mapped out.

Over the winter a movie had come out called *The Bucket List*. In it, two terminally ill aging men decide that there are just a few things they absolutely had to do before they passed. The "bucket" referred to in the title was borrowed from the phrase "kicking the bucket," which itself came from the protocol for hanging someone. The person stood on a bucket with a noose around his neck, and the executioner kicked the bucket out from under him. The movie was a hit to the point where people not necessarily ill now commonly referred to their bucket list. I had one of my own.

Of course, I wanted to return to Italy. It probably wouldn't be courtesy of boxing, but that was beside the point. Italy was and always would be my favorite place on Earth. I loved the thirty-course meals and lust for life you felt all around you just by walking the streets. The side streets were even better, with their hidden possibilities. Always the possibilities. And the men of Italy were so drop dead gorgeous. Just gazing upon them was a tonic. The thought of which gave me item number two on my bucket list.

I wanted a companion but not the kind most people thought of. No twenty-four-seven stuff for me. I had worked to too long and hard for my independence to want or need that, and the constant proximity usually only led to problems and exhaustion. Since this was my bucket list, I could have it my way. After some serious yet giddy deliberation, I decided my way was every Wednesday night, Saturday night, and all day Sunday.

Wednesday night is the middle of the week. The effects of the past weekend have worn off and the next one seems too far away. Turning a dreary Wednesday night into a fun evening seems to double life's fun and cut its troubles in half. Saturday night is date night, and why be without one? Sunday is for going to garage sales and the race track and stopping at some café you weren't even sure was an eating establishment until you took a second look into the window of that antique shop.

Next on the list was the book. I was sure how to read one though not how to write or publish one. But I knew through all the places I had been to, all the traumas I had survived including this last one, and through the good fortune of being a genuine first at something, I had a story to tell. The world was full of people who needed to hear a different voice on not giving up. Most importantly, my own life was already filled with such people. The book would be my legacy to my children.

Last and, yes, probably least on my bucket list was throwing a spiral football pass. Not many petite, educated women reaching their eighth decade of life cared much about watching football, much less playing it, but I had always wanted to throw that perfect spiral. Watching the leather missile sail and spin through the sky on a crisp autumn day seemed to be the perfection of America captured in a quick look at the sky. Whenever I tried to throw one it tumbled end over end or, at best, wobbled like a top losing its steam.

I made it out of the radiation chamber that day and all the days following. Two long Novembers after the nightmare began—November 20, 2009 to be exact—I drove down North Broad Street to one of my favorite places in the world, the stately *Blue Horizon*. I was picked to judge that evening, an event that had become increasingly rare. Mixed Martial Arts, sometimes known as Ultimate Fighting, had largely taken over, and boxing had slipped into the background. It seemed I was expected to appreciate MMA, but I didn't. I hated it. I had watched it on about five separate occasions totaling about five minutes, and it was five minutes too many. It was a TKO.

Boxing was violent. Anyone who argued otherwise was in denial or on drugs. But it was a controlled violence. There were lots of rules and lots of enforcement. No hitting below the belt. No grabbing and hitting. Large gloves limited the damage. There were two ring doctors at every fight. There was an ambulance waiting outside. Every fighter at every level had to carry around a medical passport to be presented before every fight.

This passport was not to protect the public. It was to protect the fighters from themselves. Depending on the state, a boxer was not allowed to fight within thirty days or even more after his previous fight. If he got knocked out, that restriction could be ninety days or more and require a doctor's examination. Prior to the passport system, boxers would show up wherever and whenever to make another paycheck, under an alias if they had to.

Mixed Martial Arts, however, was to me, the pits. The gutter. It was violent, ugly, and uncontrolled. Two men with no shoes and the look of wild animals released from captivity entered a big cage with one purpose—to hurt and maim each other. There didn't appear to be much officiating. The mentality was low. It was basically human cock-fighting.

Each time I peered into this world, the word "slavery" popped into my mind. Of course the fighters were there voluntarily, but at times you had to wonder. The whole endeavor had the look and flavor of the old Roman Coliseum, the one aspect of Italy I could do without. Fighters were captured from a rival province and pitted against each other. The one rule was that the loser died right there in front of Caesar and the winner got to live—and perhaps kill—another day.

Naturally, I was biased. This was evidently what the audience wanted, and they were getting it in large doses. There was once a premium on skill and athleticism and some common sense regarding when enough was enough. Now the promoters were selling pain and the people were buying.

The decline in my own career, in all fairness, couldn't be blamed entirely on Ultimate Fighting. More than anything it was Ultimate Responsibility. For many years I looked forward to that one exotic title fight per year. I didn't know where it would be or when it was coming, but I knew it was indeed coming and that I'd be ready. But by the mid-Nineties, it was more or less expected of WBA judges to travel at their own expense to conventions—in many cases held thousands of miles away—in return for assignments. While raising Larry and spread thin I could no longer justify the thousands of dollars for what was basically a working vacation. In 1996 I let my WBA membership lapse. There was no formal resignation. I just stopped mailing in my dues.

I certainly had gotten in some last licks. In 1992 I made it back to Italy for the Vasquez versus Cruz Junior Featherweight title fight, and although the bout was bumped from Naples to Novara and finally to Bergamo, it was still, after all, Italy. Then in December of 1995, I was tapped to judge the heavyweight bout between Mike Tyson and Buster Mathis Jr. This was neither a title fight nor in Italy, but judging a Mike Tyson fight in Philadelphia at the Spectrum worked for me any day of the week.

The unofficial slogan for the fight was "Presumption of Innocence." That might have referred to the hung jury at Don King's recent federal trial for wire fraud or to Mike Tyson's recent release from prison. Tyson, convicted of rape, explained to the media that in this particular case he really was innocent, but that based on the number of terrible acts he had committed over the years without being apprehended, justice had in a way been served. God had gotten him.

Or more precisely, Allah. Like so many African-American fighters before him, Tyson left the penitentiary a Black Muslim or at least a wannabe. And like so many, he looked angrier when he left prison than when he entered. That was really saying something, because Mike Tyson looked very, very angry going in.

You judge every second of every round of every fight as if it's going to mean something, even if you know it's not. Tyson-Mathis was two rounds of Mathis tying up Tyson on the ropes and one round of Tyson issuing Mathis a prison beating. Mike Tyson was still a good enough fighter to turn rage into an early round defeat of an average or even above average opponent. But it wasn't going to last forever. Mike Tyson was ripe for the taking.

Altogether I had done twenty-seven title fights. Not a bad run for someone who might have been a fluke or a novelty. In fact, this chilly November night in 2009 could have been number twenty-eight. There was a title fight in Philadelphia tonight. Francisco Rodriguez of Chicago and Teon Kennedy, direct from the City of Brotherly Love, were scheduled for a twelve round bout to determine who would go home with the vacant USBA super bantamweight title. But there would be no twenty-eighth for me. For some reason I was scheduled to judge the five preliminary bouts but not the sixth and main event.

At the moment, I had another opponent besides a touch of bad luck. Night driving was a little harder as you got older. Depth perception in the partial dark was limited, and other vehicles sometimes seemed to jump out of a picture frame. I had the additional disadvantage of two cataracts. But my vision in the ring was still good, and that was all that mattered.

Parking near the Blue Horizon in that iffy neighborhood was always a challenge, and at seventy-three I was still up to that one as well. There were a lot of vagrants and hustlers along North Broad Street, so I always tried to park along one of the side streets, like West Master or West Thompson. But there was enough activity on the side streets as well to keep me wondering between rounds if my car was being broken into. On one occasion, the leader of a small pack of street people told me he'd watch my car for five dollars. Maybe for another five dollars I should have hired someone to watch him, because when I emerged from the Blue Horizon, he was gone, though my car was still there.

My long term solution was to set up a decoy. The plan emerged organically. Weather permitting, I was regularly doing the Quakertown flea market to make a few extra dollars. On any given day I had all sorts of clothing and tchotchkes in the back and the passenger seat. My instinct was to cover it up with blankets to protect myself against both ends of the social spectrum. I didn't want the well-off thinking my vehicle housed a homeless person, and I didn't want the real homeless people spotting the goodies in the car.

So to kill at least two birds with one stone, I would pack a couple shopping bags of old clothing before a fight and leave them on the sidewalk a few feet from my parked car. I never knew for sure if this diversion worked precisely as planned, but my car was always still there and the bags were always gone.

The Blue Horizon was like an old friend. Even if you didn't see your old friend for a couple of years, you felt comfortable right away and caught up quickly and easily. And I had real old friends at the venue. Greg Sirb had been the Executive Secretary for the State Athletic Commission for many years and was always on hand to greet us. I knew just about all the other officials and the writers, whose names and faces hardly changed over the years. And somewhere in the crowd was a relatively new friend of mine. Rich, my co-author, said he would be traveling down from Easton, Pennsylvania to get another look at yours truly in action.

Once the first round bell for the first preliminary fight rang, there was no chance of my spotting Rich or any other friend. I was locked in as usual and ready as ever for a headache. But there was not much to ache over. The first two fights were four round lopsided quickies. Things started to get interesting in the six round super middleweight fight between undefeated hometown favorite Dennis Hasson and the New Englander, Eric Pinarreta. But that one was stopped in the fifth round, leaving Hasson's record unblemished and my evening still without any meaningful contribution.

The fifth fight was my last opportunity to put in a nice piece of work, and when they led Upper Darby product Big John Poore to the ring, it seemed promising. John Poore delivered on his nickname. At six-foot-three and not a pound under 240, his rock hard physique had the capacity crowd riled up before a punch was thrown and would have had any potential bar brawler thinking twice before throwing a punch of his own. Poore had begun his pro career ten years earlier with a string of victories but had begun to falter as of late, pushing forty. His opponent, Jason Barnet of St. Petersburg, was just a bit shorter and a bit lighter and entered the ring seemingly as an underdog.

There are no underdogs inside the ring. Only winners and losers and some gradations in between. John Poore swung out most of what he had in the first round and landed a blow or two. They were hard blows, but he took three for each of them. In the second round, it was all Barnett.

This was no bar brawl. There was no dramatic substitute for the stamina to go the distance, no chairs to break over people's heads, and no crowds in the midst of the fight to confuse the issue. The only crowd was surrounding the ring and up in the mezzanine, and what they saw was one man pummeling another, the latter alternately taking a wild swing and covering up like a turtle. The referee stopped the fight in the third round about a round too late, with Poor John hopefully having some time left over to stand proud and call it a career.

I had to call it a night, but I didn't want to. I was certain the best was yet to come, whether I was officially involved or not. I knew electricity, and even more than that, I knew Blue Horizon electricity. So with the super bantamweight title fight about to begin, I exchanged seats with the official behind me. He would get to put his name in the books, but I would get to do the next best thing.

At around 120 pounds soaking wet each, Rodriguez and Kennedy were similar in size, style, and quickness. The first few rounds were often a matter of feeling out the other fighter. Not these fighters on this night. They came out swinging and remained toe to toe. As quick as they were on their feet, there were plenty of chances to run around the ring and avoid the sheer punishment the other fighter had to offer. But the same way not a pound of flesh was wasted on either body, neither was a second squandered in any round.

The cheers at the conclusion of each round were getting louder. The mezzanine was in its own world, physically and emotionally. By the fifth round they were standing as the bell rang, and their collective feet lent the arena the low-pitched movement of a manmade earthquake. As for me, I had begun to score the fight in my head as if I were on duty, and for all practical purposes I was. Even though duty was imagined in this case, I could never let myself off the hook with a bunch of draws and no headache. It was three rounds to two in favor of Rodriguez and Advil later on.

The eighth round was one of a handful of the most exciting I had ever seen among countless thousands of rounds spanning almost four decades. It was toe to toe with four fists fully engaged. There were lightning fast lefts and rights coming from both sides and blows blocked with the same four fists at every angle. It was a round that should have been required viewing for every Ultimate Fighting fan in the world. By this point I had taken to scoring rounds in thirds, but the problem was it was one third of a round for Rodriguez, one third for Kennedy, and one third a draw.

Before the ninth round, the doctor climbed into the ring and grabbed a hold of Rodriguez. Maybe he had seen something I hadn't seen. Or maybe I had seen it. Rodriguez had probably taken more blows than his opponent, in particular a few more really hard ones. But since he never appeared dazed for more than a moment here and a moment there, it wasn't something that stood out in the round.

The ring doctor looked into Rodriguez's eyes for blood or dilated pupils. He asked the standard questions: What's your name? What is today's date? Where are you? Rodriguez appeared totally responsive, meaning there would probably be a ninth round. Kennedy's corner appeared to be begging for more. Over in Rodriguez's corner, which was immediately to my right, the fighter's father and two brothers, all with boxing backgrounds, fired their own questions at their son, their brother, and seemed informally to reach the same conclusion as the ring doctor.

The ninth round was a louder, wilder version of the eighth. Even the ring doctor made his rounds again, with the same result—there would be a tenth. I had it five to four Kennedy. The noise was now almost as overwhelming as the fight itself. Uncharacteristically, there was no rise in the decibel level when the long-legged blonde ring card girl held up the number 10. The crowd was already on their feet. Few rounds in boxing ended with a standing ovation. Even fewer began with one.

Somewhere in the second third of round ten, Francisco Rodriguez stopped returning punches. He wasn't backing off, and he didn't seem more than ever-so-slightly disoriented. But the referee saw something and stopped the fight. Teon Kennedy put his arms up for the first time as super bantamweight champion. The hometown crowd rocked the rafters in part for their new champion but in greater part for perhaps the best fight they had ever witnessed. It was one for the ages.

And just like that the roar subsided. Rodriguez looked more than exhausted. He appeared unbalanced. I saw someone scurry back to his corner to bring a stool out to Rodriguez. From up even closer than I was they must have determined that the fighter was not going to make it back to the corner on his own. It was odd to see a fighter sitting on a stool in the middle of the ring. A moment later they had the oxygen mask on his face, and he seemed to struggle to breathe.

I didn't see Rodriguez actually fall off the stool, but I was aware that he had fallen. At this point everyone who should and shouldn't have been in the ring was in. It was bedlam, but not the bedlam of a Don King fight gone haywire. There was no circus-like, quasi-comical atmosphere. This was grim and disturbing. I had never heard the Blue Horizon sound quite like this. People were worried.

I have always been attuned to color, and my years at ringside made this even more so. It was often the color of trunks or socks that lent me the ability to distinguish two evenly matched, similar looking fighters in furious combat. Now, when the paramedics brought in the stretcher, I was surprised. I had seen hundreds of stretchers in my time, only a few of which were actually used, and all of which had a tan fabric. This stretcher, however, consisted of plastic slats, and the slats were blood red. The color of Rodriguez's legs, meanwhile, should have been somewhat tan as well. But they were the color of clay.

The paramedics took off his shoes. Most fighters wore big thick athletic socks with brand name logos on them. But for some reason unknown, Francisco Rodriguez wore very thin, tiny white socks. That was all I could see for a moment as they lifted him onto the stretcher. A feeling of intense sadness swept over me. I heard voices from Rodriquez's corner yelling in English one word over and over again: "Breathe. *Breathe.*"

The way out of the Blue Horizon that night was unceremonious. I went to the office to get paid, and as much as I needed the money at this particular time, I didn't even care enough to check the envelope. There was usually a kind of camaraderie amongst the officials after a long night of boxing. We were exhausted but exuberant at having done our part in a tough game. But tonight there was no backslapping or war stories. We barely looked each other in the eye.

It was a rough weekend. Rodriguez was taken to Hahnemann University Hospital, and there was an information blackout. There was nothing new on his condition in Saturday's newspapers or local television news. Rich emailed me that he had indeed been at the Blue Horizon from the third fight on and witnessed a hundred times more than he had ever expected to see. He had already Googled the story and let me know he would keep doing so every few hours.

My sleep was uneasy to begin with. I was on Arimidex to cut down on estrogen production and make sure the cancer wouldn't get another foothold. I was grateful to the pharmaceutical company, AstraZeneca, for providing a fifteen-thousand-dollar-a-year drug for free. But the side effects were horrendous. My joints ached all the time. I had completed a little more than a year of this regimen and still had almost four to go. It was hell, but the alternative was worse. And my sleep was worse than ever.

I visited many places in my mind Saturday night, Sunday, and Sunday night. I went back to the radiology chamber and to the closet in my bedroom. I spent time with my medical oncologist, a beautiful woman in her thirties who was convinced she would never marry. She told me to stick it out with the Arimidex, and I told her to stop dating doctors. I woke up around 3 AM Sunday with distinct memories of serving as foreman during a week of jury duty. At the time I had just completed the second surgery and was apparently cancer-free. But the surgeon recommended I follow up with an oncologist. I ignored the surgeon. It was only during jury duty I realized that was at my own peril. It was a malpractice case. During the trial I came to understand that doctors were not babysitters. They were not obligated to keep after you. They were obligated to tell you what you needed to know exactly once.

But the most distinct dream I had was based on memories of enrolling my grandson, Larry, in Germantown Academy, a top private school. He was a little kid, all of six years old, and I wanted him to have the advantages of a boy from a well-to-do family. After I sent Larry to their summer camp one year, the director of the camp and the director of athletics were so impressed with my grandson they gave me an audience with the headmaster. I would have only a few minutes to speak on behalf of my grandson, explain why he would make such a great contribution to the academy, and then ask for financial aid. My two advocates prepped me, telling me above all no matter how deserving Larry was, not to break down and cry.

In the headmaster's office, I was as sober as a judge, and actually being one didn't hurt. My main concern, I explained, was the little things, like if Larry took a photography class how the other kids might have a Nikon and he would have a disposable. Or how he might be embarrassed on school trips by not having money to spend. A week later I received a letter from Germantown Academy stating that everything would be taken care of on Larry's behalf. It was one of the happiest moments of my life, because I knew this letter as much as anything else ensured my grandson's success. And still, I kept a stiff upper lip.

My mouse hand shook a little as I checked my email Monday morning. I clicked on an email from Rich and it was what I somehow already knew. Francisco Rodriguez was declared brain dead by the doctors over the weekend. It had taken till Sunday night for the doctors to convince his family to agree to remove life support. At 8:45 PM, they finally and reluctantly did.

I was too old and experienced for rationalizing. Of course, there was nothing I could have done to help that brave man. I wasn't even officiating at his fight. He wanted to be in that ring, and every reasonable precaution was taken within the confines of a highly regulated sport. There would be inevitable cries in the coming days to ban the sport entirely, but those of us who had lived a while knew that men would always find a path to the art of combat, and the underground version would be much uglier and far more lethal.

Here I was trying so hard not to rationalize yet doing a great job of it. The truth was there was such a thing as collective guilt. It was not punishable by a court of law, and maybe not even by God Himself, but it was real nonetheless. All of us at the Blue Horizon that night owned a little piece of that collective guilt, and trying to deny it was the ultimate rationalization.

And still, that wasn't the final truth of this tragic event. When I read that Francisco Rodriguez left behind a young wife and a five month old daughter, I was nudged closer to the truth, but I had still not arrived.

I remembered my dream about getting Larry into school, and it dawned on me that there had to be at least one moment when as a boy Francisco's parents in some way let him go, just enough for him to be a man for an hour or two. It could have been, as it was for so many of us, that moment when they left him off at school for the first time, then turned around and took a quick look back at their boy cut loose into the world.

At that instant, you don't quite know whether you want to see your child reaching out for you or not. But when the young fighter's mom said goodbye to her son at the hospital, something like this scenario had to be racing through her mind. Finally, all these years after the speech at the headmaster's office, I broke down and cried like a baby.

* * *

The irony of growing older is that even though in theory you are moving closer to death, you are at the same time even more aware of how life goes on. You are still shaken by tragedy but for shorter periods of time. Your body bounces back slower and your spirit faster. You have more respect for souls departed but more concern for the living, especially those around you.

The personal ironies of my own life, like anyone's, abound, not the least of which is the tragic conclusion of what may be the last major fight I ever see up close. I don't feel the need to do another one to erase the memory or to avoid doing another one in fear. I've learned to live with life's ironies for as long as they may last.

The only thing I really fear in my own life is the prospect of stagnating, wilting, and contributing little, and I've taken great pains to see that doesn't happen. For a person with perhaps not the best luck in the world, I am among the luckiest. I see grown children and growing grandchildren every day reminding me that not a minute was in vain. I love them all equally, but if pressed I would have to say that my grandson, Larry, is my single greatest achievement. A fight can be great, but there is always a particular round that serves as your ultimate test at a time when your strength is at its least. That is your turning point and how you define yourself. And that is really saying something coming from a woman who once complained that raising children is a lot like being slowly pecked to death by chickens.

As for the bucket list, things are looking up. You may have figured out by now that the book is coming along just fine. Three quarters of a century was a long time to wait, but it was really the fourth quarter I was worried about. Italy still beckons, but there are great deals on flights all the time. The Wednesday-Saturday-Sunday companion, I am convinced, is still out there somewhere, and if he's in Italy I may be able to kill two more birds with one stone.

Then there is the matter of the spiral. There is hope. At a recent garage sale, three teenage boys and their dad got me to buy and practice with a Nerf football. It seems as if my problem was lack of follow-through. But after a five minute training session, they all said I was really getting the hang of it. As it turns out, I might not need that companion for all of Sunday.

CAROL POLIS WISHES TO THANK

My four children and grandchildren, especially Kenny Sharp,
as he found my co-author and publisher for me.

Dr. Strickland, "The Rabbi", Richie Kates, Howard McCall,
Jim Binns, Rudy Battles, Frank Cappucino, Eva & Frank Shain,
Gilberto Mendoza, Rodrigo Sanchez, "Bullwinkle," Jeff Jowett,
Ken Hissner, Jack Obermayer, Sylvester Stallone.

Philadelphia Fighters:
Benny Briscoe, Boogaloo Watts,
Willie "The Worm" Monroe, Eugene "Cyclone" Hart.

Zach Clayton, without whom none of this would be possible.

Rich Herschlag, thank you for your tireless efforts.

Peter M. Margolis, Andrew Klein, Denny Anderson
and everyone at Velocity Publishing Group, Inc.

Former Governor Milton Shapp,
Former Pennsylvania Mayor Frank Rizzo.

Joe Frazier, Muhammad Ali, Tommy Reed, Greg Sirb,
Larry Holmes, Sugar Ray Leonard, Marvelous Marvin Hagler, "Martha,"
Dorothy & Solo Blank, Herman Taylor, Matthew Saad Muhammad,
Russell Peltz, Bert Sugar, the Blue Horizon, K.O. Becky,
Tim Witherspoon.

---

*IF YOU WOULD LIKE TO CONTACT CAROL POLIS TO
ARRANGE SPEAKING ENGAGEMENTS, PLEASE EMAIL:*
maine523@yahoo.com

RICH HERSCHLAG WISHES TO THANK

I've been fortunate to have several books published lately and, therefore, the opportunity to acknowledge a lot of deserving people. At the risk of redundancy, I will reiterate here my profound appreciation for Sue, my extraordinary bride. As we move into our second quarter century, I am ever more amazed at your courage, strength, and beauty. Our older daughter, Rachel, has brought her talent and energy to New Orleans during the school year but continues to inspire us from afar. Elise, our younger one, continues to inspire us from right here in Easton, PA. And here's to our entire spectrum of intellectually and spiritually potent family and friends. You all rock.

A special shout out to Keith Goellner for helping Sue build her dream, which is a studio of her own. We will never forget it.

I've had a few people enter my life relatively recently who have had a great impact in one way or another. Rudy Lence is someone who believes in me, and that belief will one day materialize into something tangible and awesome. Vanessa Gamboa is my long lost little sister. Ken Sharp is a fellow writer who has set the bar spectacularly high as a friend, but even more so as a son. It's good to know that no matter how long I tread on this Earth, there are always great souls I have yet to meet.

Finally, I never met Muhammad Ali, but now at least I've met someone who has. Ali has not lived a perfect life, for who has? But as I grew up he showed me what it really meant to take an unpopular position on principle and stand by it. Ali, to this day I am impressed by the blows you absorbed inside the ring, but astonished by the blows you took outside it.

RICH HERSCHLAG

Rich Herschlag's previous book, *Sinatra, Gotti and Me*, co-written with Tony Delvecchio, is a first-hand account of the rise and fall of Jilly's, the legendary New York nightclub. Herschlag's other published books include renown comedian Pat Cooper's memoir, *How Dare You Say How Dare Me* (Square One, 2010); *Before the Glory* (HCI, 2007); *The Interceptor* (Ballantine, 1998); and *Lay Low and Don't Make the Big Mistake* (Simon & Schuster, 1997). *The Lady is a Champ* is Herschlag's ninth published book.

Rich Herschlag earned a bachelor's degree in science and engineering from Princeton University in 1984. In 1991, he received his license as a professional engineer from the State of New York and went to work as Chief Borough Engineer for the Office of the Manhattan Borough President, where he stayed until early 1995. Since then he has run a consulting business, Turnkey Structural, that specializes in the rehabilitation of older residential and commercial buildings. The website is www.turnkeystructural.com

Herschlag lives in Easton, PA, with Susan, his wife of twenty-four years. They have two daughters—Rachel, 19, and Elise, 13.

PHOTO: Rachel Herschlag